ERASMUS ON HIS TIMES

ERASMUS ON HIS TIMES

A SHORTENED VERSION OF THE 'ADAGES' OF ERASMUS

BY

MARGARET MANN PHILLIPS

READER IN FRENCH, KING'S COLLEGE, LONDON

CAMBRIDGE
AT THE UNIVERSITY PRESS
1967

Published by the Syndics of the Cambridge University Press
Bentley House, 200 Euston Road, London, N.W.1
American Branch: 32 East 57th Street, New York, N.Y. 10022

Library of Congress Catalogue Card Number: 67–26071

Printed in Great Britain
at the University Printing House, Cambridge
(Brooke Crutchley, University Printer)

CONTENTS

CONTENTS

INTRODUCTION

The *Adages* is one of the world's biggest bedside books; and a great deal more. Begun in 1500 as the *Adagiorum Collectanea*, and reborn in 1508 as the *Adagiorum Chiliades*, it came to its final conclusion only with the death of Erasmus. Step by step, from the early days of its making, he had seen more clearly what a collection of proverbs could come to mean, how it might not only recall the everyday customs of our forefathers, but embody the very habits of thought of the ancient world, and finally supply a link between that world and his own. Deliberately, he left it without plan, partly because he thought a systematic arrangement of the proverbs under headings of subject-matter might be so boring as to nauseate the reader, partly because the very size of the task deterred him.[1] Perhaps there was another reason which he does not give, an intimate reason for this planned planlessness: it made it easier for him to go on adding new elements, tucking in new ideas here and there, expanding and commenting, writing in the style he loved, swift, trenchant, chatty, familiar. Everything he read contributed its quota to the snowball, and here and there groups of proverbs derived from a single author bear witness to the trend of his current reading.[2] No wonder the *Adages* was his companion throughout thirty-six years of his life. It was so much more than an anthology or even a commonplace book. It was his own, characteristic and unique. And to study it in its development and with all its accretions gives a notable picture of the mind of its creator.

The editors of the *Bibliotheca Erasmiana* rendered an immense service to students of the *Adages* by consecrating to it their first volume.[3] Thanks to this classic piece of bibliography, it is possible to find one's way easily and quickly among the many editions of the book which were published in and after Erasmus's lifetime. But only a fuller study will enable the student to pick out the important stages in the development of the *Adages*, and it is proposed here to give the salient facts which enable one to do this.

(a) The *editio princeps* of the *Adagia* is the *Collectanea* published in Paris in 1500. It is a slim volume, containing 818 proverbs, with comments of a few lines each. It was a success, and reprints followed each

---

[1] *Herculei labores*, III. I. i.
[2] E.g. III. VIII–X, from Homer; IV. IV. xxx–lxxix, Plutarch; IV. VIII. lxvii–lxxii, Pindar; V. I. i–ix, Plautus; IV. I. lxxxv–c and part of V. II. i–xxxvi, Sophocles.
[3] *Bibliotheca Erasmiana*, ed. F. van der Haeghen (Gand, 1897).

other quickly. The *Bibliotheca Erasmiana* lists twenty-seven editions dated during the lifetime of Erasmus.

(*b*) This little book was thus still being printed when Erasmus published an expanded edition, the *Adagiorum Chiliades*, at the Aldine Press in Venice in 1508. This is to all intents and purposes a new book. It contains 3260 proverbs, thus fulfilling the promise of 'thousands' in the title. Some of the early proverbs are included but they are scattered in the mass. The comments are now longer and bring much learning to bear on the questions of meaning and origin. The little Paris volume had some Greek, but very little. Now the horizon scanned is Greek as well as Latin, the proverbs are usually given in Greek, many Greek quotations are included, and the resources of the Aldine Press make the book a front-line work of the New Learning. The tone and the intention are scholarly. In a few cases only the comments are extended to include personal views, and these are on questions of humanism.

(*c*) For many reasons this collection was certain to have a much greater success than the first. It was followed very soon by the *Praise of Folly*, and Erasmus's European reputation was established. The *Chiliades* was reprinted several times, and then in 1515 he published, this time with Froben in Bâle, a new edition of the *Adages*, in which the personal note is much stronger. It seems that two causes have operated to encourage Erasmus to make his book into a personal expression of thought: the success of the expanded comments of 1508 and the confidence which his position now gives him. There are nine new long essays, three of them very long indeed (*Scarabeus*, *Sileni Alcibiadis*, *Dulce bellum inexpertis*). There are many shorter passages in which Erasmus speaks his mind. And in these it is not now a question of scholarship or learning, but of political and social reform. A further edition by Froben (1517–18) carries this process on.

(*d*) The hybrid character of the *Adages* is now determined and it does not change in any subsequent editions, but several (notably in 1520, 1526 and 1528) add personal comments. In 1533 Erasmus made the last important additions and increased the bulk of the book considerably, leaving it much as we find it today.

*   *   *   *   *   *

What kind of book is the *Adages*—one of the key books of the sixteenth century, one of the foundation stones of Erasmus's reputation, and now relegated to the limbo of scholarship?

Coming early as it did in an age enthusiastically devoted to the collection of proverbs and emblems, where did its originality lie? Was it merely a matter of being first in the field? And how much did it gain in value by the continual later divergences from its first idea?

Some of these questions, it is hoped, will find an answer in the later pages of this book. The immediate answer lies in size and scope—the magnitude of the task as Erasmus came to see it. The *Adages* was not, as he thought, the first collection of Latin proverbs, and some of the Greek collections which he used are still in existence. But no one had ever attempted to create, by way of proverbs, a window on to the ancient world—quite apart from the other massive uses to which he put his book.

To begin with a general description of the *Adages* as Erasmus left it: the final number of adages at his death was 4251. Each had a commentary, in many cases of a few lines, often of half a column in the large folio of the Leiden *Opera*. Scattered here and there are those adages which Erasmus chose as his text for the longer essays, very much in the manner of the *Essais* of Montaigne.

The proverbs themselves are taken from classical authors, the Latin form being followed immediately in most cases by the Greek, and each is traced in as many authors as Erasmus had to hand. Always an authority is given, usually several, and often a close reference giving chapter and verse, but this is not always done. The Greek extracts have their Latin translation, the verse into verse. The commentary gives the meaning of the proverb, its literal and figurative use, explains the custom or legend or geographical or historical fact which gave rise to it, and often adds a personal observation, an opinion or reminiscence of Erasmus himself.

All biographers of Erasmus have recognised the value of the longer commentaries in the *Adages*. They give a forthright and often eloquent expression of his opinions on the world of his day, dovetailing with his satirical works on the one hand and his popular evangelical writings on the other. They have been largely quoted and in some cases published separately, in the original and in translation. The bulk of the book, on the other hand, remains inaccessible to students, and looks formidable with its array of texts and authorities. The passing references, witty or scathing or humane, or sometimes simply reminiscent, tend to be lost in the mass. The *Adages* is a good example of the shift in emphasis which occurs in the reputation of a great book over several centuries. We think of it as only interesting to ourselves in what was originally a by-product, its satire. That is still alive, and applicable to problems of our own. The first intention of the book, to serve the cause of humanism, is long out of date, and that partly because of its success. The great restoration of antiquity of which it was a part, and in the advance guard at that, has turned it into a curiosity; its methods are not those of modern scholarship, its plan is personal and subjective, its resources limited, and it shares in the character of Erasmus's other writings—full of a great vision but hurried in the details. He was fond of saying that it was originally rushed together in six months. There were such infinite fields to conquer, so much to be done!

It is true that some of his generation realised at once that, valuable as the learned treatment of the proverbs was to them, the true originality of the *Adages* was in the comments.[1] And it must always have been true that the *Adages* is a hybrid work, directed not solely to the out-and-out scholar (Budé, for instance, raised his eyebrows at the many digressions) and not to a popular audience, but to something between the two. Its avowed intention was to smooth the path to knowledge of the classics for the *mediocriter literati*,[2] and Erasmus welcomed the appearance of the earliest 'Epitomes' because they catered for the purse of the young student.[3] It spoke in fact to a cultured public, much smaller than the modern one, but very like it; not to the erudite but to the general reader, interested in the classics for what light they could throw on his own life and on the choices and struggles of his own society. To redress the balance, we must try to see the *Adages* as that public saw it, a magic casement indeed, revealing and explaining so much; making the past understandable, judging the present, giving glimpses of a more rational future, and this not only in the personal comments but in the conception of the book as a whole. We cannot study the *Adagia* and leave out the adages.

In the first place, what was Erasmus's definition of a proverb, and what importance did he attach to proverbs as such? There are two places where we may seek for this information; the first Preface in which the *Collectanea* was dedicated to Lord Mountjoy,[4] and the introductory section *Quid sit paroemia* which precedes the *Adages* from 1508 onwards.

The word 'paroemia', which Erasmus uses here, meant a by-word or adage, but could also carry the sense of enigma or parable; when the disciples of Jesus said to their Master, 'Lo, now speakest thou plainly, and speakest no proverb',[5] it is the word παροιμία which is used in the Greek. The sense of mystery clung to the idea of a proverb. In his introduction Erasmus seeks a definition in the ancient authors, and finally produces one of his own. The consensus of opinion, he says, defines a proverb as a dark saying which is useful for the conduct of life; or an enigma, which means something other than what it says; or

[1] Allen, 591, line 34.   [2] Allen, 2773.   [3] Allen, 1204.
[4] Allen, 126.   [5] John XVI, 29.

a saying in which a manifest truth is wrapped in obscurity (*proverbium est sermo rem manifestam obscuritate tegens*). None of the definitions he finds seem to him to meet the case entirely, since a proverb may have no enigmatic quality and yet remain a proverb, like *Ne quid nimis* for example, or it may have the obscurity without the moral usefulness, and yet still be a proverb. For his purpose he needs to widen the scope of the word, and he chooses to define a proverb in an extremely general way, as a saying which is both well known and marked by some witty and original conception, 'pithy' as we say (*paroemia est celebre dictum, scita quapiam novitate insigne*).

He goes on to discuss what it is which differentiates the proverb from the 'sententia', or the fable, apart from mere brevity. A proverb may be a *sententia*, or a *sententia* a proverb, but they are not necessarily identical. In the Preface to Mountjoy he defines more clearly the kind of phrase he intends to collect. It may seem at first, he says, that he has just made a list of moral sayings from antiquity. Not so, for he has a clear idea of an adage: it must have some hidden kernel, either a figurative or allegorical meaning, or a problematic turn (as, 'the half is more than the whole'), or a form so compressed as to attain wit by brevity. And it must be frequently on people's lips, either from being recited in the theatre or in poetry or because it recalls some famous occasion or person. And even among these he will pick and choose, leaving aside the common sayings of the people, including nothing which is not ancient, and remarkable in itself (*aliqua gratia insignitum*).

In the light of this latter remark, it seems strange that so many of the proverbs cited by Erasmus are still in our common stock of speech today. He sometimes points out a classical proverb which is still in use in his own time, but it is not for its contemporary popularity that he includes it. A glance at the following list will show that these phrases are still on our lips; are they the common heritage of Europe? Or may it be that their continued use is partly owing to the immense fame and handling of the *Adages*?

A necessary evil (*Necessarium malum*, I. V. xlvi).
Cupboard love (*Ollae amicitia*, I. V. xxiii).
There's many a slip twixt the cup and the lip (*Multa cadunt inter calicem supremaque labra*, I. V. i).
To squeeze water out of a stone (*Aquam e pumice postulas*, I. IV. lxxv).
To leave no stone unturned (*Omnem movere lapidem*, I. IV. xxx).
Let the cobbler stick to his last (*Ne sutor ultra crepidam*, I. VI. xvi).
God helps those who help themselves (*Dii facientes adiuvant*, I. VI. xvii).
The grass is greener in the next field (*Fertilior seges est alieno in arvo*, I. VI. lxxii).
De la même farine (*Eiusdem farinae*, I. VII. xxvii).

The cart before the horse (*Plaustrum bovem ducit*, I. VII. xxviii).

'Coals to Newcastle' (*In sylvam ligna ferre, in mare deferre aquam, ululas Athenas*, I. VII. lvii).

Dog in the manger (*Canis in praesepi*, I. X. xiii).

One swallow doesn't make a summer (*Una hirundo non facit ver*, I. VII. xciv).

His heart was in his boots (*Animus in pedes decidit*, I. VIII. lxx).

A rare bird (*Rara avis*, II, I. xxi).

To have one foot in the grave (*Alterum pedem in cymba Charontis habere*, or *in sepulcro*, II. I. lii).

To be in the same boat (*In eadem es navi*, II. I. x).

I'll sleep on it (*In nocte consilium*, or *super hac re indormiam*, II. II. xliii).

To call a spade a spade (*Ligonem ligonem vocat*, II. III. v).[1]

Up to the ears (*Ad ambas usque aures*, II. III. xxvii).[2]

To break the ice (*Scindere glaciem*, III. V. xcv).

Ship-shape (*Juxta navem*, IV. I. lxvii).

To die of laughing (*Emori risu*, IV. I. lxxxvi).

To have an iron in the fire (*Nunc tuum ferrum in igni est*, IV. IV. c).

To look a gift horse in the mouth (*Equi dentes inspicere donati*, IV. V. xxiv).

Neither fish nor flesh (*Neque caro est, neque piscis*, IV. V. xliv).

Like father, like son (*Qualis pater, talis filius*, IV. V. lxiii).

Not worth a snap of the fingers (*Ne crepitu quidem digiti dignum*, IV. VII. xvii).[3]

He blows his own trumpet (*Ipse sui tibicen est*, IV. VIII. xv).

To show one's heels (*Calcaneum ostendere*, IV. X. lvi).

In another class are the proverbs which recall a classical story or event, though this may well have vanished below the surface; the person who says 'I haven't done a stroke today' is not thinking of the joke played on the painter Protogenes by his fellow artist Apelles, which Erasmus relates out of Pliny.[4] And there are other phrases familiar to us because they are part of a more literary classical heritage. Keats's name 'writ in water' and Wordsworth's light 'that never was on sea or land' are in the *Adages*.[5]

These proverbs show that Erasmus was dealing with imperishable material, the forms in which common experience has crystallised out. But this is not the point which interests him, as it might interest us today. He is more concerned to show the value and nobility of the proverb as a form of speech, its antiquity, the fact that it is used freely by Aristotle, weaving proverbs into his discussions like jewels, *ceu gemmulas*, that the divine Plato, the grave and saintly Plutarch, the poets and even the emperors of Rome did not disdain to express them-

---

[1] *Ligo* = a hoe.   [2] Erasmus explains this as referring to two-handled jars.
[3] Erasmus says the people of his own country say 'Not worth *that*!'
[4] *Nullam hodie lineam duxi*, I. IV. xii.
[5] *In aqua scribis*, I. IV. lvi; *Neque coelum neque terram attingit*, I, V. xliv.

selves in proverbs. Even Christ himself ('by their fruits ye shall know them') dignified the adage by his use of it.[1] 'And in the proverbs of the ancient world is all its wisdom enshrined.'[2]

This is the great point. The many practical uses of the proverb may be pointed out, and indeed the sermons and discussions of many generations were enriched from Erasmus's store. The book was a treasure-house of style.[3] But the essential aim was to recapture, in this handy portmanteau form, the outlook and way of life of the classical world, through its customs, legends, and social institutions, and to put within reach of a modern public the accumulated wisdom of the past.

The true significance of the *Adages* in its day was even more than this. It must have contributed more than any other one book to the growth of that sense of proportion between the present and the past which we call the sense of history. It helped to establish a perspective. We can never enter fully into the minds of our forbears, and in dealing with them we must needs remain children of our own age, but the attempt to see them clearly in the distinctive individuality of their time while yet taking for granted that the fundamental urges of human nature do not change, is a modern point of view, developed from the Renaissance. The encyclopedia or compendium of knowledge was a familiar idea to the Middle Ages, and the medieval scholar or poet might well be interested in the crossing of the Red Sea or the Trojan War, but he would see these events strictly in the mental costume of his own time, and would have no scruples about interlarding his text with passages relating to some other era altogether. However unlike a modern work of scholarship the *Adages* may be, its attitude to the past was wholly modern, and must have been a complete eye-opener to the public which acclaimed it. It made the past real and brought it within their grasp: they felt as if they were walking in the streets of Rome.

To get back to the sources, and thus establish a continuity between the classical world and his own, was one, but only one, of the great aims of Erasmus's life. To do this it was necessary to steep himself in the classics and be able to bring them sharply before his readers; but the study of the pagan world was never for him an end in itself. His whole output, and in this the *Adages* is no exception, aimed at a synthesis between classical thought and Christianity. Just as he laboured to

[1] It appears that 'the dog in the manger' figures in the newly discovered 'Sayings of Jesus' in the Luxor scrolls.

[2] Prolegomena to the *Adages*, section v.

[3] R. R. Bolgar, *The Classical Heritage*, pp. 297–300, shows how the *Adages* illustrate the method of literary study outlined in the *De Copia*. No doubt it was in this way that the *Adages* had their greatest effect on the literature of their day, by providing a store of examples to serve as a guide int he imitation of the classics.

put the learning acquired from Athens and Rome at the service of his editions of the New Testament and the Fathers, so he is continually drawing comparisons and showing the continuity of thought and usage from pre-Christian to Christian times. The revered philosophers often say the same thing, he points out, as we find in the Gospel; they saw more darkly than we who have the light of life, but they were looking in the same direction. Sometimes even they put us to shame, by being more truly Christian than we. And so the *Adages* lend themselves on the one hand to Erasmus's favourite view of learning, as an edifice of reason crowned by the revelation of God, and on the other hand to a scathing denunciation of the Europe he knew.

To make a selection from the *Adages* for translation, the ideal would be to present a balanced view of these elements. We should have to show how the book constitutes an anthology of striking passages, particularly from the poets, every Greek extract being accompanied by its Latin version, and how it reverts time after time to points of style or problems of interpretation, so that it is a lesson in understanding the past. We should also have to make extracts to show how it gives a panorama of the ancient world, drawing more on legend and custom than on history (for such is the nature of proverbs), passing lightly from marriage customs to waterclocks, coinage or the structure of the Roman army, giving pithy summaries of philosophic themes side by side with amusing stories. To get back to the starting-point of the proverb was the method, to find *fabulam proverbii parentem*. The comments involve a host of different subjects and the haphazard grouping gives the book a kind of Protean character; Erasmus apparently follows wherever his proverbs lead him. There is really considerable artistry in the seemingly artless arrangement; like is grouped with like just sufficiently for one adage to throw light upon another, and before the dominant idea becomes wearisome it gives way to the next. The effect is like that of skilfully managed conversation.

A proverb looks forward as well as backward, and it would be necessary to show how it can often be matched with a present-day saying or custom which proves the continuity of thought and of human ways. Especially this is the case when the saying presents us with a frail bridge between the pagan and the Christian worlds.

Finally there is the personal and autobiographical element in the *Adages*. A few passages in the Aldine edition of 1508 have a directly autobiographical interest, and they are concerned with scholarship. This was personal in a sense because of Erasmus's enthusiastic commitment to the revival of learning. But when he published the 1515 edition with Froben he was playing a startling trick on the reading world; the

Adages sprang to life as a political document, an attack on the abuse of power in Church and State, an exposition of the characteristic Erasmian ideal of a simple and undogmatic Christianity, a war on war. It was no longer simply the work of a northern scholar competing with Italy in the spread of the New Learning, it was the mouthpiece of a leader of thought. Later editions deepened the tone, added more personal memories, sometimes bitter reflections, but the character of the book was fixed in 1515.

These additions were made with care, often inserted between two sentences of the previous version, so that some commentaries may be patchworks of new and old. It was not only polemics that Erasmus added; he often tightened up his references or added new ones, and gave much longer quotations, particularly from the Greek. But the application of the old proverbs to new problems surprised and delighted the world.

It was a stroke of genius to transform a peaceful work of scholarship into a tract for the times, without losing a fraction of the value of the earlier book. The *Adages* went on from this point as a dual-purpose work, throwing off minor features on both sides like a catherine wheel: the purely literary or schoolbook aspect of it was often reproduced in Epitomes up to the seventeenth century, the long political essays were in some cases reprinted separately in pamphlet form. The book itself, as we have said, went on growing till Erasmus died.

The personal comments themselves have thus a history of their own; they were under review for twenty years. And it is possible to trace a difference in tone between the earlier and the later. In the first group one would classify all those comments made in the editions of 1515, 1517, 1520, 1526; energetic attacks on current abuses, often acid enough and every time a direct hit, pungent in their irony, fired with the hope of change. In the second group fall the additions of 1528 and after, when hope of altering the world, or even achieving a peaceful settlement of the pressing quarrels, has become less sanguine. Erasmus's hitting is just as hard but he expects less from it, and his tone is more querulous. It would often be possible to date these comments by the mere tone of voice. At the same time there is a vein of reminiscence, an influx of stories about places and people he had met with in his long life of travel. These memories, unlike the satirical passages, are simply pleasant and have no axe to grind.

It will be clear that the first two of these aspects of the *Adages*—the anthology and the picture of the past—are a matter of bulk and can hardly be conveyed in short extracts. The famous essays full of irony and indignation are obviously the main target of the translator. This handful of translations will therefore necessarily represent mainly the topical content of the *Adages*. For this reason we begin with a non-controversial proverb shown in its final state, to stand by itself and indicate the original function of the book, the first of its many purposes. And after the fiery topical essays we shall look for a moment at the leisurely memories of the last expanded edition of 1533.

*   *   *   *   *   *

The *Adages* was a very large pebble thrown into the European pond, and its ripples are with us still. They stem from a work highly representative of a century so passionately addicted to *devises*—in which Marguerite de Navarre embroidered *Ubi spiritus ibi libertas* on her hangings, and Montaigne had only to raise his eyes to the rafters of his study to find his own choice of proverbs. The study of the dissemination of proverbs throughout the writings of the Renaissance would be an immense task. But behind the adages themselves is the warm love of the classics and especially of poetry, the quickening of the transfusion already begun of the life-blood of Greek thought. And behind this wealth of literature and historical detail is Erasmus's own brand of quizzical reflection, his impatience with pomposity, superstition and graft, his belief in the right of the individual soul to bypass systems and meet the simple truth.

ERASMUS ON THE ADAGES[1]

So there you have a list of my little trifles, my dear Botzheim, to stimulate your appetite for buying. But, when you complain that your coffers are running low and you are forced to buy the same book twice, I should like you to argue with yourself like this. Suppose I had produced the *Adages* and died at once, as soon as the work came out; would you regret having spent money on it? I don't think so. Now suppose further that I had come to life again a few years later, and that the book was born again with me, in a better and fuller version; would you groan about the expense, or would you receive joyfully both your friend and your friend's achievement? I know quite well what you will say: 'I should certainly rejoice with the friend who was alive again— but all this is imagination.' But which do you think the happier fate, to come back from the dead or not to die at all? If it is a matter of congratulation to be resurrected, it is a greater one to have survived.

Lastly, if the later edition has nothing in it worth paying more for, you are free not to buy; if it has something, the expenditure is not loss but gain. If the first edition gave something of value, worth a moderate sum, and the second does the same, you have gained twice, not lost twice. You will say, 'Why not produce the work finished once and for all?' Well, just as we spend our life seeking to make ourselves better, so we shall not cease to make our writings richer and more accurate until we ourselves cease to live. And as no one is so good that he cannot be made better, so no book is so complete that it cannot be improved. I freely confess that I am not as diligent in this line as I ought to be; but I think others are more greatly to blame, who are much more learned than I and yet for some reason publish late, or not at all. You might have been rid of the trouble over me too, if before leaving the stage I had said to you all 'Valete et plaudite', and, believe me, it would have happened if some good wine of Burgundy had not come on the scene like a *deus ex machina*; you must decide whether you would rather have it that way, or buy a book from time to time in a revised and expanded form.

[1] Extract from letter to John Botzheim, 1523. *Opus Epistolarum Erasmi Roterodami*, ed. P. S. Allen, I, p. 27.

ON TRANSLATING ERASMUS

The passages translated here constitute the topical and largely auto-biographical element in the *Adages*. They comprise all the long topical essays, with the addition of such shorter passages as touch on the same subjects—forming a commentary on the burning questions of the day which was read *non sine cachinno* by the contemporaries of Erasmus.

But it must be emphasised that these passages were never meant to be read consecutively. The *Adages* was an anthology to be dipped into at will. For the ideas hung on the proverbial pegs to be likely to catch the eye of the casual reader, they had to be repeated more than once.

Translators of Erasmus are always faced with a dilemma. His style combines a personal raciness with the lapidary and epigrammatic qualities of Latin. Would it be better to attempt to express this raciness by telescoping and paraphrase, or try to be exact at the price of being heavy? Each method has had its adherents. Those who read him closely[1] comment on the idiosyncrasies of Erasmus's style, the malice which made him sometimes choose an unclassical word just to spite the Ciceronians, his liking for diminutives and puns, his occasional creation of a new term, the art which produced an apparent artlessness, the variety which passes from a simple conversational tone to an emphatic enumeration or an eloquence full of fire. He said that he preferred a plain straightforward style (if not *soldatesque*, as Montaigne said of his own, at least *cordata*).[2] In style as in everything else, he intended to fuse together two apparently opposing strains to achieve plenitude; here it was colloquialism and distinction, the rapid speech of every day married to a deep love of the great poets and orators of the past.

The present translation has made a bid for accuracy and attempts to say what Erasmus said, even if much of his stylistic skill must be lost in the process. As he himself said, 'I can translate the meaning of Homer, but not his genius or his grace.'[3]

---

[1] Recent studies of the Latin style of Erasmus may be found in the preface to *Dulce bellum inexpertis*, ed. Yvonne Rémy and René Dunil-Marquebreucq (1953), and in the remarkable edition of *De pueris instituendis* by J. C. Margolin (1966), pp. 465–617.

[2] Sensible, not *picta fucis* (painted with rouge: *Adages*, III. I. i).

[3] I. VII. xiii.

A TYPICAL ADAGE

I. II. xix. *Frons occipitio prior*

A proverb celebrated among the early husbandmen, and tossed about like a riddle: 'forehead before occiput', or front before back. This is the way Antiquity signified that a man's business is better looked after when he himself is present and attending to it. *Prior* here means better, more effective; anyhow, who could be ignorant that the forehead is the front part of the head and the occiput the back part? Although this riddling quality of the saying gives it a certain charm, and owing to its age it has an oracular ring. It can be found in Cato (*On Farming*, chapter 4): 'If you have built up well, the more freely and frequently you come, the better for it your farm will be, and the less likely to go wrong; you will get more fruit; forehead before occiput.' Pliny, too, says much the same thing in his *History of the World*, book 18, chapter 5: 'But the man who will be a good owner comes often into his field, and the master's forehead does it more good than the back of his head —so they say, and truly.' Again in the same book, chapter 6: 'And our forebears used to say that the master's eye was what best fertilized his field.' Aristotle in his *Economics*, book 1, seems to trace this saying to a certain Persian, connecting it with another metaphor used by a Libyan. But I had better quote his words, in case anyone would like to know them [here follows the Greek]: 'And that reply of the Persian and the Libyan is worth preserving. For the one, asked what was the best fodder for the horse, replied, the master's eye. And the other, to an enquiry as to what was the best manure, answered, the master's footsteps.'

Both of them meant that the presence of the master was the most important thing in the successful conduct of affairs. Similarly Columella thinks it is a bad thing for a farm to be often let, and a worse thing when the tenant is a townsman who intends to leave the cultivation to his household and not attend to it himself. This is rather like the story told by Gellius, about the fat sleek man with the lean stringy horse; when asked about it he said no one need be surprised if he was in better trim than his horse, since he saw to his own meals himself and the horse was looked after by a slave.

Plutarch in his work on the education of children says [here follows the Greek]: 'Here and there one finds an elegant proverb coming from the stable: that nothing fattens the horse like the King's own eye.' The same simile is used by Aeschylus in his tragedy called the *Persians*, when he calls the master's presence the eye of the house [the Greek follows, with translation]. In the same vein Livy has a happy phrase: 'There is not often much success for the things you do through the eyes of others.' Terence in his *Eunuch* has the same idea when he says 'That's what can happen when the masters are away', meaning that when the masters are absent the servants are slack in their work and lax in their morals; in a word, all these add up to the same thing: if you want a thing well done, you must do it yourself, and not trust in the diligence of others.

The person who should most take note of this is the prince, if he really has the mind of a prince and not of a pirate, that is if he has the public good at heart. But in these days bishops and kings do everything through other people's hands, ears and eyes, and think the common good is no affair of theirs, swollen up as they are with their own possessions or entirely bent on pleasure.

2

FROM THE 1508 EDITION

The two long essays translated here are mainly concerned with literary
matters, though they occasionally suggest more general topics.

In 1508 and in succeeding editions, Erasmus used as a tailpiece the
adage *Auris Batava*, on which he wrote a loyal commentary in praise
of Holland. In the final editions this becomes IV. VI. XXXV and is translated here.

(a) Festina lente[1]

Σπεῦδε βραδέως, i.e. *Festina lente*, or make haste slowly.

This proverb carries with it a pretty riddle, particularly as it consists
of contradictory terms. Thus it is to be referred to that category which
I mentioned at the beginning of this book, the class of proverbs which
go by contraries, as for instance *infelix felicitas*. It seems to me not too
far-fetched to conjecture that it was made out of that expression in the
Knights of Aristophanes,[2] σπεῦδε ταχέως, i.e. hasten with haste, so that
the person quoting, whoever it was, substituted *slowly* for *hastily*. The
interest of the idea and the wit of the allusion are enhanced by such
complete neatness and brevity, necessary in my mind to proverbs,
which should be as clear-cut as gems; it adds immensely to their charm.
If you consider the force and the significance which are contained in
the concision of these words, how fertile, how serious, how wholesome
they are and how applicable to every situation in life, you will soon
agree that there is no other in the whole range of proverbs so worthy
of use; you will feel that they should be cut on every pillar and written
over every temple porch, inscribed in gold on the double doors of
princely halls, chased on episcopal rings, engraved on royal sceptres;
that they should recur on every monument everywhere and be spread
abroad and celebrated, so that such an important thing should be so
much under the public eye that no single mortal could avoid acting on
it, especially princes, and those to whom is committed the care of
peoples, if I might quote the words of Homer.[3] Among the common
run of men, if something is left undone out of folly or done wrong out
of rashness, the loss is less important and the damage sooner repaired,
but in the case of princes it sometimes only needs a moment of idleness
or a single hasty decision to raise untold storms, and bring about the

---

[1] II. I. i; LB. 397 B.   [2] Aristophanes, *Knights*, line 495.
[3] *Iliad*, II, line 25.

3

ruin of human affairs. On the other hand, if *Make haste slowly* is the rule, that is, a wise promptness together with moderation, tempered with both vigilance and gentleness, so that nothing is done rashly and then regretted, and nothing useful to the common weal omitted out of carelessness—I ask you, what could be more happy, firm and stable than such a realm? And indeed happiness like this far outflows the boundaries of empire, and is spread abroad throughout the most far-flung peoples of the world, as Hesiod says: 'A bad neighbour is a bane, a good one a mighty aid.'[1]

Indeed I think this proverb can be called *royal*, if any can, not only for the reason I have just given, but because the minds of princes seem to be inclined to just these two failings. For everything leads that way: fortune's favour, great possessions, ready enticements to pleasure, the power of gratifying every wish at once, the dangerous cheers of the flatterers, the reception always ready for whatever is said or done, smiles, applause, congratulations—it is no wonder, say I, if this sort of thing sends some people crazy. Especially if all these excuses for easy living have youth with them, and youth's constant companion, in-experience. But, on the other hand, it sometimes happens that the vigour of mind innate in princes, and a kind of lion-like ardour, increased by fortune and encouraged by success in great undertakings, roused by anger or ambition or some such passion, urged on by bloodthirsty counsels, leads them astray, and sweeps them and their whole kingdom over the precipice. Although, if one has to go to one extreme or other, it is much better for a king to be sluggish than over-hasty. Homer appears to have portrayed Agamemnon with a too great slackness and supineness of mind, the βραδέως part of the proverb, so that no high deed or show of spirit is recorded of him except that he flew into a rage over the removal of Chryseis, and stole Briseis from Achilles. To Achilles, on the other hand, he attributes undisciplined impulses, that is the σπεῦδε part; unless it is an example of both when he draws his sword in council to fall upon the king, and is persuaded by Pallas to limit his indignation to violent abuse.[2] But that in itself was an indica-tion of lack of mental control, to pour out such abuse and revilings in the full assembly of princes against the holder of the supreme power. Alexander the Great appears to have imitated Achilles, and certainly outshone him, when he was so possessed by the violence of his spirit as to draw his sword even on his friends. Sardanapalus was an imitator of Agamemnon, but only from a great distance. It would be easy to find countless examples of the sluggishness of the one or the ferocity of the other, but you will find very few who follow this proverb and

---

[1] Hesiod, *Works and Days*, 346.   [2] *Iliad*, 1, 200.

rightly combine promptness at the opportune moment with cautious deliberation; one example will do for these, that of Fabius Maximus, who was called Cunctator, and won for himself immortal fame when by his delaying tactics he restored to Rome the power which had been forfeited by the rash haste of the other generals.

And so it does not surprise me that this proverb was a favourite with two Roman emperors, and they by far the most worthy of praise, Octavius Augustus and Titus Vespasianus. Each of them had a notable greatness of mind, and at the same time an incredible gentleness and leniency, so that they attached the affection of all by their kindliness towards the people, but they were also equally successful in dealing promptly with the greatest matters, when the situation demanded a man. Octavius, as I said, was so heartily in favour of this saying (as Aulus Gellius recounts, *Attic Nights*, book x, chapter IX,[1] and Macrobius following him, *Saturnalia*, book IV,[2]) that not only he used it often in daily speech, but often quoted it in his letters, indicating by these two words that the matter in hand was to be treated with the speed of diligence and the slowness of deliberation. Gellius thinks this can be conveyed in Latin by one word, *Matura*. For *maturare* means to do nothing over-hastily, nor later than it should be done, but at the very time. Virgil uses it in this way when he says in the *Aeneid*, book I, *Maturate fugam*,[3] hasten your flight. This word is used by the authors to mean the same thing as *festinare*, to hasten, but in such a way that you do not anticipate the appointed time. So that you might call even precipitate action *festinata*, but not *maturata*. What Suetonius says in his life of Octavius agrees with this:[4] 'He thought that nothing became an experienced general less than haste and recklessness. And so he was constantly quoting that saying,

Σπεῦδε βραδέως, ἀσφαλὴς γάρ ἐστ' ἀμείνων ἢ θρασὺς
Στρατηγός.'

Thus far Suetonius: it is a line (*trochaicus tetrameter catalecticus*) taken from some poet, I imagine, to which the emperor added στρατηγός himself. The meaning is, 'Make haste slowly, for the man who manages a matter safely and with no mistakes is better than one who is rash and overconfident.' For things are more likely to turn out well if they are managed with foresight and slowly maturing plans, than if they are hastened on by rash counsels.

It is easy to see that this saying pleased Titus Vespasianus, from the evidence of ancient coinage. Aldus Manutius showed me a silver coin,

[1] Aulus Gellius, *Attic Nights*, x, xi.
[2] Macrobius, *Saturnalia*, VI, 8, 9.
[3] *Aeneid*, I, 136.
[4] *Life of Augustus*, xxv.

of old and obviously Roman workmanship, which he said had been given him by Peter Bembo, a young Venetian nobleman, who was foremost in scholarship and a great delver into ancient literature. It was stamped as follows: on one side there was the effigy of Titus Vespasianus with an inscription, on the other an anchor, with a dolphin wound round the middle of it as if round a pole. This means nothing else than the saying of Augustus Caesar, 'hasten slowly', or so the books on hieroglyphics tell us. That is the word for the enigmatic carvings which were so much used in early times, especially among the Egyptian soothsayers and priests, who thought it wrong to exhibit the mysteries of wisdom to the vulgar in open writing, as we do; but they expressed what they thought worthy to be known by various symbols, things or animals, so that not everyone could readily interpret them. But if anyone deeply studied the qualities of each object, and the special nature and power of each creature, he would at length, by comparing and guessing what they symbolised, understand the meaning of the riddle. So when the Egyptians want to signify their Osiris, whom they identify with the sun, they carve a sceptre and in it the likeness of an eye, thus indicating that he is God, and sublime in his royal power, seeing all things, just as the ancients called the sun the eye of Jove. Macrobius mentions this in his *Saturnalia*, book I.[1]

In the same way they represented the year as a serpent curled round with its tail in its mouth, indicating the recurrence in the year of the same times and seasons. So Servius recalls the name given to the year among the Greeks, ἐνιαυτός, and Virgil was thinking of this when he wrote, 'And the year goes round treading on its own footsteps.'[2] Although Horus the Egyptian, whose two books on these symbols have survived, says the carving of the snake represents not the year, but eternity (*aevum*), the year being symbolised by Isis or by the Phoenix. Plutarch comments on these things in his book on Osiris,[3] and Chaeremon among the Greeks, as witnessed by Suidas,[4] out of whose books I suspect those examples were taken which we have recently noticed. Among them there was this very picture of a circle enclosing an anchor, round which the dolphin is curled. The circle, according to the accepted meaning, signifies eternity, because it has no end. The anchor, because it delays, slows down and stops the ship, means slowness; the dolphin represents speed, because there is no creature swifter or more agile in its onrush. So by putting these meanings together you have the phrase *Always hasten slowly*.

[1] Macrobius, *Saturnalia*, I, 21, 120. [2] *Georgics*, II, 402.
[3] Plutarch, *de Osiride*, x, page 354.
[4] Suidas, *Lexicon* (Adler edition), part II, 52, 30.

This kind of writing (i.e. in symbols) not only has great dignity, but gives no little pleasure, if only one looks deeply, as I said, into the qualities of things, and this comes partly from the skilful contemplation of things and natural causes, and partly from knowledge of the liberal disciplines. For instance, a reader of Aristotle's book on Physics may rightly understand that an analogy, a similarity, exists between space, movement and time, for these three exist each in the other. Just as time has a close connection with motion, so motion is closely connected with space. What is a point in space is a moment in time, and an impulse in motion (for it may be allowable to speak thus of something which is a very small part of motion, and indivisible). There is no need to quibble about terms if the meaning is understood. Now if you consider extension in a straight line, you find two points, of which one is only the beginning, and the other only the end, that is, the point from which length starts and the point at which it stops. Similarly, if you define motion, you will find two impulses, one from which the motion arises and one in which it ceases. The relation between these is that the initial impulse is the beginning of that motion only, and the final one the end of it and nothing else. Motion is necessarily accompanied by time, and the rule of time is that if you examine its nature separately you will see two moments (if I may put it this way), one the beginning of that space of time and one its end. Again, if you take the same line and you consider it as the points in space, the impulses in motion and the moments in time which intervene between its beginning and its end, you will find that each of them has a dual nature: with regard to the beginning they are ends, with regard to the end, beginnings. When space comes to an end, there motion ends too, and time must also finish.

That space is finite where the beginning cannot be the same as the end, where the end is such that it cannot be identified with the beginning, which happens in all figures except the circle. For in this there is no point which can properly be called the beginning, none which is an end or can receive that name, no moment or impulse. Whence it follows that, where extension is not finite, motion and time cannot be finite either. And, again, where any point may be either the beginning or the end, there we must have infinity. By the same argument, where the same impulse may be either the beginning or end of motion, there we have infinity of motion, and where any moment may be either beginning or ending of time, we have infinity of time. But the infinity of time is eternity, corresponding to perpetual motion. Eternal motion requires eternal space. These cannot be found together, except in the sphere, or circle in space. Hence some philosophers have inferred that the world is eternal, because they understood the universe and the stellar system to be spherical, and its motion to be spherical also. For the proportions of the circle not only square with this idea of space but also fit the idea of motion, as Aristotle shows in his *Physics*, book IV. Anyone who learnt these and other similar things from the systems of the philosophers will easily see why the Egyptians should express eternity by means of the circle.

Now let us look for a moment at the meaning and nature of the dolphin. Writers say that this creature leaves all others far behind in its incredible speed and force of movement. Thus Oppianus in his *Nature of Fishes*, book II, compares dolphins to no bird but the eagle: 'Just as the eagle, with regal distinction, surpasses all other swift birds, the lion is unequalled among flesh-eating wild beasts and the fierce *dracones* among snakes, so does the dolphin take first place among the fishes living in the sea.'[1] He compares it with a dart:

For they fly through the wide seas like an arrow—

Then with the wind, or rather with the hurricane—

Sometimes it whirls through the deep like a tornado.

Pliny in his *History of the World*, book IX, chapter VIII,[2] following the opinion of Aristotle, reports much the same thing, that the dolphin is the nimblest of all animals, swifter than any creature not only in the sea, but among the birds, and faster than any dart. Its extraordinary speed can be judged from this, that though its mouth is set far apart from its snout, as it were in the middle of the belly, and this must necessarily greatly delay it in hunting down fish, since it must snatch at them in a twisted and curved-back position, nevertheless there is hardly any fish which can escape its swiftness. And the creature itself is perfectly aware of this gift of nature, and sometimes, as if on purpose to show off, races with ships in full sail. For the dolphin is particularly a lover of mankind, some say a lover of boys, and on account of that it is the enemy of the crocodile, the animal most hostile to man. And thus it is not afraid of man as if he were unfriendly, but comes to meet the ships, and plays and leaps about, racing with them and sometimes passing them at full sail. Indeed, it shows finely enough, as it hunts the mullet in the lake of Laterna, what swiftness it possesses and what powers of intelligence, and how well-disposed it is to man. What shall I say about its almost incredible energy of movement? When, driven by hunger, it has followed the fish into the depths of the sea, and has held its breath for a long time, it springs up to breathe again as if shot from a bow, and often leaps over the wind-filled sails of ships. What symbol is better suited to express the ardent and dauntless activity of

[1] Oppian, *Halieutica*, II, 540, 587.   [2] *Natural History*, IX, 20.

the mind, than the dolphin? To stand for slowness and delay, there was a fitting symbol in the *echeneis* (ship-delayer) fish which the Latins call *Remora*, but since this did not seem significant enough (for apart from the fact that it is a paltry little thing, there is not much else notable about it) the symbol of the anchor was preferred; when the voyage is dangerous because of too strong following winds, it is the anchor which holds back the violent onrush of the ship.

And so this saying, 'Make haste slowly', appears to originate in the mysteries of the most antique philosophy, and from thence to be taken up by the two most admirable of Roman emperors, used by one as a maxim and by the other as a badge, and well befitting the mind and character of both. Now it has come down to Aldus Manutius of Rome, as the third heir in succession.

And not without the will and power of God.[1]

For his trade-mark, the same which pleased Titus Vespasianus once, is now not only famous but beloved wherever Good Letters are known or cherished.[2] Indeed I should not think this symbol was more illustrious when it was stamped on the imperial coinage and passing from hand to hand, than now, when it is sent out beyond the bounds of Christendom, on all kinds of books in both languages, recognised, owned and praised by all to whom liberal studies are holy; especially by those who are weary of that old, crass, barbarous doctrine and aspire to true and antique learning. This man seems born to restore it, and shaped for that destiny by the Fates themselves; all his desires are turned to one thing, all his tireless efforts are spent on it, no labour is too great, if only literature in all its glory may be restored pure and unsullied to honest minds. How much he has already succeeded in this, even, I may say, in the teeth of ill-luck, the thing itself clearly shows. If only some divinity favourable to good letters would look kindly on our Aldus's aims, noble and beautiful as they are! and if the auspices were favourable, I can promise one thing to the studious, and it would all happen in a very few years: they would possess all the works of good authors in four languages, Latin, Greek, Hebrew, and Chaldean,[3] on every kind of subject, complete and with emendations, and this would be due to this one man alone. There would be nothing wanting in the whole field of literature. As soon as this happens, it will become quite clear how many good MSS are hidden away, either pushed out of sight

[1] Imitated from Virgil, *Aeneid*, VI, 368.
[2] It is pointed out to me by my son, Mr J. F. C. Phillips, that the Aldine trade-mark reverses the emblem on the coin of Titus.
[3] The term 'Chaldean' was used for 'Aramaic' by Jerome and succeeding scholars.

by carelessness, or kept secret owing to the ambition of some people who have only one thing at heart—to seem to have the monopoly of wisdom. Then at last it will be known, how enormous are the errors scattered over the works of even thouse authors who are now thought to be textually correct. Anyone who wishes to have an illustration of this from experience, might take the edition of Pliny's *Letters* which is just coming out at the Aldine Press, and compare it with the versions already on the market; and what he sees there, he should expect to find in other authors. It is indeed a Herculean task, and worthy of a kingly spirit, to restore to the world so divine a thing, out of such complete ruin; to investigate what lay hidden, to bring to light what was concealed, to call to life what had perished, to fill up gaps and emend a text corrupted in so many ways, especially by the fault of those common printers to whom the gain of one gold piece is worth more than the whole of literature put together.

Consider as well that, however, one may sing the praises of those who by their virtue either defend or increase the glory of their country, their actions only affect worldly prosperity, and within narrow limits. But the man who sets fallen learning on its feet (and this is almost more difficult than to originate it in the first place) is building up a sacred and immortal thing, and serving not one province alone but all peoples and all generations. Once this was the task of princes, and it was the greatest glory of Ptolemy. But his library was contained between the narrow walls of its own house, and Aldus is building up a library which has no other limits than the world itself.

I do not think that by this little digression I have wandered far from the subject, because students will have more interest and pleasure in these symbols when they understand that they are found in such important authors, and when they fully comprehend what they mean; and also when they remember what good things are promised by the dolphin, if only God will prosper the valiant efforts that are being made.

I will leave this side track and go back to the main issue,[1] when I have aired my grievance about some printers who do a real disservice to literature. The grievance is not a new one, but it was never felt with more justice than when I was preparing this edition—the fourth, I think. It was in 1525. The city of Venice, so famous on many counts, is especially celebrated owing to the Aldine Press, and so whatever in the way of books is distributed from there to other countries finds a market for the sake of its place of origin alone. But this inducement is so misused by rascally printers, that from no other country do we get publications so shamelessly incorrect, and those not just of anybody's works,

[1] Passage added in 1526.

but of the greatest, Aristotle, for instance, and Cicero and Quintilian, to say nothing of the Holy Scriptures. The law sees to it that no one may make shoes or boxes without the approbation of the masters' guild, and yet authors of this stature, on whose works even religion depends, are handed out to the public by people so illiterate that they cannot even read, or so lazy that they don't trouble to go over what has been printed, or so mean that they would rather let a good book get choked up with six thousand mistakes than spend a few coins on paying someone to supervise the proof-reading.

And the ones who make the most marvellous promises on the title-page are those who make the most impudent hash of everything. If cloth has been sold as scarlet-dyed and no addition of cochineal is found in it, a fine is imposed by the authority of the law, in fact a severe punishment may be applied to anyone who cheats in this sort of merchandise. And if a man imposes books like these on so many thousand readers, he is free to enjoy his profits or rather his robbery? Formerly the same scrupulousness was applied to the copying of manuscripts as is now applied to the notary-public bound by an oath, and indeed with greater reason; and the present astonishing confusion simply results from the fact that the people employed for such a sacred trust tended to be obscure and inexperienced monks, nay, even women, employed without selection. But how small is the harm done by a careless and ignorant scribe, when you compare that done by a printer? Here the laws are nodding. One incurs a punishment for selling cloth dyed in Britain as cloth dyed in Venice, but one can enjoy the fruits of one's insolence if one sells torture and mental colic instead of good authors. You may say, it is not for the seller to be responsible to the buyer for every fault. Certainly he should, if the title-page promises care and exactitude and the book is full of errors. And there are errors which are not obvious at once even to the learned. Nowadays the innumerable crowd of printers causes confusion everywhere, especially in Germany. Not everyone may have leave to be a baker, but printing is a trade open to any mortal man. There are things it would not be safe to paint or to speak, but one is free to print anything. To what corner of the world do they not fly, these swarms of new books? It may be that one here and there contributes something worth knowing, but the very multitude of them is hurtful to scholarship, because it creates a glut, and even in good things satiety is most harmful; and there is another thing too— they act as enticing baits, luring the minds of men (flighty and curious of anything new) away from the study of the old authors, which nothing can excel, even though I do not deny that the new-fangled writers may discover some things which escaped the old. Someone may emerge who, on account of a single word, will teach something that was hidden to Aristotle, but I think no one will arise to propound the whole of Philosophy more perfectly than he. So in the study of Holy Scripture, someone may detects points which escaped the notice of Chrysostom or Jerome; but I do not think there will be anyone who will accomplish what they did over the whole field. Now these are almost out of date, and we spend our time on the rubbish written by all and sundry, and in the meantime the noble old systems of thought are lying neglected with the authors who expounded them, and ruin threatens the authority of senate, council, school, legal expert or theologian. If things go on as they have begun, the result will be that supreme power will be concentrated in the hands of a few, and we shall have as barbaric a tyranny among us as there is among the Turks. Everything will give way to the appetites of one man or of a few, and there will not remain the slightest vestige of civilised society, but all will be under the rule of military force. All noble disciplines will wither away, one law alone will operate, 'Thus saith the dictator', *sic vult* ὁ κοσμοκράτωρ. The heads of the Church will either have no influence at all, or whatever they may have in the way of wealth or dignity will go to serve those who settle everything, not by judgement, but by a nod this way or that.

How much better human interest would be served, if somehow the different elements of society could be made so to control and balance each other, as to achieve an eternal truce; thus each part of the body politic would retain its rightful authority, the people would be given their due, the councillors and magistrates would be paid the respect proper to their learning, to law and to justice; the bishops and priests would receive the honour due to them. Nor would the monks be denied what is due to them. The harmonious discord of all these, this variety tending to one and the same end, would serve the commonwealth far better than the present state of affairs, when each tries to grab everything for himself. Even a family cannot hold together, unless the husband hands over part of the administration to the wife, and unless a difference is made between children and servants, and servants themselves are treated not like beasts of burden but like men; and, finally, unless distinctions are made between one servant and another, so that those who give of their best are treated with greater indulgence, and may expect to have their freedom as a reward for good service.

Someone will say at this point, 'Hold on, crystal-gazer! What has all this to do with printers?' The fact is that no small part of the trouble comes from these fellows' unbridled licence. They fill the world with books, not just trifling things (such as I write, perhaps), but stupid, ignorant, slanderous, scandalous, raving, irreligious and seditious books, and the number of them is such that even the valuable publications lose their value. Some are rushed out without titles or, worse still, with fictitious ones. When those responsible for them are caught, they say, 'Give me enough to feed my family and I will stop printing pamphlets like these.' The thief, the impostor and the pimp might answer with less effrontery, 'Give me something to live on, and I will give up these methods'; except that it is a less serious offence to take other people's goods secretly, than to rob them in the daylight of their good fame, and less vicious to use one's own body or other people's for gain, than to attack the life of another, and what is dearer than life, his reputation.

But enough of complaining. Suppose we point out a remedy. This evil can be mitigated, if princes and magistrates will make it their own concern to expel (as far as possible) those idlers who are instrumental in provoking profiteering wars between us; next, if the really worthless, who are not restrained by reason or shame, find that the law has a big stick ready for them, unless they mend their ways; and then if those who strive to achieve what is in the public interest, but have not the means, are helped by grants from the princes, or from the bishops and abbots, or from the public funds. (It may be too much to expect any such thing from the merchant class, who have mostly dedicated themselves to the worship of Mammon.) These people promise themselves that their name will survive to posterity, because an altar or a sepulchre has been set up, or a picture hung or a statue erected—how much more lasting fame they would secure for themselves by this method! Here is one example out of many. There is hardly any author to equal St John Chrysostom as a writer on the Scriptures, or on matters relating to the functions of the preacher. And he wrote several books, of which we possess the greater part, as far as I know, but these are full of errors and some insertions have been made which have nothing to do with Chrysostom. What light would be thrown on sacred studies, if we had so great a doctor in Greek, complete and with all the emendations, or if we had him speaking Latin as he speaks Greek!

This is not the place to recall the ways in which great men spend their money, or how much of it goes on dice, lechery, drinking, unnecessary journeys, pomps, wars for gain, flatterers, jesters, players; only let some part of the wealth which is lost in shameful ways fall to benefiting the public, or increasing the owner's glory, or both. When Aldus took up this work, what scholar did not commend him? Which of them did not contribute something to help him, unequal as he was to such a task? How often old MSS have come, sent unasked for by

Hungarians and Poles, accompanied by a gift of money, so that he might give them to the world with proper attention? What Aldus was striving to do among the Italians—for he himself has met his end, though his firm still enjoys the credit of a beloved name—John Froben is trying to achieve on this side of the Alps with no less energy than Aldus, and not without success, although there is no denying that he makes less money by it. If you ask why, there may be many causes but I think this is one, that there is not the same openness of mind among us as among the Italians, at any rate in the matter of literature. And I am not afraid to say what I know by experience. At the time when I, a Dutchman, was supervising the publication of my book of proverbs in Italy, every one of the scholars who were there offered me, without being asked, copies of authors which had never been printed, and which they thought I might be able to use. Aldus himself kept nothing back among his treasures. It was the same with John Lascaris, Baptista Egnatius, Marcus Musurus, Frater Urbanus.[1] I experienced the kindness of some whom I did not know either by sight or by name. I brought nothing with me to Venice but the raw material of a future work, as yet confused and undigested, and culled only from well-known authors. It was great audacity on my part that set us both on, myself to write and Aldus to print. We broke the back of the work in nine months, more or less, and meanwhile I had had an encounter with a trouble I had not met before, the stone. Imagine how much of value I should have missed, if the scholars had not furnished me with manuscripts. Among these were the works of Plato in Greek, Plutarch's *Lives* and his *Moralia*, which began publication just as my work was ending; the *Deipnosophistai* of Atheneus, Aphthonius, Hermogenes with the commentary, the *Rhetoric* of Aristotle with the notes of Gregory Nazianzen; Aristides together with the notes, the little commentaries on Hesiod and Theocritus, the collection of proverbs which goes under the name of Plutarch, and the other called after Apostolius, which was lent me by Jerome Aleander. There were other less important things, which have either escaped my memory or need not be mentioned here. None of these had hitherto been printed.

Now listen to the fair dealing of a northern friend of mine, one of my closest in fact, and one who is still among the number, since we must learn to understand our friends' character and not to hate it. When I was preparing the Venetian edition, I happened to notice among his books a Suidas with proverbs written in the margins. The work was large, and numerous volumes had to be looked through. Wishing to save myself this bit of work, I asked him to lend me the volume just for

[1] See Renaudet, *Erasme et l'Italie* (1954), p. 84.

a few hours, long enough for my boy to copy down the notes in my book. Again and again I asked, to meet with a refusal. When no entreaty prevailed and I could not persuade him, I asked him if he was thinking of editing a book of proverbs himself, in which case I would gladly hand over the work to someone who could do it better. He swore that he had no such idea. Then what makes you act so, said I? At last, as if it were dragged out of him by torture, he admitted the reason: up to now learned men had enjoyed the admiration of the public for possessing such things as these, and now they were becoming public property. *Hinc illae lachrymae.*[1] There are old MSS lying in the colleges and monastic houses of Germany, France and England, but (with the exception of a few places) are the owners going to reveal them of their own accord? Far from it. Even when asked they will conceal them, or deny that they have them, or let them out on hire at exorbitant prices, ten times the worth of the book. The best cared-for MSS are damaged in the end by decay or insects, or stolen. Great men are so far from giving support to the world of learning, that they think no money more plainly thrown away than what is spent on such purposes; nothing satisfies them but what brings in a good interest. If the northern princes were to favour good learning as honestly as the Italians, the serpents of Froben would not be so far from the riches of Aldus's dolphins. Aldus, making haste slowly, gained both riches and fame, and deserved both; Froben, holding his staff erect, looking to nothing but usefulness to the public, not losing the simplicity of the dove while he expresses the wisdom of the serpent (better, it is true, in his trade-mark than in his actions)—Froben has amassed less money than fame.

But enough of digressions.

We must now return to the discussion of the proverb. It has a three-fold use: first, when we are giving a warning that it would be better to wait a little before tackling a matter; when a decision has been reached, then swift action can be taken, the anchor representing the period of deliberation and the dolphin speed in completion.

Here comes in that remark of Sallust's: 'before you begin, take counsel, act betimes.' Aristotle quotes the saying in his *Moralia*, book VI, as a popular one: 'they say that things over which you have deliberated should be done quickly, but the consultation should be slow.'[2] Laertius[3] says that the author of this was Bias, who used to give this advice: 'One should be slow in taking up a matter but, once taken up, it should be steadfastly persevered with'; and there is a playwright, I think it is Publianus, who says much to the purpose, 'Take a long

---

[1] Horace, *Epistles*, I, xix, 41; Terence, *Andria*, 126.
[2] Aristotle, *Moralia*, VI, 2.   [3] Laertius, I, 87 (chapter 5).

time to prepare for war, so as to conquer all the sooner.' And again: 'To think out what is useful, the safest thing is delay.' Then there is the proverb, *sleep on it*. As well as Sophocles in *Oedipus Rex*:[1] 'Unsafe is the prudence which acts with haste.' Add to these the words of Plato which we have already quoted, 'He who hurries too much at the beginning comes later to the end.' A little different, but referring to the same thing, is the remark of Quintilian: 'That precocious kind of intelligence comes not easily to maturity.'[2] And, as the common people say, children wise before their time turn out stupid in old age. Actius seems to approve of this when he says (in Gellius) that young minds should have the sharpness of green apples; both ripen in the end. Ripening brings sweetness in its own good time—the rest go bad too early.

Another way of applying this saying is when we suggest that the passions of the mind should be reined in by reason. So Plato divides the mind of man into three parts, reason, anger, desire, and he thinks the whole of philosophy rests in this, that the affections should obey reason just as if it were their king, and so he places the seat of reason in the brain, its citadel.[3]

The Peripateticians, whose standard-bearer is Aristotle, think that the affections, those impulses of the spirit, are goads which excite us to virtue, but the Stoics protest, particularly Seneca in the books he wrote for Nero on Anger.[4] For they think that these passions, far from conducing to virtue, hinder it; although even they do not deny that in the mind of their imaginary wise man there remain primitive impulses, which anticipate reason, and which you can never root out; but they are at once rejected by reason, lest assent should follow. This is what Homer means in the first book of the *Iliad*, when he shows Pallas standing behind Achilles, and restraining the hand already moving to his sword.[5] Thus you may call these violent impulses the dolphin, and the anchor is controlling wisdom.

Seneca writes that delay is useful only in anger. But indeed, whenever we have violent desires or hates, delay is salvation. Plutarch in his book on the Apophthegms of the Romans[6] tells how Athenodorus the philosopher, when he begged Octavius Augustus to let him go back to his home on account of old age, warned the emperor never to do or say anything in anger, until he had said to himself the twenty-four letters of the Greek alphabet. When Augustus heard this, he replied that he would need the philosopher to teach him the art of keeping

---

[1] *Oedipus Rex*, 617.   [2] Quintilian, *Institutes of Oratory*, I, 3.
[3] *Republic*, IV, 434 D–441 C; *Timaeus*, 44 D.   [4] Seneca, *De Ira*, I, x.
[5] *Iliad*, I, 200.   [6] Plutarch, *Sayings of the Romans*, 207, 7.

silent, and so he detained him for yet another year. Terence has the same thing in mind: *take care it isn't too hot.*[1] Some natures need the spur, others the rein. And so the ancients rightly curled the dolphin round the anchor, because one must be tempered by the other, and both united, so as to produce the kind of balanced character which Plato imagined resulting from a fusion of Music and Gymnastics, if both were practised.[2]

The third use of the saying is to point out that precipitate action should be avoided in everything, that hastiness is a fault to which some natures are especially prone, and to them any delay at all seems protracted. This kind of hurry has companions: error and repentance, according to that line celebrated among the Greeks,

> Hasty action is the cause of many ills.

Such people should have the noble maxim of Cato dinned into their ears, 'It is done soon enough if it is done well enough', which St Jerome mentions when writing to Pammachius in these words:[3] 'That word of Cato's is well known, *sat cito, si sat bene*, which we used to laugh at as boys, when it was quoted by a finished orator in a Preface. I think you remember our shared mistake, when the whole Athenaeum rang with the voices of the Scholastics saying, *Sat cito, si sat bene.*' So far Jerome. It will then fit the people who wish for fame in a hurry, and would rather have it ready-made and showy, than solid and lasting. Too early growths soon wither. Slow growing means durability. Horace says:

> From day to day like some tall tree
> Marcellus' fame grows silently.[4]

and Pindar in the *Nemean Odes*, Hymn VIII,[5]

> But virtue grows,
> Like a tree springing in the sylvan dew;
> Where men are wise and good it rises high
> To the pure air of heaven.

In short, those who go wrong out of heedlessness or ungovernable impulse, should call to mind the maxim of Octavius Caesar, the chosen symbol of Titus Vespasianus in old days, and of Aldus today, and remember the dolphin and the anchor.

---

[1] *Eunuchus*, 2, 3, 89. [2] Plato, *Republic*, III.
[3] Jerome, *Lettres*, ed. Labourt (Paris, 1953), III, lxvi, 9.
[4] *Odes*, I, xii, 45–6, trans. H. B. Mayor.
[5] Pindar, *Nemean Odes*, VIII, 40.

(b) Herculei labores[1]

Ἡράκλειοι πόνοι, i.e. the labours of Hercules, are taken in two ways. On the one hand they mean something great and manifold, which needs the strength of a Hercules, as Catullus employed the phrase: 'But to look for you would be a labour of Hercules.'[2] And Propertius: 'Then, when you have borne what legend calls the labours of Hercules',[3] or in another place: 'Not a Herculean task.' Cicero, in *De Finibus*, book II, says: 'But when you deserved praise from all the world, when you were bringing wealth and security to the needy, even to endure the toils of Hercules—for our ancestors gave the sad title of toil (*aerumna*) to those labours which could not be avoided, even in the case of a God—this would I demand from you', etc.[4]

On the other hand, those are said to be 'labours of Hercules' which are of a kind to bring the greatest advantage to others, and little or no profit to the doer, except a little fame, and a lot of envy. This is said to happen by some working of destiny, when a person is born in the fourth quarter of the moon (as has been said elsewhere).[5] Homer, in the manner of poets, puts the cause down to the goddess Ate, and to Juno, since she was an enemy of Hercules, the concubine's son, and plunged him into all these perils. And so the labours of Hercules are sung and enumerated by the poets; by far the most difficult and important being the Lernaean Hydra, a stubborn, horrible monster, and almost unconquerable even to him who had succeeded in everything. By this symbol the ancients wished to express Envy, as Horace indicates in his Epistles, when he says:

> He who crushed the fearsome Hydra,
> And subjected a notorious monster by his destined labour,
> Learnt that envy remained to be vanquished at the end of all.[6]

This most loathsome of pests has always had the habit of accompanying the fairest deeds, and following the highest virtue as a body is followed by its shadow; the phrase of Josephus in his Conquest of Judaea would fit in well here: 'There is no way of avoiding envy over deeds well done.'[7] For whoever escaped the shadow of envy, unless he had also fled from the light of virtue? These two stick together, and the best thing of all has always had as its companion the worst thing of all. It was not without reason, apparently, that Pindar wrote: 'It is the misery of envy that we get in exchange for glorious deeds.'[8]

[1] III. I. i; LB. 707 D.
[2] Catullus, *Odes*, LV, 13.
[3] Propertius, *Elegies*, II, xxiii.
[4] Cicero, *De Finibus*, II, 118.
[5] I. I. lxxvii.
[6] Horace, *Epistles*, II, i, 10–11.
[7] Josephus, *Conquest of Judaea*, I, 208.
[8] Pindar, *Pythian Odes*, VII, 19.

It was not without elegance that the old writers assigned the symbol of the Serpent to envy, primarily a sort of marsh-disease, to which those people are most subject (so say the investigators into natural causes) who are humble and abject in mind, and they are moreover those whose blood runs rather coldly. So Naso:

> Deep in the lowest vales lurks Envy's house,
> From sunshine hid, unswept by any wind,
> Gloomy, pervaded with a sluggish chill,
> Empty of fire, for ever filled with night.[1]

The creature is not one monstrosity only, but armed with a hundred heads, and if one head is struck off two more grow in its place. That is the nature of envy: if you struggle with it, you make it angrier and angrier; if you try to suppress it by the brilliance of your virtue it springs up all the more fiercely and swells out against you. If you cut it down in one place it grows higher in another. It cannot be stamped out gradually, and is hardly ever quite abolished. That is the victory of very few, and even Hercules himself barely achieved it. For though malice, like fire, leaps upward, there is a point of perfection and illustrious fame which envy cannot reach. Horace prided himself on having reached it when he says: 'Greater than envy', and again, 'And already I am less gnawed by the envious tooth.'[2]

The people who carp and slander in secret against those who are trying with the noblest efforts to do good to the world, are just spitting poison, a deadly poison at that. For to the noble and lofty mind that good fame which is being attacked is dearer and more strongly clung to than life itself. What the pagan world sought to convey by the rid- dling figure of Hercules is hinted at in Jewish history by the figure of Joseph. What Lerna[3] was to one, fraternal envy is to the other. Philo interprets it in this fashion in his book *Politikos Bios*.[4] To him Joseph represents those who hold the rudder of the ship of state. He argues that this is so, because, when Joseph was still only a shepherd, his actions, right as they were, gained him his father's favour and at the same time awoke the jealousy of his brothers. What else is it to administer a state but to be a shepherd? Hence Homer too (and Philo quotes him) calls the king the shepherd of his people; seeing that nobody gets less thanks for their benefaction than those who have served the common people. But what Hercules achieved with Greek fire, Joseph did by means of the greatness of his benefactions and the mercy of God: he

---

[1] Ovid, *Metamorphoses*, II, 760.
[2] Horace, *Odes*, II, xx; IV, iii. [3] I. III. xxvii.
[4] Philo, βίος πολιτικὸς ὅπερ ἔστι περὶ Ἰωσήφ, I, 2.

overcame envy, and saw as suppliants before him the very people who had been his jealous rivals, and those who had plotted against his life now owed their own to him. Just so, princes who have the administration of public affairs should be of this mind and follow this example, by looking only to the general good, and not using their office for themselves as if they were running a private concern. Nor should they try to involve people with the snares of the law when they think some money can be extracted that way, but seek to do good to all men, and wage a continuous war with the monsters (i.e. vice) with a clear conscience as the sufficient reward of their good deeds. But if your merit is rewarded by evil report, if secret envy hisses at you, if the Lernaean Hydra shoots poison from its three hundred heads, then it will be proof of a lofty and undaunted mind to strive none the less for immortal fame, to pursue the advantage of others at the greatest expense to oneself, and to bring forth the finest fruits of virtue by being of the greatest service to the greatest number, and thus to imitate the immortal power as far as mortal may. We can in no way pay God back by thanks or services; he, being goodness itself, shines like the sun on the just and the unjust, the thankful and the unthankful, with this one purpose, that as many as possible may share in him.

It is true that, as God cannot be rewarded for his beneficence, so he is also above the reach of ingratitude. In the case of mortals, it often happens that for all their good deeds they reap the greatest possible envy and trouble. If any human labours ever deserved to be called Herculean, it is certainly the work of those who are striving to restore the great works of ancient literature—of true literature. While, in fact, they condemn themselves to immense toil, owing to the incredible difficulty of the task, they arouse among the vulgar the greatest envy and ill-will. Great attempts always have been subject to this, and especially an attempt at anything new, not only amongst the ignorant but even with the learned. We are never more ungrateful, more jealous or more carping, or less frank, than when we are considering the work of these people, the very ones, to my mind, who can never be thanked enough. The unlearned brush them aside, the half-learned scoff, and as for the learned (with a few exceptions, and they are amongst the highest, but still they are few) some are jealous and some carp and criticise, leaving aside so much that is well said, but if the author has made a mistake once, or twice (and who never made a mistake?) that alone they point at, that alone they remember. There you are—this is the magnificent reward you are to earn with all your long vigils, your labour, your hardships. Sacrifice all the ordinary pleasures of human life, neglect your own affairs, be unsparing of your looks, your sleep, your health. Accept cheerfully the damage to your eyesight, bring on premature old age, shrug off the detriment to your own life, with no result but this: to arouse universal hatred, the deepest jealousy, and carry away a few snores as the reward of all your toil.

I should like to know who would not be frightened off by these things from engaging in such work, unless he be a real Hercules in mind, able to do and suffer anything for the sake of serving others? This thought disquiets me, to tell the truth, and in the midst of the labours I am undergoing for this book a certain sense of weariness comes over me, when I think of the great men of our time whose fame ill corresponds with their merits, and who are despised and scorned almost as soon as they are dead, by those who, as we say, couldn't hold a candle to them;[1] how ungratefully the half-learned carp at them, and how few even of the learned give them frank and generous praise. A finds an omission, B disagrees with something, C attacks the author's private life, D praises him so grudgingly that abuse would be preferable. Moreover, no one judges more unjustly than the half-learned, who measure other people's learning by their own, and think anything is to be found fault with that they have not learnt themselves; or else those scholars who have not yet tried this kind of work. These, as the Greek proverb says, judge the Achaelans from the ramparts, and are like people idly standing on the shore and watching the skill and hazards of the man who is sailing the boat. If they had a try themselves, they would read the efforts of others with less squeamishness and more indulgence. When I see what happens to the princes, nay the heroes of the world of letters, what can I expect to happen to me, knowing full well as I do that all my things are mediocre, or rather non-existent, in comparison with theirs, especially in this sort of work, which entails far more labour than can be easily imagined by anyone who has not experienced it? And then for many reasons it is easy to make mistakes in work like this, and easiest of all for anyone to notice what is left out.

For these reasons I think it is not out of place here, to digress a little further on these matters than the subject itself seems to suggest, not because I want to make a display or show off my brains and industry, but to make the reader a little more inclined to be just to me. Certainly whoever considers what immense toil and what infinite difficulties this collection of adages (however imperfect) has meant to me, will be much less impatient. The first thing you have to reckon is the great antiquity of the subject-matter itself, dating not from Evander, or from the

---

[1] *Qui illis matellam porrigant*, 'who couldn't hold out a chamber-pot to them', I. v. xciv.

Aborigines,[1] but from Κανναϰος,[2] as the Greeks say, from the age of Saturn or whatever may be older than that. And so some of them are diametrically removed, as they say,[3] from the customs of our own times. To find out the meaning of an adage you must either guess (and you will need a Delian swimmer[4] for that), or search out the interpretation in ancient authors. And in which authors? Not in this one or that one, or a certain few, as happens in other subjects. For instance, if one intends to write about the art of oratory, there are certain suitable authors, and not many at that, which can be taken as a guide. But in this work one was dealing with all and sundry, whether old or new, bad or good, in each of the ancient languages, on every kind of subject, in fact with every kind of writing, and it was necessary not only to read them but to examine and investigate with detailed thoroughness. For proverbs are like little gems, so small that they often escape the searcher's eye unless you look very carefully. They are not ready to hand but lie hidden, and it is a matter of digging them out rather than collecting them. Who can fully realise how much labour is involved in searching the whole world over, as it were,[5] for such tiny things? A lifetime would hardly be enough to explore and examine (in both languages) so many Poets, Grammarians, Orators, Dialecticians, Sophists, Historians, Mathematicians, Philosophers, Theologians (simply going over their names would weary a man out), and not once only but over and over again, as the subject requires it, one must push up the stone of Sisyphus. No one, I think, would deny that this is a huge task. And yet what proportion of our work is it? There remains something almost larger—the great bulk of commentaries; and the indolence and the lethargy of some commentators and the ignorance of others (for they are all to be looked at, as one may pick gold out of dung) added no little burden to our labours.

And now, shall I mention another thing—the bad state of the books themselves, whether Latin or Greek MSS, so corrupt that when you want to quote a passage you hardly ever find one which does not show an obvious error, or make one suspect a hidden one? Here is another labour, to examine and correct the different MSS . . . and a great many of them, so as to detect one which has a better reading, or by collating a number of them to make a guess at the true and authentic version. This must be done, if not all the time, at least whenever you quote, and quotations occur everywhere. Add to all these things this consideration, not unimportant to my mind, that the works of the ancients, the

---

[1] Evander, the Arcadian king in *Aeneid*, VIII; the Aborigines, early inhabitants of Italy.   [2] I cannot explain this allusion.
[3] I. II. lxiii.   [4] An experienced swimmer, I. VI. xxix.   [5] I. IV. xv.

sources from which the proverbs are drawn, are to a large extent
missing. Thus Greek Comedy has utterly perished, with the sole exception of Aristophanes. Latin Tragedy likewise, except for Seneca. Perhaps even this could be borne, if we possessed the works of those who
collected the proverbs from these sources and commented on them.
Among these were Aristotle, Chrysippus, Clearchus, Didymus,
Tarrhaeus, and some others of whom not the tiniest fragment has come
down to us. Some later ones we have retained, but they are lazy, un-
discriminating, scrimping and curtailed, such as Zenobius, Diogenianus, and Suidas; and I can hardly make up my mind whether we
ought to be angry with these for the way in which they have handed
down to us such bare tatters of such excellent and copious authors, or
grateful to them because it is through their care that a few remnants of
antiquity are left to us—unless one considers that it was actually owing
to the existence of their summaries of the works that the works themselves were neglected and perished. In this way some Latin writers
attribute the loss of Livy to Florus, of Pompeius Trogus to Justinus,
of the laws of the Caesars to Justinian, of Theology to the author of the
'Sentences', as they are called, and all this not without cause, in my
opinion. There is so little agreement between these authorities that they
very often write things which cancel each other out, and the additional
burden is laid on one of consulting different commentators on the same
thing, and—over and over again—of examining, comparing, ponder-
ing, and judging.

Now consider this with me; in other books there is often room for
the mind to operate, there is the pleasure of discovery or creation, there
is the possibility at any time, in any place, of completing a part of the
work by sheer mental activity, and of hastening on your project by the
quickness of your brain; here you are fettered to the treadmill, you
cannot budge an inch, as they say, from your texts. You waste your
eyesight on decaying volumes covered with mould, torn and mangled,
eaten into everywhere by worms and beetles, and often almost illegible;
in short, they are so bad that anyone who spends long over them may
easily bring on himself decay and premature old age; they may even
contain extraneous matter. How important that is I need hardly say—
those who make trial of it find that out at once. Not to speak of the
fact that if there is any pleasure in this kind of commentary it is for the
reader alone, and nothing belongs to the writer except that hateful and
monotonous business of collecting, scraping together, explaining,
translating. And yet pleasure is the one thing, as Aristotle truly said,
which makes it possible for us to persevere long in a piece of work.
Elsewhere one is allowed a little mental play, a little sporting with the

flowers of eloquence. There are pleasant digressions, in which you can dawdle when you are weary, and refresh your mind. In literature as in every other activity, variety keeps off tediousness and boredom. But in this work I have to do not with twice-cooked cabbage, as the Greek proverb says; I must look up the same things three thousand times—what the proverb means, what its origin was and how it should be used —so that this would be the place above all others for the well-worn Greek proverb about the pestle. Finally, part of the pleasure of writing is to treat subjects which treatment makes to shine, and which lend brilliance and eloquence to the author. But here, the matter treated is such that it only looks brilliant when it is being used, not when it is being talked about; proverbs only show their real beauty when they are seen inserted like jewels into the right place in a speech. Separate, they are lifeless, and seem petty, flimsy little things. Another thing is that in other kinds of writing the whole work is taken into account, and the reader makes an effort as well as the writer; but this kind is dipped into here and there—the reader turns his whole attention on to one proverb, some idly, it may be, some with eagerness, no doubt, others with scorn. Think what a difficult situation I am in, when I have to manage in each proverb to occupy the idle, satisfy the eager and content the critical! Added to this is the labour of translating all the Greek, which everyone agrees to be a most difficult business—except the people who have never tried turning good Greek into good Latin. Think of the variety of authors, each to be rendered in his own style; of the different kinds of poem, among the immense mass used in this book (I think it cannot be less than ten thousand); as if anyone who only translated so many poems into Latin, in the few months we spent on this edition, and into Latin verse too, could be continually accused of idleness. What other people may think of this I don't know. For my part, just knowing where you are in such an immense number of adages, simply remembering what you said where, and not getting lost in the mass of facts, seems an achievement in itself. And, when anyone is dealing with so many difficulties that they can hardly be numbered, is it any wonder if he makes a slip sometimes in his great hurry? Why I had to hurry so much is a point I shall soon explain.

If Horace says about subjects which have not these problems 'Excuse those errors which come from negligence or which human nature is not proof against',[1] and thinks that in a long piece of work it is not surprising that sleep overtakes one, if Homer nods now and then without rousing indignation,[2] why should we fly into a rage if a few mistakes creep into a work like this, in which, as well as all the ordinary

---

[1] Horace, *Ars Poetica*, 352–3.   [2] *Ibid.* 359.

reasons for going astray, there is the additional difficulty that one cannot do the work by oneself, and must have guides who continually lead one wrong? Not to speak of the errors in the MSS, which cause trouble to the best scholars, not to mention the weariness which saps the vigour of the brain, or the hotch-potch of varied topics which call the mind hither and thither in so many directions that it hardly ever seems to be present to itself.

It remains to say a few words in reply to those who, I believe, would wish to find a little more care and industry in this collection of mine. I know there are people who measure a book not by its scholarship but by its size, and only think it is complete when nothing can be added and much is superfluous; nothing is enough for them without over-expenditure of effort, only repeating things to the point of satiety seems to them being full enough. One of these will say that I might have treated some parts more fully and copiously. Somebody comes across a passage in his reading which may be a proverb, or may not be a proverb but looks like one to him, and he will immediately throw it up at us that we have missed it. I wonder who would dare, who would have the arrogance to make a statement like that. Who would be so unjust as to expect nothing to be left out in a work of this sort? To expect, in fact, that one should have read everything, made notes on everything, prepared all the ground, and that in such an immense flood of facts the right thing should immediately come to mind in the right place? How unmanageable that diligence would be, if one were to hunt out everything that could apply in every way to the development of a proverb! Take 'a Sardonic smile', for instance. What end or limit would there be to the volumes needed to explain it, if I were to look up in all the Geographers the details about this island, its situation, the history of its people, and go into it from top to toe, as they say, and then deal with the kind of grass which is mentioned, its appearance and its power, scraping together whatever can be found in medical books about it; how it produces a smile, why that smile should be found on the faces of the dying, according to all the writings of the doctors, and what can be found in the works of all the historians about the people to whom that smile was a familiar thing? Then why such a smile ill befits a good man; and what the moral philosophers and the poets have said about this smile in praise or censure—putting all this together into a heap? And supposing I were to get everything together which could be applied to the amplification of this adage, every maxim, everything elegantly said or memorably done, every fable or story, every wise-crack either in favour or against? Isn't it obvious that if I had tried to do this every adage could have been made into a volume? This would be no less absurd than if I were to recount the whole of the Trojan War (beginning from the double egg, as Horace says) to illustrate the proverb 'an Iliad of woes', or explain 'the wiles of Odysseus' by retelling the whole story of the Odyssey! Then, how often does one come across sayings on everyday topics, on life and death, friendship, rivalry, good men and bad? I am foolish to start giving a list of them, because there are as many of these as there are proverbs, and it would not be difficult to enrich the text-books of oratory with them so that every saying reached the size of a volume. But that kind of diligence would not only be stupid, it would be beyond the power of anyone writing Chiliades, and beyond the endurance of anyone reading them. And so I have thought it best in this work to seek moderation rather than completeness, to look at the end rather than try to extend it. However, if as we pushed along something struck my mind in passing which was worth knowing, and not inapplicable to the proverb, I did not hesitate to put it in as an addition. Finally, there are some places— why should I not tell the truth?—but not very many of them, in which we ourselves felt something lacking, and yet we did not think they should be passed over in silence, even though we were not satisfied by what we could find out about them in our authorities. The idea was to mention them so that an opportunity might be given to others with more leisure, better library facilities or better memories, or richer in learning, to investigate further, and we said like the comic writer, 'Not as we would, but as we can.'

I saw that it would be possible to arrange the book in some sort of order, if one followed a scheme of like and unlike, agreement and contradiction, introduced a good many sub-titles and classed each proverb in its place. However, I intentionally avoided this, partly because of a feeling that in a miscellany like this it was better not to have an order, partly because I saw that, if I arranged all remarks of the same nature in the same class, the resultant monotony would produce such boredom for the reader as to sicken him (and make him say 'Twice-cooked cabbage is poison', and 'Corinthus son of Jove is in the book').[1] Partly I was deterred by the immensity of the work. Why conceal the fact? I saw that it could not be done without remaking the whole book from end to end, and that I could not think of publishing until the last paragraph had been added; it would need the nine years of Horace. But as it was, I could add things even during the printing, if anything came to hand which should not be left out.

[1] A proverbial expression. Pindar, *Nemean Odes*, VII, 105; Plato, *Euthydemus*, 292 e. See *Adages*, II. 1. l: 'said of those who are always saying or doing the same thing.'

I can hardly believe that there will be anyone so unfair (and yet I think in the future there will be) as to expect even eloquence from a Dutchman, i.e. a Boeotian or worse, and I am not joking—and in a work which is entirely directed to teaching, and teaching things like these, not unworthy of notice, but so tiny, so humble, that not only do they not attract ornaments of speech and fluent writing but they repel everything of the sort. In a medley like this, with the constant enumeration of the names of authors, even modest ones, which I had to persevere in with dull stolidity for the sake of teaching, with the frequent interspersion of Greek and the recurring translations, what room was there for brilliance or elegance, or for maintaining the style, or for flow of oratory? Tully does not require eloquence from a philosopher, and is anyone going to ask it from a proverb-writer? Seneca never recommends it except when it comes easily or is there of its own accord, so as to treat great subjects in the great manner, and if I were to pretend to the paraphernalia of the Rhetors would it not be a case for quoting the proverb about 'Perfume in the pease-porridge'?

For myself, though I don't despise eloquence in other people, I have never much sought it in my own case, preferring, I don't know why, a sensible style to a highly coloured one, as long as it was not vulgar, and really expressed my thought. Whatever ease of writing I had managed to acquire would soon have had to vanish in such a long, varied and hurried perusal of Greek and Latin authors. Indeed, as Cicero says, richness of style must dry up if there is the slightest interruption; if the matter in hand really called for flowers of rhetoric, I had no time for them. And time would always be short for so much looking up, commenting, and memorising. Although I think that the achievement of expressing these things in not ill-chosen words will seem to be part of eloquence in itself, to anyone who knows what it is. I say nothing of those people (I might call them the apes of eloquence) who judge the art of speaking by a childish jingle of words, and when they have (by dint of many days' toil) interwoven a few flowers of speech into their writings, and scattered over four phrases from Cicero and as many from Sallust, think they have reached the peak of Roman eloquence. They don't think much of the style of St Jerome, they recoil from Prudentius, anything seems inelegant, dumb and stuttering to them unless it holds those four bits of Cicero. If these people ever experienced what it is to chase apparent trifles like these through books, they would perhaps recognise their own lack of fluency and be less impudent in scorning the eloquence of others.

Some critic very well worth listening to might say to me, 'Yes, but it is just that which would have been elegant, to add some amplitude to these small things by way of stylistic art, to give these humble things dignity, and as Virgil says: "To small trifles add this honour."[1] And indeed there would have been time for that, if you had separated the work of collecting from that of polishing, and had left a proper interval between. What need was there (in Plautus's phrase) to suck in and blow out at the same time?[2] Who was forcing you to hurry on with the printing, and finish a book so large and laborious in a year and a half and publish it at once? If you had taken the advice of Horace and kept on your studies for nine years, you might not only have added the grace of eloquence, but brought out a book both fuller and more correct, so that you would have had nothing to regret nor to add. Either the task ought not to have been undertaken at all, or once undertaken it ought to have been fully completed.'

Here—I am not one to oppose the truth—I must admit my short-comings. I was quite aware that this work required not a Theologian, who dips into the literature of antiquity briefly and as it were hurrying past, but one who has spent his whole life turning over the pages of these authors, interpreting and investigating them, who has the right not only to dally but to die[3] over work like this. I saw clearly that this was not work for one man, nor one library, nor for a few years—this work that I finished alone, unaided, in less than eighteen months, with the help of one library—though that was Aldus's, and a large one, richer than any other in good books, especially Greek, and from this library as from a fountain-head all other good libraries all over the world are coming to birth and increasing. I don't deny that it was copious, but it was the only one.

There really are reasons which may lessen my fault, if not purge it altogether. First, it was not deliberate intention but chance which started me on this book, and I was incited to it by the requests of my friends; I was never good at refusing at any time, and especially it was that Maecenas of mine, William Mountjoy, one of the foremost noblemen of the English court, who begged me for it, a friend so deserving and so beloved that I had to comply with his wishes, even if it meant putting everything else second. The creeds of the Philosophers admit that we may be slightly deflected from the right way for the sake of our friends, and so I think I may be excused, if in order to please such a friend as this I undertook a piece of work which was attractive in itself, though perhaps not very suited to me—especially as I saw that no one among the learned was taking it in hand; not, I think, because they felt

---

[1] Virgil, *Georgics*, III, 289.
[2] Plautus, *Mostellaria*, III, i, 101. See *Adages*, II. II. lxxx.
[3] Play on *immorari* and *immori*.

themselves unequal to it, but because they saw and recoiled from the amount of work it would entail, especially because they knew it would bring them much more labour than joy.

Then when the work was begun, I saw that there was really no end to it, and I decided to impose a limitation measured not by the matter itself but by my other occupations, and to spend on it not the amount of work it required, but the amount I could spare from my studies without being at fault. And so I rather hurried to finish it, partly because it was not my line of country, partly because, once this was done, I could return with my whole heart to the work which belongs to my own profession, and which I had laid aside for a few months, less by personal choice than to please a friend.

I am not particularly worried about Horace's advice. He meant it for those who write for intellectual glory, but I had nothing in view but usefulness to the reader. He was addressing writers of poetry, which more than anything else has need of eloquence (see Pliny),[1] while I was putting together notes on the adages. And then that nine years' work, which he himself certainly did not give to his poetry, might be given by someone to a hundred items; but to do the same when you come to thousands, would be immensely difficult. To exact it would be inhuman, when it is so arduous to produce thousands at all, without the labour of perpetual revision which is hardly less than writing in the first place. I think the care which Horace calls for must be measured by industry and not by time. As far as that goes I can testify that I have done my best to make up for the lack of time by my care and perseverance, so that I hope the candid reader will not miss too much on this score. For, if you only count the actual time spent, we did do it in a great rush; but, if you think of the nights and days spent toiling in unwearying study, our haste was a ripening too. It may be that our attention did not always meet the needs of the book, but one thing will remain true, that of all those who have tried to write Proverbs in Greek or Latin (I am speaking of those of which commentaries survive) I have been much more persevering than any. Anyway, since the job is endless, and contributes to the general good, what is to prevent our sharing out the labour and finishing our work by our joint efforts? I have done my stint and I am handing on the torch. Let someone take up the succession. I have supplied an anthology, not a bad one in my opinion; now let others come to chisel and polish and variegate it. I have done the part which means most hard work and least glory; others need not hesitate to add what is both easiest and most creditable. It does not matter under what name my works are read, I shall not trouble

---

[1] Pliny, *Letters*, v, 8.

myself about who gets the glory as long as we have given students the opportunity to possess a thing of such value. Neither shall I be in the least offended if a better scholar comes along and corrects my work, if a more diligent author fills it out, a more accurate one rearranges it, someone with more eloquence gives it lustre, someone with more leisure polishes it, some luckier man appropriates it, as long as all this is done for the good of the reading public, which has been our only aim in this work—to the extent of neglecting our own. I could easily have chosen, like other people, a line of work which would have caused me far less toil and brought me much more glory. Who would not have thought it a much more glorious achievement if I had translated the whole of Demosthenes, of Plato or someone like that into Latin? And yet it is hard to say how much less time, night-watches and midnight oil I should have had to spend on a book like that, than on collecting these trifles, as they seem to be. I could have selected two or three hundred out of all this number, and turned all my energy to polishing, developing and elaborating them, which would certainly not have meant much less of a seed-time of hard work, but which would have brought me in a much greater harvest of fame. But that would have been to work for my own advantage, not for that of others who love learning. In my opinion, anyone who cares for the restoration of literature must have a truly 'Herculean' spirit, that is, he must not let any hardship to himself prevent him from contributing to the general good, or slacken his efforts.

But enough of this, and more than enough—I am afraid it will be a Herculean task to read the lengthy speech that the 'labours of Hercules' have led me to write!

So I will make an end, but after adding this: that when this was first in process of publication I had beaten all the labours of Hercules. For he, unconquered up to then, could not fight two monsters at once, and thought it better to run away and leave us the proverb,[1] than try the contest, preferring to be laughed at in safety than praised when dead. At that time we had a battle on hand with two huge monsters, each of them such a business that it needed many Hercules, instead of both being tackled together by one humble individual. For the printing was going on at Bâle of the *Adagiorum Chiliades*, so amended and increased that the new edition cost me as much trouble as the previous one which had been produced in Venice by Aldus Manutius, and at the same time they were printing the complete works of St Jerome[2] in which I had undertaken the largest and most difficult part, i.e. the Letters. It was no light task, by the Muses! if only for the number of volumes

---

[1] *Ne Hercules quidem contra duos*, I. v. xxxix.

[2] Jerome, *Opera Omnia* (Froben, Bâle, 1516), vol. 1–4, *Epistolae*.

which had to be looked through. Now, heavens above! what a struggle I had with the monstrous scribal errors which were swarming throughout the text! What a business it was to restore the passages in Greek, which our great author had mixed in everywhere—for mostly they had either dropped out or were wrongly reinserted. Another thing added no little to my labours: those famous Notes (*Scholia*) which we added with their arguments. There were two reasons for this: first, because, being the first editor to do this, I had no one to follow, no one to turn to for help, and, secondly, because Jerome is a bit like Romulus, who was said to be as good an advertiser of his own great deeds as a doer of them. Just so Jerome, who had in his mind a rich store derived from all sorts of writers and subjects of study, was by far the best commentator on his own doctrine. In fact it is with a sort of saintly boasting that he triumphantly hands out everything he has found concealed in the Old or New Testament, everything he has ferreted out in legend or history, in Greek or Hebrew literature, cramming it all into his pages. The task of bringing order into the work of an author who has been so much jumbled by various hands may not redound to one's glory, but it does mean a great deal of trouble. All this mass of work had to be the share of this one poor individual. Except that in dealing with some of the Hebrew, since my acquaintance with that language was only superficial (only a taste, as we say), I did have the help of Bruno Amerbach, a young man as learned as he is modest. We exchanged with each other, he taking over this part of the work and I taking care of the emendations in Greek and Latin. I need hardly add that it was quite a difficult business to detect those passages which had been added to the works of Jerome, some of a learned kind, some ignorant and childish, some apparently with a touch of madness; we picked these out by likely conjecture or traces of origin, and, when we had abstracted them, we restored them to their right places. Then we rewrote the life of this great saint, using his own works as authority— a life which has been so inaccurately reported by others, in such a foolish and insipid way. The nature of this kind of work is that it brings profit to everyone, and the only person to suffer hardship is the one who undertakes to do it. The reader who freely runs through all these books does not realise that sometimes we were held up for days by a single word. Nor does he understand, or if he understands he does not remember, what difficulties have gone to create the facility with which he reads, or how many troubles one must go through to save others from trouble. And so it seems to me that I really was born in the fourth quarter of the moon, since by some inexplicable fate I have been plunged into these more than Herculean labours.

(c) Auris Batava[1]

Just as the Greeks say βοιώτιον οὖς, i.e. the Boeotian ear, meaning dull and gross, so Martial in his *Epigrams*, book VI, says that *Batavam aurem* means an ear which is rustic, untutored, boorish:

> It is you, you he means, that Martial
> Whose naughty jokes are plainly understood
> By one who has not a Batavian ear.[2]

So Domitius Calderinus reads, though some alter the reading *Batavam* to *severam*.

The Batavi were a German tribe, part of the Catti, who migrated owing to internal dissensions and occupied the extreme tip of the coast of Gaul, then unoccupied, and also at the same time an island situated between two stretches of water, washed by the ocean in front and by the river Rhine at the back and sides.[3] As a people they were strong fighters, with much experience in the Germanic wars, but also powerful through their wealth, so that the Roman military power could not be exhausted while these people were allies of the Empire and contributed to it both arms and men; how generously, Cornelius Tacitus tells us in his book XX. Most scholars agree, and the guess seems uncontradicted, that this island mentioned by Tacitus is what we now call Holland, a country I must always praise and venerate, since to her I owe my life's beginning. And I would that I could bring as much honour to her, as I have little regret in being her son! For as to that accusation of boorishness which Martial levels against her, and Lucan's charge of savagery, I think that either they have nothing to do with us at all, or both can be turned into praise. For which people has not been uncultured at one time? And when was the Roman people more praiseworthy than when they knew no arts except farming and fighting? If anyone argues that the criticisms levelled at the Batavi long ago still hold good today, what better tribute could be paid to my dear Holland, than to have it said that she recoils from Martial's pleasantries, which he himself calls vile? If only all Christians had 'Dutch ears', so that they would not take in the pestilential jests of that poet, or at least not be infected by them, if understood. If you call that rusticity, we freely admit the impeachment, in company with the virtuous Spartans, the primitive Sabines, the noble Catos. But Lucan, I imagine, calls the Batavi 'savage' much as Virgil calls the Romans 'sharp' (*acer*).

If you look at the manners of everyday life, there is no race more

---

[1] IV. VI. XXXV, LB. 1083 F.   [2] Martial, VI, lxxxii.
[3] Tacitus, *Annals*, IV, xii.

open to humanity and kindness, or less given to wildness or ferocious behaviour. It is a straightforward nature, without treachery or deceit, and not prone to any serious vices, except that it is a little given to pleasure, especially to feasting. The reason for this is, I think, the wonderful supply of everything which can tempt one to enjoyment; due partly to the ease of importing goods (since the country stands at the mouth of two noble rivers, the Rhine and the Meuse, and is washed on one side by the sea), and partly to the native fertility of the region, intersected as it is by navigable rivers full of fish, and abounding in rich pastures. And there is a plentiful supply of birds from the marshes and heaths. They say that there is no other country which holds so many towns in a small space, not large towns it is true, but incredibly civilised. As for domestic furniture, Holland is unsurpassed in neatness and elegance—or so say those merchants who travel over most of the globe. In no country are there more people who have a tincture of learning than in Holland. If there are few deeply learned scholars, especially in the classics, this may be due to the luxury of life there, or it may be that they think more of moral excellence than of excellence in scholarship. For it is certain, and many things go to prove it, that they are not wanting in intellectual power, though I myself have it only in a modest degree, not to say scanty—like the rest of my endowments.[1]

[1] There is an affectionate reference in a comment of 1526 (I. IV. lii, *Arenae mandas semina*) to *nostra Brabantia*, where he says there are husbandmen so energetic that they can compel the thirstiest sands to grow wheat.

3

FROM THE 1515 EDITION

The long essays in the 1515 *Adages* range freely over a number of topics, and any arrangement of them must be a little arbitrary. But they can be grouped for the present purpose under three headings: protest against tyranny in various forms; criticism of the contemporary representatives of Christianity, together with the defence of learning and the ideal of a pure religion; the exposure of the futility and the evils of war.

To these we may add some shorter passages dealing with Erasmus's memories of individual people.

I. MONEY AND POWER

The subject of the right choice and education of a ruler, and of the right way to rule, recurred often to Erasmus's thoughts. Scattered among the *Adages* there are a number of warnings, to the princes and bishops who neglect their responsibilities and are content to delegate them to inferiors,[1] who expect moral behaviour from others but not from themselves:

and everyone who is set in a position of responsibility ought to make it his first concern to fulfil his own office worthily, before he exacts work from others. But now you may see some princes who require obedience to the law from their people while they live themselves as if exempt from all law; they expect integrity from the magistrates, while they themselves openly sell government posts or make them a matter of favouritism. You may see some bishops who demand religion and piety from their flock and are far from any piety themselves.[2]

With these we may class allusions to the tyranny of money, whether in the form of extortionate taxation or undue profits. Erasmus was not respectful of mercantile wealth:

The merchant class hold nothing sacred except financial profit, to which they devote themselves entirely as if to God. By this alone they assess godliness, friendship, honour, reputation, everything either in heaven or earth. The rest is nonsense (*nugae*).[3]

[1] *Frons occipitio prior*, I. II. xix (1520).
[2] *Bonus dux bonum reddit comitem*, I. VIII. c (1515).
[3] *Simul et da et accipe*, I. VIII. viii (1515).

34

Would that all mortals, and especially merchants, would inscribe this maxim not only on their boxes but on their hearts, and would think that profit no profit at all which is gained by the loss of a good conscience; and nothing useful that is not honest.[1]

One passage about debt reveals the bitterness of his early struggles for independence:

Whoever has not experienced this, let him read Plutarch's commentary *On avoiding usury*, and he will easily understand how wretched it is to be in debt. What could be a worse fate than to be always blushing, scratching one's face (*perfricare frontem*, to lose the sense of shame), fleeing, hiding, lying, cheating; now begging, now demanding; to be openly accused, avoided, pointed at; in short, never to be your own master? For these, and many other troubles, are brought about by debt.[2]

The chief essays on these topics are *Aut fatuum aut regem nasci oportere* (I. III. i), *A mortuo tributum exigere* (I. IX. xii), and the long *Scarabeus aquilam quaerit* (III. VII. i).

(a) *Aut fatuum aut regem nasci oportere*[3]
[Kings and fools are born, not made]

Annaeus Seneca was a man, as Tacitus said, of a very pleasant wit; this is clear from that amusing book which he wrote against Claudius Caesar, and which has recently come to light in Germany. In his book he mentions an adage, *One must be born a king or a fool.* It is best to give his very words: 'As for me,' he says, 'I know I have gained my freedom from the fact that the end has come for that man who proved the truth of the proverb, *One must be born a king or a fool.*' And again in the same book, 'He killed in one and the same house Crassus, Magnus, Scribonia, Bassonia, the Assarii, although they were noble. Crassus indeed was such a fool that he might have reigned.'[4] In another place, though the allusion is less clear, he refers to the same thing in his line 'He snapped the royal thread of a stupid life'.[5] If Hesiod is right in saying that a popular saying is never meaningless, perhaps it would not be beside the point to inquire what can have given rise to this proverb, uniting as it does two such dissimilar things—a king and a fool—with the obvious intention of drawing a parallel between the two. Especially as it is the

---

[1] *Lucrum malum, aequale dispendio*, III. III. lii (1515).
[2] *Felix qui nihil debet*, II. VII. xcviii (1515).
[3] 'Kings and fools are born, not made', I. III. i, LB. 106 c. (One contemporary translation of this adage into German exists. It was made by George Spalatinus (Burckhardt) and published at Mainz about 1520.)
[4] *Divi Claudii Apocolocyntosis*, I, i; XI, ii.   [5] *Ibid.* IV, i.

particular distinction of kings (and the only true royal one) to surpass others in wisdom, prudence, and watchfulness.

Well, everyone agrees that those famous kings of old time were for the most part well endowed with stark stupidity; one can see this in the fables of the poets on the one hand, in the writings of the historians on the other. Homer, for instance (and the writers of tragedy after him), makes his Agamemnon ambitious rather than wise. What could be more stupid than to purchase the title of commander-in-chief by the cruel slaughtering of an only daughter? What could be more idiotic than to be up in arms like a little boy for the sake of a little girl from a foreign land, and then, when he couldn't keep his sweetheart, to filch one from Achilles, and put the whole army in danger? And then there is Achilles himself—how foolishly he rages when bereft of his lady-love and how childishly he goes crying to his mother![1] And yet he is the one whom the poet sets before us as the perfect example of an excellent prince. Look at Ajax, and his unwise anger; look at Priam, and his senile maunderings when he embraces Helen—that shameless creature—and calls her his daughter, and declares he has no regrets for that war which brought him such disasters, bereaved him of so many children, plunged him into such mourning—and all so that Paris should not fail to get possession of his girl. Why say more? the whole of the *Iliad*, long as it is, has nothing in it, as Horace says in an elegant line, but the passions of foolish kings and foolish peoples.[2] The *Odyssey* also has its dense and stupid kings, its suitors and Alcinous. Even Hercules himself is described as sturdy and spirited, but heavy and doltish in mind. Indeed Hesiod (whom some think older than Homer) calls princes 'gift-greedy'[3] and childish—I suppose on account of their small wisdom in government, and the way they strain after the accumulation of riches by fair means and foul, rather than after the public good. So they imagine that old Midas, wearing his ass's ears as a mark of stupidity. And I don't know whether this is the place to mention how the earliest theologians—that is, the poets—attribute wisdom to Apollo and to Minerva, but to Jove, the ruler of gods and men, they leave nothing but the three-forked lightning, and that nod and that eyebrow which makes all Olympus tremble. Moreover, what profligate, what buffoon ever fooled so foolishly, or was more vilely vile, than this character whom they make ruler of the world? He deceives his wife with tricks, turning himself into a swan, a bull, a shower of gold; he rigs up traps for women, suborns Ganymede, fills heaven with bastards. In the same way Neptune and Pluto are painted as fierce and ruthless, but they are not credited with wisdom.

[1] *Iliad*, book I.   [2] *Epistles*, I, ii.   [3] *Works and Days*, 39.

But suppose we dismiss the legends and turn to more recent times, to history: how much sense do you think Croesus King of Lydia had, if he was truly such as Herodotus paints him,[1] so relying on his treasure of jewels and gold that he was angry with Solon for refusing him the name of 'fortunate'? Or what could be imagined more idiotic than Xerxes, when he sent messengers to Mount Athos, to terrify it with scornful and threatening letters, or ordered so many lashes to be given to the Hellespont? Alexander the Great showed no less kingly stupidity when he renounced his father and commanded that he should be greeted as the son of Jove, when he strove in his cups, when he allowed himself to be worshipped as God by the flatterers in his banquets, when he complained that this world was too small for his victories, and took to the ocean to find other worlds to conquer. I leave aside all the others, the Dionysiuses, the Ptolemies, the Juliuses, the Neros, the Tiberiuses, the Caligulas, the Heliogabaluses, the Commoduses, and the Domitians[2]—among whom one arrogated to himself the name of God when he was unworthy of the name of man, another exposed himself to be laughed to scorn by his very flatterers, another urged by ambition shook the whole world with meaningless wars.

But I look rather silly myself when I embark on this catalogue, and, as they say, carry water to the sea. You merely have to turn over the chronicles of the ancients and the moderns, and you will find that in several centuries there have been barely one or two princes who did not by sheer stupidity bring disaster to human affairs. A prince, indeed, is either a fool to the immense detriment of the whole world, or a wise man to the immense benefit of all; although it is easier to do harm than good, and calamity creeps along or rather pervades everything quicker than useful effort. But nowadays we see some princes who aspire to anything except the one thing which would make them deserve the name of prince; and stupid subjects, who look for everything in their kings except the one thing needful. 'He is young'; that would recommend him as a bridegroom to a bride, not as a prince to the state. 'He is good-looking'; that is the right praise for a woman. 'He is broad-shouldered'; if you were praising an athlete, that would be the way to do it. 'He is strong and can stand hard toil'; that is a testimonial for a batman or a houseboy. 'He has a large store of gold'; you are describing an active moneylender. 'He is eloquent'; that's what dazzles me in a sophist. 'He sings well, he dances well'; that is the way to praise flute-players and actors, not kings. 'He has no equal in drinking'—for

---

[1] Herodotus, *History*, book i.
[2] Erasmus writes 'Domitios': his eighteenth-century editor, Leclerc, suggests 'Domitianos'.

former princes actually delighted in this commendation! It would be fitter praise for a sponge. 'He is tall, and stands head and shoulders above the rest'; that's splendid, if one wants to reach something down from a high place. As for saying 'He's a skilled dice player, he's good at chess', that is praise shared with the lowest idlers, and a prince should be ashamed of it. You may heap up everything—public adoration, gold and jewels, statues, a pedigree drawn from Hercules (or from Codrus or Cecrops if you prefer), but unless you tell me of a mind far removed from vulgar foolishness, free from sordid desires for worthless things, and from the prejudices of the herd, I have not heard any praise worthy of a king.

For it was not ill-advisedly that the divine Plato[1] wrote that the only way for a state to attain happiness was for the supreme command to be given to philosophers, or else, inversely, that those who govern should themselves follow philosophy. And to follow philosophy is not just to wear a mantle and to carry a bag round, or let your beard grow. What is it then? It is to despise those things which the common herd goggles at, and to think quite differently from the opinions of the majority. And I don't see how it is possible for a man who thinks he is free to do just what he likes, who marvels at riches as if they were important, who thinks any legal rights may be set aside for the sake of power, who is captivated by empty glory, who is a slave to shameful lust, who is terrified of death—I just can't see how such a man can play the part of a beneficent king.

The first requisite is to judge rightly about each matter, because opinions are like sources from which all the actions of life flow, and when they are infected everything must needs be mismanaged. The next essential is to recoil from evil and to be led towards good. For true wisdom consists not only in the knowledge of truth, but in the love and eager striving for what is good. You may well find (among rulers) one who can see that it is not possible to go to war without grave disaster to human affairs, and that an old obsolete claim to sovereignty is not very important—and yet he will plunge everything into war merely out of ambition. There may be one who can see that the greatest curse of a state comes from appointing as magistrates not those who can be of the most use to the public weal by their prudence, experience and integrity, but those who can bid the highest sums—and yet he will be impelled by avarice to look after the treasury and let the abuse go on. And there is another who understands that the duty of a prince, who takes taxes from all, is to consult the advantage of all—to preside over trials, to stamp out crime, to respect the magistrature, to amend useless

[1] *Republic*, book VI.

38

laws. And yet he is called away from this business by pleasure, which does not give him the time to attend to matters worthy of a ruler. Another is conscious that he has it in his power to confer a great benefit on the human race, but at the risk of his life; and anyone who thinks it is the most terrible thing to die, will fail in duty to the state at this point. And so first of all the mind of the prince must be freed from all false ideas, so that he can see what is truly good, truly glorious, truly splendid. The next thing is to instil the hatred of what is base, the love of what is good, so that he can see clearly what is becoming to a prince, and wish for nothing but what is worthy of a good and beneficent ruler. Let him recognise the good where it may be found, and always measure everything by it, never varying from this aim. This is what is meant by wisdom, and it is in this that the prince must so far excel other mortals, as he excels them in dignity, in wealth, in splendour, and in power.

If only all Christian princes would copy that wisest of all kings,[1] who when he was given a free choice of a boon from him to whom nothing is impossible, wished for wisdom alone, and that wisdom by which he might rightly govern his people! And pray what did he teach his own son, but the love and following of wisdom? It is for this reason that the Egyptians make a symbolic representation of a prince by drawing an eye and a sceptre.[2] Indeed what the eye is to the body, so is a true prince to the body politic. As the sun to the sky, so is the prince to the people; the sun is the eye of the world, the prince the eye of the multitude. As the mind is to the body, so is the prince to the state; the mind knows, the body obeys. And, if the mind commands the body, it is for the body's good; it does not rule for itself like a tyrant, but for that which is in its charge. Above all, the good ruler is the living portrayal of God, who rules the universe. And the closer the prince conforms to the lines of the original, the more magnificent he is. God is all-seeing, all-feeling, and swayed by no passions. He is greatest in power, just as he is greatest in goodness. He does good to all, even the unworthy. He deals no punishments, except rarely and when he must. He governs this world for us and not for himself. All the reward he asks is to do good. But the evil prince, on the contrary, seems to be the copy of the devil, and to act in his stead. Either he knows nothing, or what he knows is how to bring about public disaster. What power he has, he uses to harm the state. And though it is in his power to do a great deal of harm to everybody, he would like to do even more than he can.

Nothing is nobler than a good king, nothing better, nothing nearer God; equally, nothing is worse than a bad prince, nothing viler,

---

[1] 1 Kings III, 5–15.   [2] Plutarch, *De Osiride*, X, page 354.

nothing more like the devil. There is something divine about a beneficent prince, but no wild beast is more destructive than a tyrant. And a
tyrant is whoever wields power for himself, whatever name his paint-
ings and statues give him. It is not for us to pass judgement, as it were,
upon the great ones of the earth, but yet we are obliged—not without
sorrow—to feel the lack in Christian princes of that high wisdom of
which we have spoken. All these revolutions, treaties made and broken,
frequent risings, battle and slaughter, all these threats and quarrels,
what do they arise from but stupidity? And I rather think that some
part of this is due to our own fault. We do not hand over the rudder of
the ship to anyone but a skilled steersman, when nothing is at stake but
four passengers or a small cargo; but we hand over the state, in which
so many thousands of people are in peril, to the first comer. If anyone
is to be a coachman, he learns the art, spends care and thought; but, for
anyone to be a king, we think it is enough for him to be born. And yet
to rule a kingdom well, as it is the finest of all employments, is also the
most difficult by far. You choose the man who is to have charge of a
ship; but you do not choose the man to whom you are entrusting so
many cities, so many human lives? But there it is, the thing is so established that it is impossible to root it out.[1] Kings are born, and whoever
may have been picked on by chance, whether he be good or bad,
stupid or wise, sane or clouded in mind, as long as he looks like a
human being, he is to be entrusted with supreme power in the state.
By his will the world is to be thrown into an uproar with wars
and slaughter, all things sacred and profane are to be turned upside
down.

But if this is a thing we cannot change, the next best plan would be
to improve matters by careful education; and, if we may not choose a
suitable person to be our ruler, it is important to try to make that person
suitable whom fate has given us. We see with what care and solicitude
and watchfulness a father brings up his son, who is the future master of
one estate. How much more care, then, should be spent on the education of one who, if good, will be so to the immense benefit of all, and, if
bad, will bring about the ruin of all—one on whose nod hangs the
safety or the destruction of the world? With what rules and precepts of
philosophy must that mind be fortified, not only against such great
calamities as may arise in a state, but against the favour of fortune, so
often accompanied by pride and stupidity; against pleasures, which can

---

[1] Here there is plain indication of Erasmus's preference for an elective monarchy.
But, being essentially practical, he accepts the necessities of his day. The hereditary monarch must be fitted for his work by education, and restricted by the
existence of constitutional controls (cf. *Education of a Christian Prince*).

corrupt the best natures; still more against the dangerous fawning of
flatterers, and those poisonous cheers of applause which they are most
prodigal with when the prince is acting most like a madman. It seems
to me that he should have attached to him, while still an infant, some
skilful educator; for no one can truly be fashioned into a prince, except
long before he knows that is what he is. In the early days, I say, a pre-
ceptor should be appointed, and we should take all the more care in
choosing him because we are not free to choose our prince—but we are
free to educate him. Let him instil into this childish mind, as yet blank
and malleable, opinions worthy of a prince; arm it with the best
principles of conduct, show it the difference between a true prince and
a tyrant, and lay before its very eyes what a god-like thing is a beneficent ruler, what a loathsome hateful brute is a tyrant. He will explain
that a ruler who wields power for himself and not for the state is no
prince, but a robber; that there is no difference between pirates and
pirate-minded princes, except that the latter are more powerful and can
bring so much more disaster on human affairs. He will impress on his
pupil that he can be of use to so many thousands of people—nay, to the
whole world—by simply behaving as one good and wise man. He will
teach that among Christians supreme rule means administration of the
state, and not dominion. It may bear the name of supreme rule, but he
must remember that he is ruling over free men, and over Christians,
that is, people who are twice free. In addition, for a person to be a
prince it is not enough to be born, to have ancestral statues, the sceptre
and the crown. What makes a prince is a mind distinguished for its
wisdom, a mind always occupied with the safety of the state, and looking to nothing but the common good. He will warn his pupil not to
judge himself by the plaudits of the stupid populace or the praise of
flatterers, not to do anything on the impulsion of hatred, love, or anger,
or at the urge of any passion. When he appoints magistrates, creates
laws, or in his other duties, he must work for one end only, for good,
and for the people's benefit. It is not enough if he himself does harm
to no one—the prince is also the guarantor of the uprightness of his
officials. The glory of a prince does not lie in extending his sway, in
pushing back his frontiers by force of arms; but, if he happens to acquire
the sovereignty of a region, he must make it flourish by justice, by wise
economy, and the other arts of peace. The teacher will recommend him
to be particularly inclined to serve the cause of good men, to be ready
to pardon, and with the attitude towards punishment of a friendly
doctor, who amputates or cauterises the limb which he despairs of
healing; to be careful to avoid everything from which he can foresee
the danger of evil to the state. Above all, he is to shun war in every way;

other things give rise to this or that calamity, but war lets loose at one go a whole army of wrongs. These principles and others like them should be impressed on the child's mind, with the help of the maxims of the ancients and the examples of virtuous princes.

What actually happens is that no kind of man is more corruptly or carelessly brought up than those whose education is of such importance to so many people. The baby who is to rule the world is handed over to foolish womenfolk who are so far from instilling anything in his mind worthy of a prince, that they pooh-pooh whatever the tutor rightly advises, or whatever inclination to gentleness the child may have in himself—and they teach him to act like a prince, that is like a tyrant. Then no one fails to fawn and flatter. The courtiers applaud, the servants obey his every whim, even the tutor is obsequious; and he is not doing this to make the prince more beneficial to his country, but to ensure a splendid future for himself. The cleric who is popularly called his confessor, is obsequious too—he has some bishopric in mind. There is flattery from the judges, flattery from playmates and companions; so that Carneades[1] was right when he said that the only art kings could learn properly was the art of riding, because only a horse makes no distinction between prince and peasant and is unable to flatter. He just tosses off the rider who is not skilful enough to stay on his back, no matter who it may be.

One of the earliest lessons is pomp and pride; he is taught that whatever he wants he can have. He hears that the property of everyone belongs to the prince, that he is above the law; that the whole paraphernalia of government, laws and policies exist stored in the prince's mind. He hears the terms *sacred majesty*, *serene highness*, *divinity*, *god on earth*, and other such superb titles. In short, while he is yet a boy, all he learns to play at is being a tyrant. Then he is caught up among the girls; they all allure and admire and defer to him. The effeminate crew of young friends is there, and they have no other topic for jokes or conversation but girls. Next there are other diversions—gaming, dancing, feasting, lute-playing, gadding about; the best years of his life are used up like this. If he takes a fancy to beguile his leisure by reading, he reads old wives' tales or, what is worse, historical stories. His mind is not in the least equipped with any antidote, and he imbibes from them an enthusiasm—what the Greeks call *ȝeal*—for some pernicious hero, say Julius Caesar or Xerxes or Alexander the Great. And what suits him best in them is the worst. They furnish the worst example, they foster the craziest urges. Now imagine, if you please, an intelligence not selected from among many, as should be the case, but a

[1] The second-century Greek sceptic philosopher.

very ordinary mind, and an education so corrupt that it would corrupt the mentality of an Aristides;[1] then imagine the poison of flattery, frolic and pleasure (which don't agree very well with wisdom), luxurious living, wealth and magnificence, the sense of power; all this at an age of ruthlessness and inclined naturally to bad courses. Add finally the tainting of the mind by false ideas. And can you wonder if, coming from this early environment to the administration of a kingdom, he doesn't do it very wisely?

'But never mind,' they say, 'he's young, he'll learn by experience.' But the prince must never be young, even if he is young in years. Any prudence which is won from experience is of a sorry kind, and sorriest of all in a prince. The prince's prudence will be too dearly bought by the country, if he only learns by waging war that war is the thing he must avoid at all costs; or if he fails to understand that public offices must be given to upright men, until he sees the state tottering through the audacity of evildoers. Don't tell me that those who wish to learn to sing to the lute will spoil several lutes in the process, before they learn the art, as Xenophon said; that would mean that the prince would only learn to administer his state by the ruin of the state.

It is not therefore much to be wondered at, if we see things going absolutely contrary to the way they should; when, instead of the passions which arise from the body being controlled by the mind, the disturbances in the mind spread out into the body, when the eye sees less than the rest of the body sees, when the person who is most pernicious and harmful to the public is the very person who should be beneficial to all, acting in place of God. Do we not see fine cities, created by the people, overthrown by the princes? Or a state enriched by the toil of its citizens, and looted by the princes' greed? Plebeian lawyers make good laws, princes violate them; the people seek for peace, the princes stir up war.

I think these are the things which gave rise to this proverb, from which somehow or other we have digressed a long way; but now we return to it. So it is said, *Kings and fools are born, not made*, because the primitive kings were of that sort, as the ancients tell—and may the princes of our day be altogether different! For everything is permitted to fools, because of the weakness of their minds. And everything in the way of praise is awarded to kings, because of their power. There is perhaps another way of understanding the saying, in reference to the equal happiness of kings and fools; because whatever a king wants is provided by fortune, and fools are no less fortunate because of their self-satisfaction; it allows them to think they have no lack of good

[1] Athenian statesman (*c.* 530–468 B.C.) called 'the Just'.

gifts.[1] On the other hand, the proverb seems to have originated among the Romans, who hated the name of king as barbaric and tyrannous, and contrary to political freedom, of which they at that time were the most enthusiastic supporters.

(b) A mortuo tributum exigere[2]

Ἀπὸ νεκροῦ φορολογεῖν, i.e. *a mortuo tributum exigere*, is applied to those who heap up riches by fair means or foul. Aristotle quotes in the second book of his Rhetoric κἄν ἀπὸ νεκροῦ φέρει, i.e. 'he makes a profit even on the dead',[3] explaining that this is usually said of people who squeeze profits out of the meanest and most squalid things, as Vespasian did out of urine;[4] or from shameful things, such as the trade of a pander and the sale of one's body; or in the cases of extortion practised on anyone, on the poor, on beggars, finally on the dead. It was counted shame to the rulers of Rome when they broke into the monuments of the Corinthians and took away the Corinthian bronze, and the shamefulness of the deed was reflected in the word to which it gave rise, for things removed in this way are called *necrocorinthia*. In the Attic tongue they call φόρος, or tribute, any proceeds or interest which are made on any affair, even in the way of money. Anyone who collects booty of this kind they call φορολόγος, a race of men who are hated by all, and rightly so. However φόρος comes from the verb φέρειν, which means *ferre*, to bring in, and the same root gave the Latins the word *foenus* (interest), which the ancients only used with reference to the produce of the earth—for she, like a grateful debtor, sometimes gave back a hundred grains for one. And indeed it is against nature, as Aristotle said in his *Politics*, for money to breed money.[5] But now this thing is so widely accepted among Christians, that, while the tillers of the soil are despised (though no kind of men are more innocuous or more indispensable to the community), usurers, on the other hand, are considered to be among the pillars of the Church. And yet usury was condemned by the earliest of the human race, regulated and controlled by the laws of the Gentiles, absolutely banned by those of the Jews, fulminated against in the decrees of the Popes, and censured by them in every way. Not that I am particularly against usurers, whose skill I can see some reason for defending, if it had not been condemned by the authority of the Fathers. Especially if one considers the morals of our own times, I would sooner approve of a usurer than

[1] This suggests a reference to the *Praise of Folly*.
[2] 'To exact dues from the dead', I. IX. xii, LB. 336 E.
[3] Aristotle, *Rhetoric*, II, 6.
[4] Suetonius, *Life of Vespasian*, xxiii.   [5] Aristotle, *Politics*, book I.

of this niggardly class of dealers who are on the hunt for profits from every possible source, by trickery, by lies, by fraud, by cheating, buying up here what they sell for more than double there, and robbing the wretched poor with their monopolies—and yet these people, who never do anything else than this in their lives, are the ones we think almost the only people worthy of honour.

I think this proverb is either the same as, or closely related to, the one we have quoted elsewhere, 'he even asks the very statues for flour.'[1] It is jokingly that *farina* (powder or flour) is here spoken of as a tax, because everything comes back to food, and the statues were put up to the memory of the dead, so that anyone who scratched a bit of profit off them seems to be extorting it from the defunct. Among the ancients, however, there was great respect for burial, and graves were held to be inviolable. Nowadays the rage for possession has got to such a pitch that there is nothing in the realm of nature, whether sacred or profane, out of which profit cannot be squeezed, and that not only by princes, but even by priests. In old days, even under the tyrants (when they were as yet untutored and did not know what tyranny really was) certain things were common to all—the seas, the rivers, the highways, the wild game. Now the great lords arrogate everything to themselves, as if they alone were men, or rather gods. The most poverty-stricken mariner is obliged to change his course, even to his peril, and to do and suffer all sorts of things at the will of an insolent robber, as if it were not enough misfortune for him to have to struggle with winds and waves, without these other storms. He reaches the harbour, and something is extorted from him; there is a bridge to cross, toll must be paid; a river to cross, and you will encounter the rights of the prince; suppose you have a small piece of luggage, you must pay dues to get it out of the hands of these impious fellows; and, what is much more cruel, the common people, wretched as they are, are defrauded of their means of existence, and all these tithes and taxes gnaw away the livelihood of the poor. You may not carry the corn from your own fields, without paying a tenth. If you grind or mill it, another bit is nibbled off. Wines cannot be imported without being tithed over and over again. You may get the wine into your cellar, but not before you have parted with half or at least a quarter of the value to these rascally harpies. In some cases more than half of what they call *cervisia*[2] is set aside for the overlord. You may not kill a beast without counting out coin to the tax-gatherers, nor sell a horse bought with your own money without paying out something. When I was living in the country near Bologna, at the time when the city was in the power of Julius,[3] I saw peasants of

---

[1] III. II. lxxxix.   [2] Beer.   [3] Julius II.

the utmost poverty, whose whole living consisted of two oxen, and who did not succeed in keeping their whole family with the labours of these two, but still they had to pay out a ducat on each beast. In some places it is not allowable to contract a legal marriage without paying tax.

But why should I try to catalogue single instances? The greed of these people outstrips the power of words. There is nothing in the world from which they do not squeeze some gain. There is no measure and no limit; every day they think out new ways of getting money, and, once they have managed by chance to establish a precedent, they stick to it fiercely. These performances are hateful enough in themselves, but when they are put through by agents who are even more hateful this arouses much resentment against the rulers. But they think anything beseems them which brings in cash, that is, which increases the hunger of the poor and nourishes the luxury of the nobles (or rather the bandits). And there are even some who make a tidy pile out of the deeds of criminals, using the law as their fishing-net. Now what magistrate's post or governorship is there, which is not for sale in several quarters? And finally, since all these many expedients cannot fill a leaky barrel, i.e. the prince's royal treasury, someone thinks up a reason for going to war, the generals get their heads together, the unhappy population has the very marrow sucked out of its bones, just as if kingship were nothing but a vast profit-making concern.[1]

It may be nauseating to see Christian princes acting thus with more inhumanity than was ever shown by pagan tyrants, but even this is a little less detestable than the fact that among priests too—among the people who ought to despise money, and freely give what they have freely received—there is nothing which is not on the market, nothing inviolable. What an outcry they raise about their tithes, how they harass the miserable peasantry! You can't be baptised, that is made a Christian, without paying for it, and under these glorious auspices you enter the portals of the Church. They don't bless your marriage unless you pay; they only hear your confession because they hope to make money by it. They say the services for pay, they won't sing gratis, nor lay on hands gratis. They can hardly be got to make the sign of benediction from a distance, unless they have been paid. They must have the fee before they will consecrate a foundation stone or a chalice. As to the real duty of priesthood, that of teaching the people, the profit motive corrupts that. Finally, they will not communicate the Body of Christ, except for money. Without mentioning what a harvest they reap from lawsuits, from dispensations (so-called), from remissions of sin which

---

[1] Cf. the humorous picture of the council of the king of France in the first book of *Utopia*.

the common people call indulgences, from the conferring of Orders and institution of bishops and abbots. But why should anything be free of charge, among people who sell the right of burial, even in ground which is not theirs? Among the heathen there was a common burying-ground for the poor, there was at least a place where you could bury your dead without having to pay. Among Christians it is not permitted to dig a hole in the earth for the dead, unless you have leased a little bit of ground from the priest, and if you pay more (but only then) you can have a larger and grander place. If you have paid a great deal, you may lie and rot in the church near the high altar; if you have given stingily, you can be rained on with the common herd outside. It would be shameful enough if they accepted the price as an offering; but now they call it their right, and the audacity with which they insist on it is amazing. Hebron, who was both a Gentile and an untutored man, offered his unknown guest Abraham the courtesy of a free sepulchre, and could hardly be brought by pleading to accept the money offered;[1] and do we, who are priests, sell the right of burial in others' land? Or rather do we turn to private profit what belongs to the public? And no one reaps this kind of harvest more greedily than those who do nothing for the people, but live entirely for themselves, or at most for the prince. Some of them sing us the old song, *the labourer is worthy of his hire*,[2] as if there were no difference between a bishop and a hired soldier, or a labourer. Menial labour is paid with wages. But the duties of princes and priests are beyond price.

(c) Scarabeus aquilam quaerit[3]

Κάνθαρος ἀετὸν μαίεται, i.e. *Scarabeus aquilam quaerit*, the beetle searches for the eagle: when the feebler and weaker seeks to do harm to a far more powerful enemy, and hatches a plot against him. There is another reading, and that a more correct one to my mind, ὁ κάνθαρος ἀετὸν μαιεύεται, i.e. the beetle is midwife to the eagle. The sense is much the same, whether you read μαίεται or μαιεύεται. For it applies to a man, weak in himself, who devises the ruin of one who vastly exceeds him in strength, by means of malicious plots and secret wiles.

[1] See Gen. XXIII, 3–20.   [2] Luke, X, 7.
[3] 'The beetle searches for the eagle', III. VII. i, LB. 869 A. This was one of the proverbs to be printed separately, first by Froben together with the *Sileni Alcibiadis*, in April 1517, and subsequently by Thierry Martens, Louvain, in September 1517. Two other separate editions appeared at Leipzig, 1521, and at Strasbourg, 1522. It was not however translated into any modern language. The only author to have paid great attention to it appears to be R. B. Drummond, who gives a close paraphrase of the proverb in his *Erasmus, his life and character* (London, 1873), I, p. 299.

Aristophanes, in the *Lysistrata*:[1] 'I am furiously angry with you, I am the beetle to your eagle, when you lay an egg I will be the midwife.' There is a fable on this subject among the Greeks, and not without charm; Lucian ascribes it to Aesop, when he says in *Icaromenippus*[2] that Aesop related how once upon a time the beetles and the camels went up to heaven. As to what concerns the fable of the beetle and the eagle, it goes like this:

For a long time there has been war between the race of eagles and the entire population of beetles, an old longstanding enmity, in fact what the Greeks call ἄσπονδος πόλεμος.[3] For they hated each other with a more than Vatinian hatred, so much so that Jupiter himself, οὗ κράτος ἐστὶ μέγιστον[4] and at whose nod Olympus trembles, was unable to make peace between them and end their strife, if the fables tell true.

In fact they got on no better than the noblemen, those gods of our own day, get on with the humble folk in their obscurity.

But there may be someone who is unfamiliar with, and ἀνήκοος[5] of the fables of Aesop, and who will wonder what kind of business an eagle can possibly have with a beetle. What acquaintance or contact or affinity can exist between two such different creatures? For it is when they are linked by something of this sort that discords arise, especially between princes. And whatever could be the cause of this deadly hatred? And then where did the beetle find the courage to open hostilities against the eagle-race? Again, what humiliation could it be which so affected the splendid spirit of the eagle, θυμὸς ἀγήνωρ,[6] that he did not despise so petty an adversary and judge it unworthy even of his hate?

Clearly this is a mighty subject, the outrage one of long duration, and all the circumstances following it are long too, and the whole affair is beyond the eloquence of man. But if the Muses who were willing to dictate to Homer the *Battle of the Frogs and Mice* will aid me too—although it is so long since I deserted Helicon—I will apply my greatest efforts to giving a summary account of the matter. For if he has the favour of the Muses, what may a man not dare?

But to bring the matter into a clearer light, before I come to discuss the affair itself I will describe in as few words as I can the characters of the two protagonists, their habits, their appearance, their nature and their abilities.

First of all, it occurs to me to wonder what came into the heads of

---

[1] *Lysistrata*, 693–4. [2] Lucian, *Icaromenippus*, x.
[3] 'Implacable war'.
[4] 'Whose is supreme power.' *Odium Vatinianum* (II. II. xciv) refers to Vatinius, spoken against by Cicero; Catullus, 14, 3.
[5] 'Ignorant'. [6] 'Splendid soul'.

the Romans—sensible people in other respects—when they treated this bird as they did, using it as a symbol for extolling themselves above other nations and counting themselves next to the gods, winning so many victories and holding so many triumphs under the standard of the eagle, and yet—far from showing gratitude—repaying it with an intolerable insult. For they make it feminine! Not being so very masculine themselves, they unsex and castrate that bird, of all birds the most vigorous and the most male, and turn it into a sort of Tiresias;[1] although *aetos* in Greek is certainly masculine. And that seems to me much more suitable to the eagle, to whom the Father of gods and men gave dominion over the wandering birds—had not Jupiter found him faithful in the matter of flaxen-haired Ganymede, the only creature who dares hand to angry Jove his trident, while the other gods sit aloof (not for him to be frightened by the proverb, 'far from Jove is far from the thunderbolt')? I think it is not without good reason that among all the nations and tribes of the birds the eagle has been found the suitable candidate to be elected king, not only by the φρῆτραι[2] of the birds, but by the *senatus populusque* of the poets and by universal acclaim. As far as the decision lay with the birds the majority of them were inclined to hand over the supremacy to the peacock; that seemed to be its due, by virtue of its beauty, magnificence, exalted character and regal splendour. And the voting would have gone that way at once, if some shrewd birds of long experience, such as the crows and ravens, had not foreseen what would happen after the peacock's election—just what has happened in the case of certain kings for a good many years now! The peacock would have acted the part of king, but only in name and noise, and the eagle would have ruled just the same, even without the votes of his subjects. And indeed I think the poets (wisest of men) were quite aware that no better image could be found to describe the life and conduct of kings. I am speaking of most of them, not of all. In every kind of thing, there has always been and always will be a scarcity of the good. And a new age brings with it new men.

But let us put both sides of the argument in a few words. If there is anything to be augured from a name (and there certainly is), the Greeks were certainly right to call the eagle *aetos*, by connection with *aisso*, which means roughly to dart, to be carried swiftly along. Some birds are naturally mild and gentle, and others which are wild can be tamed by care and skill, and become quiet. Only the eagle is not amenable to any training, nor can be tamed by any efforts. It is simply driven headlong by the force of nature, and whatever it wants it

---

[1] Tiresias, in Greek legend, was turned into a girl.
[2] Clans, or brotherhoods.

demands as by right. Would you like to see a chick with the spirit of an eagle? Horace has drawn a graphic picture:

> Like to the lightning's winged guard . . .
> From his first cradle in the nest
> Courage ingrained and youthful zest
> Drive him of hardships unaware,
> And winds of March, that from the air
> Have swept the storm-clouds, guide aright
> His timid wings in venturous flight;
> Now on the sheep-folds far below
> Sudden he stoops, a mortal foe,
> And urged by love of feast and fray
> Soon makes the writhing snake his prey.[1]

This riddle is better understood by those regions which have experienced how great misfortunes may arise from the unbridled violence of young princes. It is for philosophers to discipline the passions and follow in all things the leading of reason. But as the Satirist says,[2] 'Nothing has more violence than the ear of a tyrant, always ready with the words, I want, I order, my will is the reason why.' I may add that, while there are six kinds of eagles known, I think,[3] they all have something in common, strongly hooked beaks and no less hooked claws, so that from the very appearance of the creature you could tell it for a carnivorous bird, an enemy of peace and quiet, born for fighting, rapine and plunder. And as if it were not enough to be carnivorous, there are some which are said to be bone-crushers—and so they are.

But here, gentle reader, I hear you silently saying to me: what has this metaphor to do with a king? A king's highest glory is to be merciful, and, being all-powerful himself, to wish to hurt no one; to lack a sting alone of all the hive, to devote himself entirely to the well-being of his people, so truly that when that wisest of sages Niloxenus was asked, 'What is the most useful of all things?' he replied, *Rex*. He meant to say by that, that it is the mark of the true prince, to hurt no one, to be of benefit to all, as far as in him lies, and to be the best rather than the greatest. In reality he can only be greatest by being best, that is by being the most beneficent of all. For my part, I admire the pattern monarch which the philosophers skilfully paint for us, and I hardly think such princes are to be found ruling the state in the city of Plato. Certainly in the annals of history one could not find more than

---

[1] Horace, *Odes*, IV, IV (trans. H. B. Mayor).
[2] *ait Satyra*, added after 1520. Juvenal, *Satires*, VI, 223.
[3] Pliny, *Natural History*, book x, 6.

one or two whom one would dare to compare with this model. Moreover, if one were to consider the princes of more recent times, I am
afraid that one would not find in exactly every case that one could not
apply the horrible reproach which Achilles, in Homer, hurls against
Agamemnon, 'People-devouring King'.[1] And Hesiod uses the word
δωροφάγος[2] where he should more properly say παμφάγος.[3] Aristotle
would take as an obvious means of distinguishing between king and
tyrant, that the latter only thinks of his private advantage, whereas the
former consults the good of the people; but to some of them the title
of king is not enough! That title seemed excessive to the early (and
truly great) rulers of Rome, and rather to be avoided for fear of envy,
but now you must add to it a long string of magnificent lies; they must
be called Gods who are scarcely men, Invincible, who never came out
of a battle except defeated, Magnificent, when they are midgets,[4] Most
Serene, when they shake the world with the tumults of war and senseless political struggles, Most Illustrious, when they are darkened by the
profoundest ignorance of all that is good, Catholic, when they have in
mind anything but Christ. And if these gods, these heroes, these
triumphal leaders have any leisure left over from dicing, drinking,
hunting and whoring, they do give every bit of it to truly regal con-
siderations. Their one and only care is this, to utilise laws, edicts, wars
and truces, treaties and councils, acts of justice, everything sacred and
profane, for the purpose of diverting the whole wealth of the whole
community into their own treasury, that is collecting it into a leaky
barrel; and just like eagles, they cram themselves and their young with
the entrails of harmless birds.

Come now, any one who is at all practised in reading faces, let him
have a good look at the very features of the eagle, the greedy, evil eyes,
the cruel *rictus*, the grim cheeks, the fierce brows, and lastly the thing
which Cyrus the king of the Persians was so delighted to see in a
prince, the hook-nose:[5] does not all this call up the very image of a
king, full of splendour and majesty? And then there is the deathly
colour, hideous and ill-omened, filthily dark. Indeed that is why we
call anything dusky and blackish 'aquiline'.[6] Then there is the voice,
the unpleasant, terrifying, paralysing voice, with its threatening screech,
which frightens the life out of every kind of creature. This symbol too
will be recognised at once by anyone who has experienced or merely
witnessed how terrifying the threats of princes can be, even uttered in
jest, and how a shudder of fear goes round when the eagle-voice

[1] *Iliad*, book I.   [2] 'Greedy for presents', Hesiod, *Works and Days*, 39.
[3] 'Greedy for everything'.   [4] A play of words on *Augusti* and *angusta*.
[5] γρυπός.   [6] *aquilus*.

screeches out: 'If they will not give me a fresh prize, I shall help myself to yours, or I shall walk off with Odysseus's. And what an angry man I shall leave behind me!'[1] Or that no less kingly saying: 'Sit there in silence and be ruled by me, or all the gods in Olympus will not be strong enough to keep me off and save you from my unconquerable hands.'[2] At this screech of the eagle, I declare, the common people tremble, the senators huddle together, the nobles pay heed, the judges become obsequious, the churchmen are silent, the lawyers bow in assent, the laws give way, immemorial custom gives way too; nothing can stand up against it, neither right, nor duty, nor justice, nor compassion. And though there are many birds with speaking voices, and many tuneful ones, with such a variety of song and music that they might move the heart of a stone, yet there is less power in them than in that harsh unmusical cry of the eagle.

There is, however, one kind of eagle which pleased Aristotle particularly, perhaps because he wanted his own little chick Alexander to resemble it; no less greedy and no less a bird of prey, it is a little more moderate and quiet, with a milder nature, if only because it brings up its young itself.[3] (The others do what wicked parents usually do, they abandon their young, though even tigers take care of their cubs.) For this reason it is called γνήσιον, as if one should say true and natural. Homer saw this kind, blind as he was. For he calls it μελάνωτον and θηρευτήν, i.e. black-backed, hunter-kind, names which would quite well suit such princes as Nero and Caligula and too many more. There are some of these, how much nearer, ye gods! to the true eagle, or more than aquiline—who, next to the Gods though they may be, yet can stoop sometimes to use their sceptres and the statues of their ancestors to flatter the little common man, and act like spongers, always providing there is a not unattractive booty to be gained.

We are told in literature that the eagle is long-lived. But when it arrives at extreme old age it thirsts for nothing but blood, and by sucking blood it prolongs a life universally hated; in fact the upper part of its beak grows so long that it cannot tear flesh. And hence comes the very well-known proverb Αετοῦ γῆρας[4] applied to drunken old men, because all the other birds of the crooked-talon variety either do not drink at all or very rarely, if we are to believe Aristotle. And when they do drink, they drink water. Only the eagle thirsts for blood. Nature is not always an unkind step-mother! By making this incurved beak she seems to be thinking of the good of the other creatures, and

[1] *Iliad*, book 1 (trans. E. V. Rieu).   [2] *Ibid*. 1.
[3] Pliny, *Natural History*, book x, 6.   [4] 'the old age of an eagle', 1. ix. lvii.

setting a term to this insatiable greed. Likewise with similar foresight she does not allow the eagle to lay more than three eggs, or to bring up more than two chicks. In fact if we are to believe the line of Musaeus quoted by Aristotle,[1] 'It hatches two, lays three, brings up one.' And during the days when they are sitting on the eggs (for they sit for thirty days) careful nature sees to it that they have no food, by turning back their talons, otherwise they would snatch the young of all the wild creatures. During this time their plumes turn white with hunger.[2] And hence they hate their own young. (One might wish to see this among the Roman eagles, but one does not—for of their pillaging of the peasantry there is no limit nor measure. With them the thirst for spoil increases with age, and they never lean more heavily than when they have hatched a chick. Then indeed the population is stricken with one contribution after another.) As well as all this, nature gave the one creature several enemies, of whom more hereafter. And no one will wonder at this careful dispensation of nature, if what Pliny writes is accepted as true, when he relates an extraordinary marvel of voracity (hardly to be credited even on the word of a Democritus, and even though Plutarch, one of the most serious of writers, tells it as an established fact): namely, that eagles' very feathers, if mixed with the feathers of other birds, will eat them up, slowly reducing them to nothing. Such is the power of inborn greed. I think myself that the same thing would happen, if the bones of tyrants were mixed with the bones of humble folk, and that their blood could no more be mingled than that of Aegithus and Florus.

Now just consider with me whether all this does not agree pretty well with the character of some princes. I am not talking about the good and upright ones, and having once said this I should like the reader to remember it. One single pair of eagles needs a large tract of country to devastate, and they will not allow any other plunderer near them, so they settle the limits of their territory. Among our eagles, on the other hand, how important each considers his sway to be! What ambition there is to extend his dominion far and wide! What a struggle with the neighbouring eagles or kites about the limits of his kingdom, or rather of his plundering-space! Perhaps as a matter of fact the comparison is not quite apt, because the bird of prey, rapacious as it may be, does not attack its neighbour, possibly because the harm it does might return on its own head, and instead it seeks its prey from far away; but tyrants do not spare even their own friends, and do not keep their greedy claws off their own kindred and household—nay indeed one is

[1] Aristotle, *Historia Animalium*, VI, 6 (see Pliny, *Natural History*, X, 13).
[2] Pliny, *Natural History*, book X, 13.

in the greater danger, the nearer one stands to the prince, as if to Jove and the thunderbolt.

This inborn and hereditary greed for plunder is much increased by upbringing. Just as eagles push their barely fledged young out of the nest to go hunting, so that they may learn from their earliest youth (from their tender claws, as the proverb says)[1] to live by robbery and to rely on their own talons. But in the case of some princes, heavens above! what incentives are added to natural rapacity! As well as the most corrupt education, there are such swarms of flatterers, so many unprincipled ministers, dishonest counsellors, stupid followers and profligate companions, who get great personal satisfaction from what does harm to the public. Add to these pomps and pleasures, luxury and pastimes for which no booty can ever be enough. Add silliness and inexperience, the most intractable of all things if it is combined with good fortune. Since the most promising minds can be spoilt by these things, what do you think will happen if they are heaped on a greedy and worthless character, like fuel to fire?[2]

But the eagle would not be equipped in kingly fashion[3] enough if it had only hooked talons and hooked beak to arm it for hunting its prey, and had not eyes sharper than Lynceus's,[4] able to gaze unblinking on the sun; it is said that by this quality it is able to detect whether its young are its own. And so these birds watch from far away the prey that they intend to seize. The king of birds, however, has only two eyes, one beak, few claws, and only one maw. But our eagles, wonderful to relate, have goodness knows how many ears (of eavesdroppers),[5] eyes (of spies), claws (of officialdom), beaks (of governors), bellies (of judges and lawyers), the latter practically insatiable, so that nothing is enough for them, nothing is safe from them, not even what is hidden in the most private chambers or the most secret papers.

To continue, the eagle would perhaps be less harmful if it were not that its weapons and bodily strength are reinforced by a crafty mind; as a blade, murderous enough in itself, is tipped with poison. When it walks it draws in its claws, clearly so that their points may not be blunted for plundering; it has this in common with the lion.[6] It does not attack all and sundry, but only those creatures it believes weaker than itself. And it does not swoop suddenly towards the earth, as other birds do, when it is after its prey, but sinks gradually, so as not to startle it by a violent attack. Even a hare, its favourite prey, it will not attack unless it perceives that the animal has come down to level

---

[1] Ad., I. VII. lii.
[2] I. II. ix.
[3] βασιλικῶς.
[4] II. I. liv.
[5] corycaeus, I. II. xliv.
[6] Pliny, Natural History, VIII, 41.

ground. Nor does it lie in wait at all hours—no one is going to catch it at a moment of weariness!—it flies out hunting from breakfast-time to noon, and then for the rest of the time it sits idle, while the market-places fill with thronging people.[1] Then, when it has killed, it does not immediately devour the prey, lest a swift attack should find it feeding and off its guard. It rests and makes sure of its strength, and then it carries off the prey to its nest as if to a fortress. By what arts it captures a stag, so much superior to itself, I shall soon relate. There is a par-ticularly memorable proof of its cleverness, the way it snatches up a tortoise, rises high and picks out a suitable place below, and drops the tortoise on a rock, so that it can eat the flesh from the broken shell. Although there was nothing very eagle-eyed about the one which mistook the shining bald head of Aeschylus for a stone and dropped a tortoise on it, thus killing the poor man, and so making itself hated by all the race of poets, and with good reason. And it goes on doing the same thing now, as if by right. What it actually did was to persuade the tortoise in its wily way that it was going to teach the poor shell to fly. And, when the tortoise was buoyed up by this hope, the eagle dashed it down upon a stone, just like a tyrant taking pleasure in another's disaster. Anyone who ponders over the various arts, plots and schemes and juggling tricks by which bad rulers arm themselves for the despoil-ing of the people—levies, fines, false honours, pretence of war, use of informers, family alliances—anyone who considers all this will almost declare that the eagle is unworthy of being taken as an example of kingly rule.

It remains for us to describe the kind of enemies this aristocratic brigand has to meet. For what the proverbs say is true—the eagle does not catch flies, or look for worms. It ignores the booty which seems unworthy of its regal claws—unless there are some who are related to Vespasian, who thought money smelt good wherever it came from.[2] There are in fact some degenerate eagles who live by fishing, and who will not disdain a carcass already killed. But the nobler sort, like tyrants, leave something for pirates and robbers, though there is nothing which distinguished them from these gentry, as that lofty-minded pirate said in the presence of Alexander of Macedon, barring the fact that they have greater forces and a bigger fleet to harass a larger part of the world with their plunderings. So the eagles leave small fry to the other birds of prey, and themselves attack four-footed beasts, not without danger, but not without the hope of victory, as becomes an energetic leader. Among these is particularly the hare, as I said, which is hunted by the

[1] Much of this is taken literally from Pliny, *Natural History*, book x, iv.
[2] Suetonius, *Life of Vespasian*, 23.

eagle, and so one kind is called the hare-eagle, as a general may be called Africanus or Numantinus.[1] It does not despise the unwarlike foe, but wants to eat it, and so although victory does not bring much glory it brings no little profit. But sometimes it happens that, when the eagle is hardest in pursuit of the hare, it is most likely to be caught itself, hit by a feathered arrow—as the proverb says, *killed by its own feathers*.[2] It dares even to fight with the stag, but is likely to be beaten unless it puts on a wolf's skin. For craft steps in where strength runs low. Before rushing into battle, it rolls itself in the dust, and then alighting on the antlers of the stag it shakes the dust collected on its feathers into the animal's eyes, and beats on its face with its wings, so that in the end the stag is blinded and driven against the rocks. But with the snake there is a keener fight, of which the outcome is much more uncertain— it may even be in the air. The snake hunts for the eagle's eggs with deadly cunning, and the eagle in turn snatches up its enemy whenever it sees one.[3]

That there should be war to the death between the fox and the eagle will surprise no one who knows what a kingly reception the one gave the other in old days. Once the eagle was friendly with her neighbour the fox, but, when she was sitting on her eggs and had no food, she stole the cubs from her neighbour and took them to her nest. The fox came home and saw the mangled remains of her offspring. All she could do was to call upon the gods, and especially on Jupiter φίλιος, the avenger of violated friendship. And some god seems to have heard her prayer. It happened a few days afterwards that the eagle carelessly carried into her nest a live coal which was clinging to the flesh of a sacrifice. And then, when the eagle went away again, the wind gently fanned the fire and the nest burst into flames. The terrified chicks threw themselves out, although not yet fledged. The fox picked them up, took them to her hole and devoured them. From that time onwards, there has been no possibility of agreement between the eagle and the fox, and the foxes have suffered no little from this; though I am not sure that they deserved it, since they once refused to join in alliance with the hares, who were begging for reinforcements against the eagles (see 'The Annals of the Beasts', from which Homer got his *Battle of the Frogs and the Mice*).

Then there is deep enmity also between the eagle and the vulture, a creature who may be said to work on the same lines, a runner-up in gluttony, though for this reason it is more cruel, while the eagle is nobler, because it eats only what it has killed, and does not settle lazily on carcasses killed by others.

---

[1] 'Britannicus or Germanicus', all editions before 1533.
[2] In Greek, see *Adages*, I. VI. lii.   [3] Pliny, *Natural History*, X, 17.

The eagle has reason to hate the nuthatch, which uses cunning wiles to break the eagle's eggs; and it fights with the heron, which even when it is being carried away in the eagle's claws is not afraid to turn on it and do battle so fiercely that it dies in the struggle. Nor is it strange that there should be enmity between the eagle and the swan, truly the bird of poetry; what is strange is that the swans often get the better of so fierce a creature. The race of poets is apt to be unpopular with kings whose consciences are not too clear, for it is a free and plain-speaking race, which sometimes prefers, like Philoxenus, to be taken back to prison[1] rather than be silent. For if they have a grievance, they write it down in their black books, and let out the secrets of kings to the kings' own descendants.

There is bad feeling too between eagles and cranes, I think because the latter greatly appreciate democracy, so hated by kings; and they beat the eagles by intelligent behaviour. For when they migrate from Cilicia and have to cross the mountains of Taurus, the haunt of eagles, they take up big stones in their beaks, thus preventing themselves from making any sound, and fly across silently by night, and so they cross in safety and cheat the eagles.

But there is a special enmity between the eagle and the wren as it is called, for no other reason (or so says that famous old rambler)[2] than that it is also called by the name of king or counsellor.[3] This is particularly among the Latins. And so the eagle visits deadly hatred upon it as a pretender to the throne. And yet it is not an enemy whose might is to be feared by the eagle. For the wren is a tiny little flitting thing, yet endowed with such sense and quickness that it hides in thickets and deep places, so that it cannot easily be caught by a more powerful adversary. In old days when it embarked on a flying contest with the eagle, it won, more by craft than by strength.

Finally, the eagle wages deadly warfare with the Cybindus, so unremitting that they are frequently caught locked together. The Cybindus, however, is a night hawk. And there is no kind of man more hated by tyrants than those who can see quite clearly in the dark—who disagree completely with the common opinion.

But would it not be ridiculous for me to go on enumerating the enemies of a creature which is at war with everyone? In the case of other species of living creatures there is war on one hand and friendship on the other; the fox has many foes, but it has a friend in the raven, who gave it help against the bird Aesalon attacking the fox-cubs. It also gets on well with snakes, as they are both fond of rabbits. The crocodile has

---

[1] *in lapidicinas* (1515, 1520, etc.); *in Latomias* (1533).
[2] Aristotle: referring to the word 'Peripatetic'.   [3] βουληφόρος.

an enemy in the ichneumon[1] but a close intimacy with the wagtail, so close that the bird is allowed to hop unharmed into the great beast's jaws. It is the eagle alone which has no friendship nor kinship with any living creature, no comradeship, no daily intercourse, neither treaty nor truce. It is the enemy of all, and all are its enemies. Obviously a creature cannot fail to be the enemy of all others, when it lives and fattens on all others' distress. And therefore, with an evil conscience, it nests not in the plain but among rugged and lofty rocks, sometimes in trees, but only in the tallest, like a tyrant muttering to himself, *Let them hate me as long as they fear*.[2] And so it happens that, while storks are sacred to the Egyptians, so that it is a capital offence to kill one, geese were sacred to the Romans, no one among the Britons will harm a kite, the Jews do not kill pigs, and the ancients refrained from hunting the dolphin (it was forbidden to harm them, but if people had made a mistake while hunting they were given a few strokes of the whip like boys); against the eagle there is the same law all over the world, as against wolves and tyrants—it is a deed of merit to kill the common enemy of all. Thus the eagle loves none and is loved by none, no more than evil rulers are loved, who rule for themselves and to the great disaster of the state.

Perhaps these affections belong only to ordinary people; these great satraps are so estranged from them that sometimes they do not even love their own children, apart from the profit they can make out of them, and often they hold them in suspicion and hatred. That an animal as savage as a lion should retain a sense of gratitude to a man who had been kind to it, and should save the life of the person who had healed its paw, is a story almost everyone believes. Many people believe in the snake which used to protect its master and come at the call of the familiar voice. Then there is the story of the viper which used to come every day to a certain man's table: when it found that one of its offspring had stung and killed the son of its host, it killed its own child, to avenge the outrage against hospitality, and never came back into that house out of pure shame. Philarchus tells this tale and there are some who credit it; Demetrius Physicus thought it worth writing and Pliny took the trouble to repeat it.[3] There was a panther whose cubs a man had rescued from a pit; it obligingly led the way for him until he had got out of the wilderness and into the open road.[4] Aristophanes the Grammarian was the lover of a girl of Stephanopolis, and his rival was an elephant; Plutarch says this was well known and much talked about. He also speaks of a snake which passionately loved an Aetolian girl.[5]

---

[1] The Nile rat.   [2] Seneca, *De Clementia*, I, 12, II, 2; *De Ira*, I, 10.
[3] Another story (not this one) is told by Pliny, *Natural History*, VIII, 61.
[4] *Ibid*. VIII, 60.   [5] *Ibid*. VIII.

As for the dolphin and its love for human beings, there is no doubt about that; it saved the life of Arion, brought Hesiod to shore, rescued the virgin Lesbia with her lover, carried a boy backwards and forwards out of kindness. But even those who believe everything do not believe a girl could be loved by an eagle. You can judge what a deadly hatred this creature has, towards men too, by the fact that it was chosen to be the tormentor of Prometheus, of all the gods the greatest lover of humanity, on Mount Caucasus.

And yet there is something to be praised, among such a multitude of vices. The most rapacious of creatures are the least given to drink or lust. When the eagle carried away Ganymede, it was for Jove and not for itself. But you may see some of our eagle-hearted gentry carrying off for themselves, not one Ganymede, but girls and married women, and this activity makes them almost more intolerable than their pillaging, which above all is not to be borne.

And so we may say that there are many kinds of birds, some to be admired for their rich and brightly coloured plumage, like the peacock; some remarkable for snowy whiteness like the swan; some on the contrary of a beautiful shining black, like the raven; some of extraordinary height like the ostrich; some famous for legendary marvels like the phoenix; some praised for their fertility like the dove; some appreciated for the pleasures of the table, like partridges and pheasants, some merry talkers, like parrots, some wonderful singers, like nightingales, some notable for their courage, like cocks; some born to be pets, like sparrows; but, out of them all, the eagle alone has seemed suitable in the eyes of wise men to represent the symbol of a king—the eagle, neither beautiful, nor songful, nor good to eat, but carnivorous, greedy, predatory, ravaging, warring, solitary, hated by all, a universal pest, the creature who can do the most harm and would like to do even more than it can.

It is exactly on the same grounds that the lion is appointed king of the animals—when there is no other great beast which is fiercer or more noisome. Dogs are useful for a great many things, and especially for keeping watch over people's possessions. Oxen till the soil. Horses and elephants go to war. Mules and donkeys are useful for carrying loads. A monkey can fawn and cling. Even the serpent has its use—for showing the value of marathrus for improving the eyesight. The lion is nothing except a tyrant, the enemy and devourer of all, never safe but for its strength and the fear it inspires; obviously it must be a royal creature, just like the eagle.

This seems to have been well understood by those who emblazon those aristocratic shields with lions gaping their widest and spreading out their claws for their prey. Pyrrhus, who liked to be called the Eagle, was apparently more perceptive in this than Antiochus, who rejoiced in the name of Hawk. But there is no need to be surprised that the lion was chosen as king of the beasts, since even among the gods of the poets it was Jove who was considered most fitted to administer the kingdom—Jove, the unfilial son who persecuted and drove out his own father, the incestuous husband of his own sister, embellished with so many instances of debauchery, adultery, and rape, and after all this 'with darkest frown and smouldering thunderbolt', striking terror to all. For it is all very well to sing the praises of the republic of the bees, in which only the ruler may carry no sting, many may praise it but no one copies it, any more than they copy Plato's.

To come back to the eagle: on account of the qualities which I have described, so truly royal, and the excellent services it renders to the whole range of living creatures, the senate and people of poetry have decreed by a large majority, first that it should be given the title of king universal, and even deified; then that it should have a decent enough place among the constellations, and they decorated it with a few little stars; and lastly that it should be awarded the honour (among all the heavenly beings) of bringing to angry Jove the weapons with which he shakes the whole earth. So that this could be done with impunity, they gave also another gift: of all living beings, the eagle is the one who fears not the thunderbolt and is never harmed by it, but gazes on the lightning with the same unblinking stare that it turns upon the sun. An addition to all this was made by those sage old pristine Romans, who arranged that the eagle should have first place among the standards of their legions, and be as it were the ensign bearer of all the standards, all the others following after—even the wolves, the nurses of the Roman race, and the minotaurs and boars, not beasts of the greatest rapacity, and finally the horses. For in old days the standards bearing the signs of these four beasts followed the eagle; soon afterwards, it not only outdistanced its companions but left them in camp, and it alone was carried into battle. This creature alone, I repeat, was considered worthy to be the mark of everything belonging to the monarch of the whole world; it adorned his sceptres, banners, shields, houses, clothes and dinner-service and livery, although unless I am mistaken it was on the augury of the vultures that Rome was founded and not on that of the eagles. The college of augurs added another point, that if an eagle were to perch on somebody's house, or drop a cap on his head, it was a portent of imperial rule.

So much for one of the contending generals; now I will turn to the beetle. It is an animal (or perhaps scarcely an animal at all, since it lacks several senses) belonging to the lowest species of insect, which the Greeks call by a notorious name, κάνθαρος, and the Latins *scarabeus*; horrid to look at, horrider to smell, and horridest of all by its buzzing noise, with wings covered by a scaly sheath. Indeed, the whole beetle is nothing but a shell. It is born in excrement, that is in the dung of animals, and in that it lives, and makes its home, takes its pleasure and wallows with delight. Its chief occupation is to make balls, as large as possible, like pastilles, only they are not made of scented stuff but of dung, preferably goats' dung; for that to the beetle has the fragrance of marjoram. It rolls them along backwards with tremendous efforts, pushing up with its back legs (they are very long) and with its head touching the ground. If, as sometimes happens, they push their burden up some slope, and the balls continually slip and come rolling back again, you would think you saw Sisyphus rolling his stone. They are never tired, they never rest, so great is their keenness for the work, until they have got the stuff into their holes. In these balls they themselves were born and they bring up their young the same way, and keep them warm while they are young, nestling against the winter's cold.

I know the beetle is well known to everybody, as it is to be met with everywhere except where there is no dirt at all. But there is more than one kind. There are some whose shell has a kind of greenish-black shine. Some are rough, horribly black. There are others which are larger, armed with very long two-pronged horns, with the tip shaped like pincers, and when they wish they close them to nip or squeeze. Some are reddish, and they are very large indeed; they dig into dry soil and make their nests there. Some make a terrifying buzz and dreadful booming noise as they fly, and frighten the unwary quite badly. There are other variations. But one thing is certainly common to them all: from dung they come, on dung they feed, in dung is their life and their delight.[1]

I imagine someone—an earnest supporter of the Roman generals— is going to bewail the evil fate of the eagle, who has to contend with such a humble and low-born enemy; so regal a bird, against an opponent like that, in conquering whom there would be no glory, while to be beaten by him would be most shameful! The mere fact of confronting the eagle would give him enormous credit, even were he to be beaten in the field. According to the poets, Ajax was ashamed of having so unwarlike an opponent as Ulysses,[2] and is the eagle to be forced to contend with the beetle? Again, someone else will wonder wherever such a vile insect got such spirit and audacity as not to be afraid of

---

[1] Pliny, *Natural History*, XI, 98–9.   [2] *Odyssey*, book XI.

entering on a war with the most warlike of birds. And where did it find the resources, the strength, the means and the allies necessary to carry on the war for so many years?

But in reality anyone who opens this Silenus-image,[1] and looks at this despised creature more closely and as it were sees it at home, will find it endowed with so many unusual qualities, that, all things carefully considered, he would decide that he would rather be a beetle than an eagle. Now let no one raise a shout or contradict me until he knows the facts. First of all, the beetle is superior to the eagle in this, that every year he sloughs off his old age and immediately renews his youth. This in itself is so important, that I imagine even some of the Roman Pontiffs—they who may go straight to heaven because they have the Keys—when they arrive at unloved old age, which must resign all pleasures, would rather cast their skins with the beetle, than have a sevenfold crown instead of their triple one. Then, in so small a body, what valour of spirit the beetle has! What mental power, worthy of heroes! What vigour in the attack! Homer's fly[2] is nothing compared to the beetle. It is for this reason, I think, that some beetles are nick-named bulls. Even lions will not rashly come into conflict with bulls, and eagles still less.

It is also endowed with no common brains, unless we are to think that the Greek proverb 'wiser than the beetle' is without foundation, either in origin or in its wide acceptance; it seems to refer to some special and unique wisdom. It makes no difference if someone sneers at the way it is housed, and says that its home is disgusting. As far as physical beauty goes, if you consider the matter without vulgar prejudice, the beetle is really not to be despised. For, if the Philosophers say true, that the figure we call a sphere is not only the most beautiful, but in every way the best, and that it and no other was chosen by the great creator to be the shape of heaven, the fairest of all things—why should not the beetle seem beautiful, since it approaches much nearer to this shape than the eagle? And if a horse is beautiful in his kind, and a dog in his, why should not the beetle have its own beauty? Unless we are to measure everything by ourselves, and judge everything deformed which does not conform to human shape. As to colour, no one, I think, will criticise the beetle for that, as it is a hue which graces some gems. The fact that he uses the dung of animals for his own purposes is a point which does credit to his brains, not a fault. As if doctors did not do exactly the same thing, when they use animals' dung or even human

---

[1] See explanation in *Sileni Alcibiadis*.
[2] Does Erasmus refer to 'Virgil's' *Culex*, in imitation of 'Homer's' mock-epic, *The Battle of the Frogs and Mice*? Or to the gadfly of *Iliad*, XXIV, 532?

excrement not only in making ointments, but as medicine in disease.
The alchemists (godlike men, obviously) are not ashamed to use ordure
in their search for what they call the quintessence. Farmers, who used
to be the most honoured of the human race, are not averse either to
enriching their fields with manure. There are some people who use
dung to plaster the walls of their houses; and they pound it and dry it
in the sun, and then use it to keep the fires going, like wood. The
Cypriots fatten their oxen on human ordure, and not only fatten them
but doctor them with it. But, you say, a disgusting thing like that smells
sweet to him. Well, it would be stupid to expect a beetle to have the
nose of a man. Indeed, it is a peculiarity of the human race to dislike
the smell of its own excrement; it is not so with any other creature. So
the beetle is better off than we are, not dirtier. As a matter of fact, in the
case of men too it is not so much the thing which disgusts them, but the
idea; for to the earliest mortals the thing itself was not so disgusting as
it is to us, or they would never have given it the auspicious name of
laetamen and they did not hesitate to call the god Saturn by the nick-
name of Sterculeus, and it was a compliment too, if we are to believe
Macrobius. According to Pliny[1] Stercutus the son of Faunus gained
from this not only his name, but his immortality throughout Italy; and
in Greece the same thing brought glory to two kings, that is to Augeas
who thought it out, and to Hercules who made it famous. And there is a
memory that will never perish, preserved to posterity by Homer because of the very thing which is the beetle's delight: the picture of the
royal old man (as Cicero mentions in his book on Cato)[2] spreading
manure on the fields with his own hands. There was a Roman emperor
who did not mind a stench if there was money attached to it,[3] and why
should the beetle be scared of a thing of so many uses by so slight an
inconvenience, if it be one at all? And finally, when we see the beetle
keeping clean in the midst of its dung, with its shell always shining, and
the eagle smelling bad even in the air, well, I ask you, which of them is
the cleaner? Indeed I think this is the origin of the name, the beetle
being called *cantharos* or *catharos* (clean), unless you like to derive it
from the Centaurs. You must not think that the beetle is debarred by
its squalid nature from liking luxurious living, for it seems according to
Pliny that it has a particular love for roses, and covets them above
everything.

These endowments may seem slight and common, but there is one
which no one will deny to be magnificent, a real feather in his cap: the
fact that in old days the beetle had pride of place among divine images

[1] *Natural History*, XVII, 50.   [2] *Odyssey*, XXIV; Cicero, *De Senectute*, XV.
[3] Suetonius, *Life of Vespasian*, XXIII.

and priestly rites, as the most fitting symbol for an excellent warrior. Plutarch tells us, in his commentary on Isis and Osiris,[1] that in the Egyptian hieroglyphics the sign for a king was an eye, with the addition of a sceptre, which signified watchfulness allied to the right and just administration of the state. For in those days, I believe, there were still kings of this sort very unlike eagles. The same author says that at Thebes they kept certain statues without hands, representing judges, who must be as far as possible from all bribery, and among these there was one which also lacked eyes, and signified the president of the court, because for him the important thing was to be without personal preference, and to see only the matter in hand, without seeing the individual concerned. And there among the sacred images (not, as the proverb says, a weed among the vegetables) was the beetle, carved on a seal. And what did the sage theologians intend to signify by this new symbol? Apparently something not at all common—an eminent and invincible military leader. This, by the way, is also mentioned by Plutarch, in case anyone should think I have invented it as allegories are often trumped up by ignorant theologians.

Some uninformed person may ask, what has a beetle to do with generalship? There are many points of agreement. In the first place, you see how the beetle shines all over with armour, and there is no part of its body which is not protected with scales and plates, so that the Mars of Homer in all his panoply would not seem better armed. Then there is the warlike onset, with terrifying panic trump, and truly military music. For what is harsher than the sound of trumpets, or ruder than the roll of drums? The song of the trumpets, indeed, which now delights kings so much, was unendurable to the Busiritae of old, because it sounded like an ass's bray, and among those people the ass was detested.

Then you have the beetle's patience in its labour of rolling burdens along, its invincible perseverance, and the way it takes no account of its own life. They say, I may add, that there are no females in the beetle kind, but all are male. I ask you, what could better suit a mighty emperor? There is also a perfect fitness in the fact mentioned by the same Plutarch, that they use those delightful balls of theirs which I have described for the birth, nurture, food and bringing-up of their young; birthplace and victuals are one and the same thing. It is not very easy for me to explain this mystery. Those who could expound it better are the soldiers under the general's command,[2] who know what it is to be 'the guest of one's shield, to sleep on the ground', who have often during a sharp siege borne hard winters and harder hunger, who have

---

[1] Plutarch, *De Osiride*, XI, 354.   [2] *imperatorii milites.*

dragged out a life of ill-health from eating not only roots but rotten food, who have spent months at sea. Compared with the filthiness of this life, the beetle is clean; compared with its wretchedness he is enviable. But this is really the fate and manner of life of the most brilliant commanders—in case anyone happens to sneer at it. Only it is permissible to wonder why our rampart-stormers prefer to put on their escutcheons (on which they think their whole title to nobility rests) either leopards, or lions, or dogs, or dragons, or wolves, or some other animal which chance has thrown in their way or which they have chosen to adopt, when the really suitable symbol is the beetle; and when it is not only perfectly apt, but attested and consecrated by that very antiquity which is the one and only begetter of aristocracy.

Finally, no one will think the beetle altogether to be despised, on considering that doctors and learned leeches draw remedies from this creature for the greatest ills of mankind. Indeed the horns of the Lucani (for so they call this sort) are not only carried in purses but hung round people's necks, sometimes set in gold, as a remedy against all infantile diseases. Would it surprise you if the beetle were to claim equal power with the eagle in the most successful cures (and the least credible too, if the authority were not Pliny)? That is to say, a certain particular beetle, carved on an emerald; for, as the proverb says, you can't carve a Mercury out of any kind of wood, and the beetle does not regard every gem as worthy of him, but if he is carved on an emerald, the brightest of gems, as I said, and hung round the neck (on apes' hair, remember, or swallows' feathers), he will prove an immediate cure for poison of all kinds, and as effective as that herb Moly which Mercury gave to Ulysses.[1] Not only is he useful for this, but he brings no common luck to anyone preparing to seek audience of a king; so a ring of this kind is the one to be worn by those who have decided to petition a king for some fat benefice, an archdeaconry or a bishopric, for so they are called. Likewise it keeps away headaches—no small trouble, upon my word, especially to heavy drinkers. In the matter of these cures, remarkable as they are, the sage physicians make no difference between the eagle and the beetle. So who can scorn the said beetle, whose very image carved on a stone has such virtue? The mention of gems reminds me to add another thing, that if the eagle prides itself on having given a name to a jewel (Aetite) the beetle does not yield to him in this. For to him the *cantharias* owes its name, imitating the whole appearance of the creature, so you would think that it was not the moulded form, but the true and living beetle imprisoned in the jewel.

To conclude (if there is anything in this), the dung-descended beetle

---

[1] *Odyssey*, book x.

is distinguished by as many proverbs as the eagle, the king of birds. If any adherent of the eagle party wishes to deny that the beetle can stand comparison on this score, on the grounds that the Thebans (thick-headed fellows) used to place the eagle among their gods, well, I will not deny it, but let him remember that the eagle shared this honour with crocodiles and tailed apes, together with onions and the breaking of wind, since among the Egyptians all these wonders had divine honours. And, if there is any value left after these comparisons in the empty name of divinity, there are not lacking those who would attribute divine honours to the beetle as well.

There we have the portraits of both generals. Our remaining task is to examine the causes of such a ferocious war. Once upon a time on Mount Etna, an eagle was in hot pursuit of a certain hare, and was so near pouncing with tense claws upon its prey, that the animal—timid by nature and now breathless with fright—fled for refuge to the nearest beetle's hole. So it is that at a critical moment, when things are desperate, one seeks for shelter anywhere and hopes to get it. This beetle, however, was, in the words of Homer, 'good and great'. For in that mountain the beetle kind is said to be of particularly triumphant stock, so that the 'beetle of Etna' has passed into a proverb, apparently from its majestic proportions. And so the hare took refuge in the beetle's cave, and flung itself as a suppliant at his feet, begging and praying his household gods to protect its life against the savage enemy. The beetle found it quite flattering that there should be anyone in existence who wished to owe life to him, and who believed that he could supply so great a gift. And then to think that his hole, which all human beings were apt to pass by holding their noses and using bad language, should seem fit to be a place of refuge, to be fled to like the altar of sanctuary or the statue of a prince!

The beetle immediately flew to meet the eagle, and tried to mollify the raging creature with these words:

The greater your power, the more it becomes you to spare the harmless. Please do not bring mourning into my home with the death of an innocent animal. And thus may your own nest be safeguarded from a similar disaster. It is the mark of a noble and kingly spirit to forgive even the unworthy: and the guiltless—surely they should be protected by respect for the home, which must be safe and inviolate for everyone; so justice demands, so law allows, so custom decrees. If your suppliant lacks importance, at least he has zeal— let it influence you.

> Though you may scorn the Beetle race, yet still
> The Gods remember deeds of good and ill.[1]

[1] A parody of Virgil, *Aeneid*, 1, 541–2.

If you are not afraid of the fate of those who violate the heart of home—a deed which may turn back on to your own head—at least respect mighty Jove, whom you are offending in three ways by one single act: this is my guest, you are wronging the laws of hospitality, he is my suppliant, and I am yours, you are flouting the law of the olive branch, and lastly I pray as a friend for a friend, you are violating the law of friendship. You know well what sure anger Jupiter conceives in his wrathful heart, how sharp is his revenge when injured, of course you know, you carry his weapons to him as he rages. He does not allow his own people free rein in everything, he does not condone every kind of conduct in those he loves.

The beetle would have said more, but the eagle beat him with her wings and threw him contemptuously to the ground. The hare begged in vain; the eagle killed it before the beetle's eyes, tore it up and carried away the mangled remains to her savage eyrie; neither the prayers nor the threats of the beetle were of the slightest avail. The eagle would not have scorned the beetle in this fashion if her good sense had been equal to her strength and audacity, or if she had happened to remember the tale of the lion who was saved by a mouse when in the direst peril of its life—the king of all the beasts accepting on occasion a gift which is almost beyond the power of the gods, from a humble and despised little animal. Or she might have considered the case of the ant inspired by gratitude to save the life of the dove, by stinging the bird-catcher's heel. It is so true that there is no creature of so humble and so low a kind that it cannot on occasion be useful as a friend and harmful as an enemy, even to the most powerful foe. But at that time nothing of all this occurred to the eagle; she simply took over the prey that came to hand and enjoyed it.

That humiliation sank deeper into the heart of the lofty-minded beetle than anyone would have dreamed. It roused his sublime and titanic soul. It made him feel shame, that his influence should be of so little weight in so just a cause; pity, for a harmless and peaceful animal, torn to pieces in such a ruthless way; and chagrin at being so helpless under the eagle's fierce contempt, when he did not feel that he deserved contempt at all. Indeed no one seems to himself to be without dignity. And then it occurred to him that the whole race of beetles would be put to shame, if once that deed of the eagle's were to pass unpunished.

At this point the beetle, powerless to avenge himself, yet showed something regal in his behaviour. The same thing as was meant by Calchas speaking of Agamemnon to the other kings: 'Even if the king swallows his anger for the moment, he will nurse his grievance till the day when he can settle the account.'[1] He called up before his mind all

---

[1] *Iliad*, book I, trans. E. V. Rieu.

sorts of arts and schemes. It was no common penalty which he was preparing; it was extermination and utter ruin that he was turning over in his mind.

But he did not think it safe to plunge straight into open war with such a fierce enemy as the eagle. Not only because his forces were inferior, but because Mars is a stupid and senseless god, as blind as Plutus himself, or Cupid, and often favours the worst cause. Even if it were not so—if forces were equal and the best man was sure to win— he could still see a way in which he could cause more torment to the eagle and secure a better vengeance to satisfy his hate, if by taking away the hope of posterity he were to make the eagle, living and feeling, die a long lingering death. There is no severer way to torture parents than through their children. Those who will endure the most cruel torments in their own body, cannot bear to see their children tortured. He had seen asses rush into the fire to save their colts, careless of their own lives, and many other instances of this behaviour in other animals. He thought that the eagle was no different from others in these affec- tions. And then he thought it would be safer for his own race if he could wipe out such a tenacious enemy root and branch, so to speak. I think he must have heard the well-known proverb: 'You may kill the father, the children will be left.' A certain alluring hope was also tickling his fancy—when the deed was done, and the eagle overthrown, perhaps he might become king himself.

Suffering not only makes people strong and fearless, it also makes them wise. So he sought industriously to find out where the enemy hid her hope of posterity. When he had discovered this, he went to Vulcan, who was rather a friend of his on account of their similarity in colour. He begged him to hammer out a suit of armour, not too heavy to fly in, but strong enough to protect him against an average attack. Vulcan armed the beetle from top to toe, in the very armour which he still wears (for before that he was unarmed, like a fly).

The eyrie was far away, on a lofty, rugged crag, surrounded by a defensive barricade of branches and brushwood. Thither forthwith goes our remarkable beetle, whether by flying or creeping along his- tory does not relate, but he arrived. Some say that he was carried up clinging to the feathers of the unconscious eagle, and deposited by her unawares in the nest. Anyhow, the beetle managed to find a way into a place where man, the most cunning of all animals and the cleverest at doing harm, has never penetrated. He laid wait, hidden among the brushwood, and seizing a propitious moment, pushed the eagle's eggs out of the nest one after the other, till there was not one left. They were smashed by the fall, and the yet unformed chicks dashed pitifully against the rocks, deprived of life before they had consciously lived at all. The beetle's resentment was not satisfied by this dreadful punishment; it added another. There is a precious stone, a gem of the greatest value, which the Greeks call Aetite from the name of the eagle; it is not unlike an egg, and one sex can be told from another, for in the female you can see a foetus enclosed rather like a chicken. It has a wonderful power of aiding delivery at birth. For this reason it is placed on women in labour to this day, to make delivery easy. It is usual for the eagle to place a couple of this kind in its nest, otherwise it could not lay eggs, or certainly not hatch them. This was the great treasure which the beetle threw out of the nest, so as to destroy all hope of future parenthood. The stones shattered into fragments on the pointed rocks below.

But the beetle's rage was not assuaged even by this. It would be too slight a disaster, unless he could enjoy the grief, and so he hid again in the bushes.

The eagle came back, saw the recent calamity which had struck her family, and the mangled remains of her offspring; she saw the loss of the priceless jewel; she wailed, she cried, the howled, she shrieked, she lamented, she called on the gods—and with those famous eyes of hers, made even sharper by grief, she looked round to find the mighty enemy. As she thought it over anything and everything came into her mind, rather than the despised beetle. Terrible were her threats, terrible her curses, against the author of such a disaster, whoever it might be. Can you imagine what pleasure filled the beetle's heart as he listened? What could the wretched eagle do? She must fly off again to the Fortunate Isles, for only from there could she bring back the eagle-stone. Another couple of stones must be found. The nest was removed to a much loftier and remoter position. Again the eggs were laid, and the unknown enemy penetrated there too, just the same; everything was ruined, the same tragedy was re-enacted. Once again the eagle removed to a safer stronghold, laid more eggs, collected more eagle-stones. But once again the beetle was there.

Over and over again the one fled and the other followed, until the bird, wearied out by so many fatalities, decided to appeal for divine protection, and, instead of relying on her own powers, to turn for help to the ruler of the gods. She went to Jove, described the whole sequence of her tragedies, and how she had an enemy who was most powerful, and (worst of all) anonymous; so that, after enduring so much, there was no hope of revenge. She added that the ruin which threatened her was a matter which affected Jove, too, because the imperial office which he had bestowed would come to an end and he would have to find another armour-bearer, if the enemy succeeded in finishing what it had begun; she added that there was some value in having known and familiar servants, even if the new arrival of Ganymede had been a pleasant change. Jove was moved by the danger in which his attendant stood, especially since he still felt grateful about the recent kidnapping of Ganymede. He commanded the eagle, if she so wished, to lay her eggs in his very bosom. There, if anywhere, they would be safe. The eagle produced the eggs, and laid in the bosom of mighty Jove the last hope of her race, entreating him, by that blessed egg which Leda brought forth to him long ago, to guard them well.

What will not deep-seated grief do? I am afraid the facts will seem hardly credible. The unconquerable beetle flew up to the very strong-hold of mighty Jove, with the help of some occult power. He deposited in Jove's bosom a ball expressly made for the purpose out of dung. Now Jupiter is unaccustomed to squalor, dwelling as he does in the purest region of the universe, far removed from the contagion of earth; and so he was disgusted by the offensive smell and tried to shake off the dirt from his bosom, thus inadvertently throwing out the eagle's eggs, which fell from such a height that they perished before touching the ground. And so at length it came out that the beetle was the author of all these calamities, and he had his final touch of bliss. He was delighted to be acknowledged. It was a heavy addition to the eagle's discomfiture—for Jove learnt all the facts from the beetle himself—that the cause of her disasters was so contemptible a creature. It is no small consolation, if one is vanquished by a noble foe.

Hence the war broke out between them afresh, and the eagle attacked the beetle kind with all her might wherever she came across them, harrying them, carrying them off, crushing them, destroying them. The beetle on the other hand strained every nerve to ruin the eagle. And so they went on, without truce or respite, preying on each other, laying wait and killing, and there seemed to be no possible outcome except the final destruction of both species, a Cadmean victory as one might say; with such gladiatorial fury did they each try to intercept the other. The eagle could not gain the victory, the beetle did not know the name of defeat.

In the end Jupiter thought it necessary to intervene in such a dangerous condition of things, and attempted privately to reach an understanding between them. The harder he tried, the more violent their hatred became, their passion blazed up and their battles grew fiercer. Without doubt the god himself had a leaning to the eagle's side; on the other hand, it was setting a most harmful example if anyone were to be allowed to flout the laws of sanctuary, of friendship, and of hospitality. And so he did what he usually does at critical moments—he assembled the council of the gods; and in a few words he explained to them the course of the affair. Speaking through the herald Mercury, he threw the matter open to discussion, and invited them to declare their opinions. There was some divergence in their inclinations. The smaller gods were almost all on the side of the beetle, and, among the greatest even, Juno strongly supported him, out of hatred to Ganymede—she was hostile to the eagle's cause. Finally, all had to agree with a decision announced in a clear voice by Mercury and graven in bronze by Vulcan, that the eagle and the beetle were to go on according to their wish waging eternal war. Whatever loss befell either party, he could not complain in law, it was to be considered the fortune of war, and whatever either seized he was to hold by right of conquest; only the gods did not favour the complete extermination of either race. For this reason there was to be an armistice kept for thirty days, with no hostilities, while the eagle was sitting on her eggs. During that time no beetle was allowed to appear in public, so that the eagle should not have to cope with the fatigue of war as well as with fasting and the care of a brood. Jupiter added another thing owing to his partiality for the eagle (and not without arousing some protest): 'It is only right', said he, 'that out of the vast expanse of the earth some tiny corner should be reserved for my own servant, as a place of sanctuary where she could be safe from the attacks of the beetles. And this is no new idea which I am suggesting. There are places where wolves are unknown, where poisons cannot enter, where moles cannot live. I myself will measure out a tract of land in Thrace, near Olynthus, and, if any beetle sets foot there, for any reason, whether prudent or imprudent, willing or unwilling, let him die the death; once he has got in he shall never get out again, but there he shall writhe until he dies. That place shall be given the name of Beetle-lessia[1] so that by that very word the beetle may know it will be the end of him if he dares to break into that place against our express command. The eagle is banished from Rhodes, lest anyone should think it hard to banish the beetle from Olynthus.'

He spoke; Olympus trembled at his nod.

A murmur ran through all the assembly of the gods.

This decree holds good to this very day, and always will. A war to the death goes on between the eagles and the beetles but, during those days when the eagle is sitting, the sons of the beetle are nowhere to be seen. The place which Jupiter assigned is most carefully avoided by them; if one is taken there, it dies at once. If any reader desires confirmation of this fact, he will find it in Pliny, book IX, chapter 28. And

[1] *Cantharolethrus.*

also in Plutarch, a weightier author, in his commentary on the Tranquillity of the Mind.[1]

But I know very well that you have been saying to yourself for a long time, dear reader, 'whatever is this man thinking about, to deluge us with nonsense about nothing at all—not making an elephant out of a fly, as they say, but a giant out of a beetle? As if it were not enough trouble to get through all these thousands of adages, without his wearing us out with all this rambling twaddle.' Let me say a word. Everyone has his own opinion, and to some people I seem scanty in my comments on the adages, and meagre. For they think the only grand thing is to extend a volume to an immense size. I wanted to show them that in the rest of the book I have made an effort to be brief; otherwise there would have been no lack of matter to enrich it with, if I had thought more of showing off my abundance than of giving pleasure to the reader.

But let us get back to the proverb. Aristophanes the comic poet has an allusion to this fable in *Irene*, in the following lines:[2]

> It is the only living thing with wings,
> So Aesop says, that ever reached the Gods.
> O father, father, that's too good a story
> That such a stinking brute should enter heaven!
> It went to take revenge upon the eagle,
> And break her eggs, a many years ago.

The story teaches us that no enemy is to be despised, however humble he may be. For there are some tiny men, of a very low sort but extremely pernicious, no less black than beetles and no less evil-smelling and contemptible, and yet by the persistent cunning of their hearts (although they can do no good to any mortal creature) they can often bring trouble even to great men. Their blackness is terrifying, their noise drowns everything, their stench is a nuisance, they fly round and round, won't be shaken off and wait their chance—so that it is far preferable to compete with great men sometimes than to irritate these beetles, whom one is ashamed of mastering; it is impossible either to shake them off or to struggle with them without coming away defiled.

II. THE CHURCH

Under this heading we may group a number of essays in the *Adages* which placed it, in 1515, alongside Erasmus's other works contributing to reform within the Church. Criticism of contemporary behaviour

[1] Plutarch, *On the Tranquillity of the Mind*, xv.
[2] Aristophanes, *Peace*, 129–34, trans. B. B. Rogers.

among ecclesiastics took two forms in the *Adages*: on the one hand it was part of the campaign against obscurantism, and especially against the resistance to the New Learning, and on the other it went deeper and attacked the clergy on moral issues.

There are a number of digs at the enemies of Good Letters. *Impossibilia captas*[1] is illustrated by the folly of attempting to find peace of mind in wealth or vulgar pleasures, or 'true learning without the knowledge of languages'. *Elephantus non capit murem*[2] has a plain straightforward comment in 1508: 'The noble and distinguished mind does not trouble about vile booty or small profits. A man of true learning does not carry on attacks against those minute creatures who ape the really educated. A man of real power is not worried by the pinpricks of small fry.' But in 1515 an additional note brings in a new idea:

In these days a ridiculous use has been made of this adage by our mock philosophers and would-be theologians, when owing to their ignorance of Greek and Latin they make some horrible mistake (which they do all the time): 'An eagle', they say, 'doesn't catch flies', as if they were eagles, indeed, when they babble out their silly sophistries, or as if the knowledge of languages were not the greater part of learning.

The charming adage about the rarity of friendship between hedgehogs,[3] *Prius duo echini amicitiam ineant*, suggests that 'there is little agreement between the prickles of the theologians and good letters', and a caustic note on 'perishing like the last bean', *tam perit, quam extrema faba*,[4] explains the last bean is in danger of being trodden underfoot or nipped off by passers-by, and the image may be applied to a man or a thing exposed to injuries from all sides, 'or one might say that Theology is *perishing like the last bean* because everywhere it is being handled by the most ignorant people (*Sophists* in 1515), and thus destroyed.'

Between the 1515 and 1517 editions Erasmus made two notes expressing his distrust of Aristotelian teaching and influence. The first is a mere aside, a straw showing the direction of the wind; on *Croeso, Crasso ditior*[5] he remarks that some names are given by Pliny, xxxiii, iii and x, of people who possessed inordinate riches, 'and among these is Aristotle, that holy philosopher, almost a God for the theologians of our times.' But in another place he expresses this distrust more fully:

Try for the highest, and you may obtain a moderate success ... But today some Aristotelian theologians teach how far one may go in permitting wealth, in gambling, in making war or seeking revenge. It would be far better to shun

[1] I. X. vii. [2] I. IX. lxx. [3] II. IV. lxxxiii (1517).
[4] IV. IV. lxxii (1515). [5] I. VI. lxxiv.

the appetite for riches, war and pleasure altogether. Then we might manage to pursue them with moderation. But now, when we are satisfied with the mediocre, we fall far below mediocrity.[1]

But it is not only for lack of learning or for false ideals that the contemporary churchmen deserve censure. They are Pharisees, aptly illustrated by the adage *suum cuique pulchrum*:[2] 'those who arrogate piety to themselves more proudly than ever the Pharisees did; imbued as they are with intolerable and unmentionable vices, they rage with extraordinary arrogance against the lives of others.' The fable of Bacchus descending to the lower regions with the lion-skin of Hercules over his delicate womanish tunic, *Leonis exuvium super crocoton*,[3] is turned into a dig at hypocrisy: 'This may aptly be applied to some monks or scholastics who wear the dress of their order in public, but in private behave like soldiery, or who are forbidding in appearance and effeminate in their lives.' He is caustic about the 'diseases of good men', *Hic bonorum virorum est morbus*:[4]

(used) ironically about some harsh and gloomy vices, which although they are among the most hateful do not lead to dishonour because important and respected men suffer from them. Who does not condemn a thief? And yet adultery is much worse, and great nobles make it a matter of pride. To be envious, to be a backbiter, to concentrate on amassing wealth—this is much worse than to have a girl to sleep with for fear of the dark, as St Jerome says. But a priest who does this is called a good-for-nothing, a cess-pit, while others are held to be upright and holy, who swell with ambition or consume away with avarice, or breathe the poisonous stench of envy on to everyone else; these, if you please, are the diseases of good men.

The chief essay on these topics is the long *Sileni Alcibiadis*. This essay, one of the most important of the 1515 edition, was carefully edited and expanded by Erasmus in later editions. His modifications are of three kinds: (*a*) precautionary measures, including several toning-down passages and one omission; (*b*) reinforcement of the argument; (*c*) a final summing-up inserted before the last paragraph, which may stand with other writings as part of the effort he was making in his last days to appeal for the unity of the Church. There are also two shorter pieces which may find a place here: they are attached to the proverbs *Illotis manibus*, *Ignavis semper feriae sunt*.

[1] II. III. xxv (1517), *Summum cape, et medium habebis*.　[2] I. II. xv (1520).
[3] III. V. xcviii (1515).　[4] III. VII. lxxiv (1515).

(d) Illotis manibus[1]

Illotis manibus, with unwashed hands, ἀνίπτοις χερσίν, is mentioned by Diogenianus as meaning irreverently and without due preparation; it is borrowed from the idea of purification for sacred ceremonies. Hesiod, in *Works and Days*,[2] forbids anyone to pour a morning libation to Jove with unwashed hands.

> Nor shall you ever, in your eagerness, pour a morning libation to Jove
> With unwashed hands, nor to any other of the gods.

Similarly, he gives a warning against stepping into a stream or a spring *manibus illotis*. Hence there is frequent mention in Homer of χέρνιβες. This expression means exactly *washing of hands*, a rite always observed in old times before divine service, and even before a feast, considered a sacred thing. Gregory (called the Theologian) joins both of these terms in his *Apology concerning his flight to Pontus*: 'With unwashed hands, as the saying is, and profane feet, they break into the sacred mysteries.'[3] Gaius, LI, pandect I, entitled *On the Origin of Law*, says: 'If it is apparently an abomination, so to say, for those who plead causes in public to explain their affair directly to the judge without any prefatory speech, how much more improper is it for those who promise an interpretation, to plunge straight into the matter of the interpretation itself, without any opening stages, without delving into origins, and, so to speak, with unwashed hands?'[4]

Both proverbs [i.e. this and the preceding *illotis pedibus*] are to be used of those who rush into an undertaking either recklessly, or else without sufficient knowledge of the important facts; as if someone were to seize the office of a prince without possessing virtue or wisdom or the experience of public affairs. Or as if an attempt to interpret Divine Scripture were made by one who was unschooled and ignorant of Greek, Latin, and Hebrew, and of the whole of antiquity—things without which it is not only stupid, but impious, to take on oneself to treat the mysteries of Theology. And yet—terrible to relate—this is done everywhere by numbers of people, who have learnt some trivial syllogisms and childish sophistries and then, heavens above, what will they not dare? What will they not teach? What will they not decide? If they could only know what amusement, or rather what sorrow they arouse in those who know languages and the classics—what howlers they produce and what scandalous errors they fall into—they would

---

[1] I. IX. lv; LB. 354 C.   [2] *Works and Days*, 740–1.
[3] Gregory Theologus, *Apologetica*, VIII; *Oratio*, II.
[4] Gaius, *Digest*, book I, title 2, *de origine iuris*, fragment I.

certainly be ashamed of their rashness and would go back (even as old men) to the first steps of learning their letters. Plenty of people judge rightly without knowing the rules of logic, to say nothing of the quibbles of the schoolmen. There were wise men on the earth before Aristotle (the god of those people) was born. No one ever understood any other person's opinion without knowing the language in which that opinion was expressed. And so what did Saint Jerome do, when he had decided to expound Holy Scripture, and did not wish to set about it with unwashed hands, as they say? Did he fill his head with nonsensical sophistries? Or with the rules of Aristotle? Or with nonsense even more frivolous than this? Not he. What then did he do? With incalculable toil, he made himself master of the three tongues. He who is ignorant of them is no theologian, but a violator of Theology. Truly *with hands and feet unwashed*, he is taking the most sacred thing of all, not to treat it, but to profane it, pollute it and do it violence.

(e) *Ignavis semper feriae sunt*[1]

Those who are idle and at leisure are said to keep holiday (*feriari*) and the words *feriati* (holidaymakers) and *feriae* (holidays) are metaphors which have become proverbial. Theocritus in his *Bucolics* says 'it is always holiday for the idle'.[2] For on festive days the pagans abstained from worldly business. Those who are shy of work long for feast-days, when they may be idle and indulge their appetites. And so of old the peasants were given some feast-days to recreate their weary selves in play, but religion was mingled with it so that their sports might be kept within bounds. Nowadays, however, the Christian multitude spends those 'holydays', which were instituted of old for piety's sake, in drinking, lechery, dicing, quarrelling, and fighting. There is no time when more offences are committed, than on these days when people ought specially to abstain from offending. We are never better at imitating the heathen, than at the very times when we ought to be most Christian! And since it is perfectly clear, that a thing devised for the benefit of religion is becoming the destruction of religion, I cannot imagine why the Popes go on adding feast-day to feast-day, when it would be better to copy good physicians who change their remedies according to the course of the disease, having only one thing in mind, the re-establishment of good health. So when they see a thing which was valuable for the times in which it was instituted becoming a plague to religion, now that the ways of Christians are changed, why should it

[1] 'For the lazy it is always holiday', II. IV. xii; LB. 586 F.
[2] *Idylls*, xv, 26, see Plutarch, *On Tranquillity of the Mind*, xx.

be an offence against religion to change the custom, for the very same reason for which our ancestors established it? What I say about saints' days can be applied to many other things. Not that I want to condemn Christian festivals, but I don't want to see them increase indefinitely; and I should like to see those few which were instituted by the authority of early times returning to the purpose for which they were invented. For to true Christians every day is a feast-day; but to the wrong sort (the great majority) holidays are profane rather than holy.

But, to return to the proverb, it may well be applied to those who will find an excuse in everything, to allow them to be idle: those who find learning disagreeable, for instance, will excuse themselves on the grounds of health, or of domestic business, or say the winter is too cold, or the summer too hot, and the autumn weather is particularly dangerous. The beauty of spring, so soon to fade, calls them away from their books. They say there must be no reading after dinner, before the meal has been digested; before dinner they are far too hungry! It's lazy, they say, to stay in the house by daylight; and sitting up by candle-light hurts the eyes. If they are comfortably off, why bother with learning, they say? If not—well, a poor man can hardly be a philosopher. The young man says he is not going to spend the flower of his youth on elderly cares. The greybeard says he must take care of his health.

(f) Sileni Alcibiadis[1]

Σειληνοὶ 'Αλκιβιάδου, i.e. the Sileni of Alcibiades, seem to have become proverbial among the learned; at any rate they are quoted as a proverb in the Greek collections; used either with reference to a thing which in appearance (at first blush, as they say) seems ridiculous and contemptible, but on closer and deeper examination proves to be admirable, or else with reference to a person whose looks and dress do not correspond at all to what he conceals in his soul. For it seems that the Sileni were small images divided in half, and so constructed that they could be opened out and displayed; when closed they represented some ridiculous, ugly flute-player, but when opened they suddenly revealed the figure of a god, so that the amusing deception would show off the art of the carver. The subject of these statuettes is taken from that ridiculous old Silenus, the schoolmaster of Bacchus, whom the poets call the jester of the gods (they have their buffoons like the

---

[1] 'The Sileni of Alcibiades', III. III. i; LB. 770 C–782 C. *Sileni Alcibiadis* was published separately by Froben in 1517, and the *Bibliotheca Erasmiana* lists six other separate editions in Latin, three in Spanish, one in German, five in Dutch, and one in English. This last was printed by John Goughe, London, *s.d.* but probably 1543.

princes of our time). Thus in *Athenaeus*, book v, the youth Critobulus jeers at the old misshapen Socrates, calling him *more deformed than Silenus*—the place is to be found in Xenophon, the *Banquet*.

Socrates: You boast as if you were the more beautiful.
Critobulus: Yes, by Jupiter! otherwise I should be the ugliest of all Sileni among the Satyrs.

And, in the *Symposium* of Plato, Alcibiades starts his speech in praise of Socrates by drawing a comparison between him and the Sileni, because he looked quite different to the eye of an intent observer from what he had seemed at first appearance. Anyone who took him at his face value, as they say, would not have offered a farthing for him. He had a yokel's face, with a bovine look about it, and a snub nose always running; you would have thought him some stupid, thick-headed clown. He took no care of his appearance, and his language was plain, unvarnished, and unpretentious, as befits a man who was always talking about charioteers, workmen, fullers, and blacksmiths. For it was usually from these that he took the terms with which he pressed his arguments home. His wealth was small, and his wife was such as the lowest collier would refuse to put up with. He seemed to admire the beauty of youth, he seemed to know love and jealousy, though even Alcibiades learnt how far Socrates was from these emotions. In short his eternal jesting gave him the air of a clown. In those days it was all the rage, among stupid people, to want to appear clever, and Gorgias was not the only one to declare there was nothing he did not know: fusspots of that kind have always abounded! Socrates alone said that he was sure of one thing only, that he knew nothing. He was apparently unfitted for any public office, so much so that one day when he stood up to do something or other in public he was booed out.

But once you have opened out this Silenus, absurd as it is, you find a god rather than a man, a great, lofty and truly philosophic soul, despising all those things for which other mortals jostle and steer, sweat and dispute and struggle—one who rose above all insults, over whom fortune had no power, and who feared nothing, so that he treated lightly even death, which all men fear; drinking the hemlock with as cheerful a face as he wore when drinking wine, and joking with his friend Phaedo even as he lay dying. 'You had better sacrifice a cock to Aesculapius to liberate yourself from your vow,' he said, 'since when I have drunk this medicine I shall feel the benefit of true health'—leaving the body, from which arise all the many maladies of the soul. So it was not unjust that, in a time when philosophers abounded, this jester alone should have been declared by the oracle to be wise, and to

78

know more—he who said he knew nothing—than those who prided themselves on knowing everything. In fact that was the very reason for his being judged to know more than the others, because he alone of them all knew nothing whatever.

Another Silenus of this kind was Antisthenes, grander with his stick, his wallet and his cloak than all the riches of the greatest kings. Another Silenus was Diogenes, whom the mob considered a dog. But it was about this dog that a divine observation was made by Alexander the Great, the fine flower of princes, it seems, when in his admiration for so great a soul he said 'If I were not Alexander, I would wish to be Diogenes'; though he ought all the more to have wished for the soul of Diogenes, for the very reason that he was Alexander.

Epictetus was another of these Sileni, a slave, and poor, and crippled, as his epitaph tells; but, greatest fortune of all, he was dear to the gods, something which can only be attained by purity of life combined with wisdom. Indeed, this is the nature of truly noble things; what is most valuable in them is hidden away in secret, what is worthless is exposed to view, and they hide their treasure under a miserable covering rather than show it to profane eyes. But the commonplace and the trivial have a very different approach: they please at the outset and put all their finest wares in the shop-window but, if you examine more deeply, you find they are anything but what their style and appearance led you to expect.

But is not Christ the most extraordinary Silenus of all? If it is permissible to speak of him in this way—and I cannot see why all who rejoice in the name of Christians should not do their best to imitate it. If you look on the face only of the Silenus-image, what could be lower or more contemptible, measured by popular standards? Obscure and poverty-stricken parents, a humble home; poor himself, he has a few poor men for disciples, chosen not from king's palaces, not from the learned seats of the Pharisees or the schools of the Philosophers, but from the customs-house and the fisherman's nets. Then think of his life, how far removed from any pleasure, the life in which he came through hunger and weariness, accusation and mockery to the cross. The mystic prophet was contemplating him from this angle when he wrote, 'He hath no form nor comeliness; and when we shall see him, there is no beauty that we should desire him. He is despised and rejected of men', and much more in this vein.[1] But if one may attain to a closer look at this Silenus-image, that is if he deigns to show himself to the purified eyes of the soul, what unspeakable riches you will find there: in such service to mankind, there is a pearl of great price, in such

[1] Isa. LIII, 2–3.

humility, what grandeur! in such poverty, what riches! in such weakness what immeasurable strength! in such shame, what glory! in such labours, what utter peace! And lastly in that bitter death there is the source of everlasting life. Why do the very people who boast of his name shrink from this picture? Of course, it would have been easy for Christ to have set up his throne over all the earth, and to possess it, as the old rulers of Rome vainly claimed to do; to surround himself with more troops than Xerxes, to surpass the riches of Croesus, to impose silence on all the philosophers and overthrow the emptiness of the Sophists. But this was the only pattern that pleased him, and which he set before the eyes of his disciples and friends—that is to say, Christians. He chose that philosophy in particular, which is utterly different from the rules of the philosophers and from the doctrine of the world; that philosophy which alone of all others really does bring what everyone is trying to get, in some way or another—happiness.

The prophets were Sileni of this kind in old time, exiles, wandering in the wilderness, dwelling with the wild beasts, living on wretched herbs, clothed in the skins of sheep and goats. But one had looked right into these Silenus-images when he said, *Of whom the world was not worthy.*[1] Such a Silenus was John the Baptist, who with his robe of camel-hair and his belt of hide outshone all the purple and jewels of kings, and with his dinner of locusts surpassed all the dainties of princes. Indeed, One perceived the treasure hidden beneath the rough cloak when he summed up all his praises in that wonderful testimony, saying, *Among them that are born of women there hath not arisen a greater than John the Baptist.*[2] Such Sileni were the Apostles, poor, unschooled, unlettered, base-born, powerless, lowest of the low—the objects of everyone's scorn, ridiculed, hated, accursed—in fact the public laughing-stock and abomination of the world. But just open the Silenus-image, and what tyrant could possibly claim to equal the power of these men who commanded demons, quieted the raging sea with a nod, brought back the dead to life with a word? What Croesus would not seem poor beside them, as the mere falling of their shadow gives health to the sick, and the touch of their hands imparts the Holy Spirit? What Aristotle would not seem stupid, ignorant, trivial, compared to them, who draw from the very spring that heavenly wisdom beside which all human wisdom is mere stupidity? No offence is meant to those who think that it is a shocking and criminal thing to detract in any way from the authority of Aristotle. I grant that he was a man of most consummate learning, but what light is so bright that it is not dimmed by being compared with Christ? The kingdom of heaven has

[1] Heb XI, 38.   [2] Matt. XI, 11.

as its symbol a grain of mustard seed, small and contemptible in appearance, mighty in power; and diametrically opposite to this, as I have said, is the reckoning of the world.

Such a Silenus, scorned and ridiculed, was the great Bishop Martin, and such were those bishops of old, sublime in their humility, rich in their poverty, glorious in their forgetfulness of glory. There are still today some hidden good Sileni, but alas, how few! The greater part of mankind are like Sileni inside out. Anyone who looks closely at the inward nature and essence will find that nobody is further from true wisdom than those people with their grand titles, learned bonnets, splendid sashes and bejewelled rings, who profess to be wisdom's peak. In fact you may often find more true authentic wisdom in one obscure individual, generally thought simple-minded and half-crazy, whose mind has not been taught by a Scotus (the subtle as they say) but by the heavenly spirit of Christ, than in many strutting characters acting the theologian, three or four times Doctor So-and-so, blown up with their Aristotle and stuffed full of learned definitions, conclusions, and propositions. I would not say this of all, but alas, of how many! In the same way you would find in no one less real nobility than in those Thrasos with their long pedigrees and collars of gold and grand titles, who brag of their noble blood; and no one is further from true courage than those who pass for valiant and invincible just because they are rash and quarrelsome. There is no one more abject and enslaved than those who think themselves next to the gods, as they say, and masters of all. None are in such trouble as those who think themselves most fortunate; the world grovels before some men because they are rich, but they are really the poorest of the poor. No one is less bishop-like than those who hold first rank among bishops. Again and again I beg you, reader, not to think that I mean this as an insult to any particular person: I am talking of the thing itself, not the people. Let us hope there are none whom the cap fits! And if there are none now—which the Lord grant—there have been such in the past, and there will be in the future. I wish it were also not true, that those who are furthest from true religion are just the people who claim to be the most religious— in name, in costume, and in external appearance of sanctity. And so it is always the same: what is excellent in any way is always the least showy.

In trees, it is the flowers and leaves which are beautiful to the eye: their spreading bulk is visible far and wide. But the seed, in which lies the power of it all, how tiny a thing it is! how secret, how far from flattering the sight or showing itself off! Gold and gems are hidden by nature in the deepest recesses of the earth. Among what they call the elements, the most important are those furthest removed from the senses, like air and fire. In living things, what is best and most vital is secreted in the inward parts. In man, what is most divine and immortal is what cannot be seen. In every kind of thing, the material of which it is made is the baser part, most apparent to the senses, and the essence and value of it is felt through its usefulness, and yet that is far from sense-impressions. So, in the organisation of the body, phlegm and blood are familiar and palpable to the senses, but the most important thing for life—breath—is least observable. Lastly, in the universe, the greatest things are those not seen, like substances, which are called separate. And at the highest point of these there stands what is furthest removed from the senses, namely God, further than our understanding or our knowing, the single source of all things. Indeed one may find some similarity with the Sileni in the Sacraments of the Church. Let no one be offended by this. You see the water, the salt and the oil, you hear the spoken words, these are like the face of the Silenus; you cannot hear or see the power of God, without which all these things would be but mockeries.

The very Scriptures themselves have their own Sileni. If you remain on the surface, a thing may sometimes appear absurd; if you pierce through to the spiritual meaning, you will adore the divine wisdom. Speaking of the Old Testament, for instance, if you look at nothing but the story, and you hear of Adam being made from mud, his little wife being abstracted secretly from his flank as he slept, the serpent enticing the woman with the bait of an apple, God walking in the cool of the day, the sword set at the gates of Paradise lest the exiles should return —would you not think all this a fable from Homer's workshop? If you read of the incest of Lot, the whole story of Samson (which Saint Jerome judging by the externals calls a fable), the adultery of David and the girl lying in the old man's arms to warm him, the meretricious marriage of Hosea—would not anyone with chaste ears turn away as from an immoral story? And yet under these veils, great heaven what wonderful wisdom lies hidden! The parables of the Gospel, if you take them at face value—who would not think that they came from a simple ignorant man? And yet, if you crack the nut, you find inside that profound wisdom, truly divine, a touch of something which is clearly like Christ himself. It would be too discursive to go on piling up examples; suffice it to say that, in both the domains of nature and faith you will find the most excellent things are the deepest hidden, and the furthest removed from profane eyes. In the same way, when it is a matter of knowledge, the real truth always lies deeply hidden, not to be understood easily or by many people. The stupid generality of men often blunder into wrong judgements, because they judge everything from the evidence of the bodily senses, and they are deceived by false imitations of the good and the evil; it is the inside-out Sileni which they marvel at and admire. I would speak here of the bad, I would not insult the good—nor the bad either for that matter. After all, a general discussion about moral faults does not lead to the injury of any individual —and would that there were fewer to whom these words could apply. When you see the sceptre, the badges of rank, the bodyguards, and when you hear those titles—'Your Serene Highness, Most Clement, Most Illustrious'—do you not revere the prince like a god on earth, and think you are looking at something more than human? But open the reversed Silenus, and you find a tyrant, sometimes the enemy of his people, a hater of public peace, a sower of discord, an oppressor of the good, a curse to the judicial system, an overturner of cities, a plunderer of the Church, given to robbery, sacrilege, incest, gambling—in short, as the Greek proverb has it, an Iliad of evils. There are those who in name and appearance impose themselves as magistrates and guardians of the common weal, when in reality they are wolves and prey upon the state. There are those whom you would venerate as priests if you only looked at their tonsure, but, if you look into the Silenus, you will find them more than laymen. Perhaps you will find some bishops too in the same case—if you watch that solemn consecration of theirs, if you contemplate them in their new robes, the mitre gleaming with jewels and gold, the crozier likewise encrusted with gems, the whole mystic panoply which clothes them from head to foot,[1] you would take them to be divine beings, something more than human. But open the Silenus, and you find nothing but a soldier, a trader, or finally a despot, and you will decide that all those splendid insignia were pure comedy. There are those—and I wish they were not to be met with so frequently—who, judging by their flowing beards, pale faces, hoods, bowed heads, girdles, and proud truculent expressions, might be taken for Serapio and St Paul; but open them up, and you find mere buffoons, gluttons, vagabonds, libertines, nay, robbers and oppressors, but in another way, I dare say more poisonous because it is more concealed—in fact, as they say, *the treasure turns out to be a lump of coal*.[2] Again I must warn you that no one need be offended by these remarks, since no one is alluded to by name. Anyone who is not like this may consider it has nothing to do with him; anyone who recognises his own weakness, may take the admonition to himself. Let the first congratulate himself, and the second give me thanks.

Among all kinds of men, there are those everywhere to be found whose physical appearance would make you think they were not only

----

[1] In Greek.   [2] Greek proverb.

men, but noble examples of mankind: but, if you open up the Silenus, you will perhaps find a pig, or a lion, or a bear, or an ass. Something has happened to them which is different from what the poets' fables tell of Circe and her magic potions. In her house they had the shape of beasts and the minds of men; but these people look like men, and inside are worse than beasts. On the other hand, there are those who on the face of it, as they say, hardly resemble men, and yet in the depths of their heart they hide an angel.

Here then lies the difference between the follower of the world and the follower of Christ; the first admires and chases after the worthless things which strike the eye at once, while the second strives only for the things which are least obvious at a glance, and furthest from the physical world—and the rest he passes over altogether, or holds them lightly, judging everything by its inner value. Among the 'good things' (as Aristotle calls them)[1] which are not a natural property of man, come first and foremost riches. But with the common people, nay, with almost everyone, the man who has got hold of them by hook or by crook is regarded most highly. The whole world hunts for them over hill and dale. The thing next in order of importance is noble birth—though, if nothing else goes with it, it is simply laughable, an empty name. Is it sensible to half-worship a man who can trace his descent from Codrus King of Athens, or from the Trojan Brutus (was he ever born, I wonder?) or from the Hercules of legend, and call the man obscure who has won fame by his learning and his merit? Is one man to be illustrious because his great-grandfather made a great slaughter in war, and another common, with no statues erected to his name, when he benefited the whole world with the riches of his soul? In the third place come the gifts of the body; anyone who happens to be tall, hardy, handsome, and powerful is included among the number of the lucky ones, but all the same riches come first and birth second—the last thing to be thought of is the mind. If you divide man according to St Paul into three parts, body, soul, and spirit (I am using his very words),[2] it is true that the common people value highest what is most obvious—the lowest part, condemned by the Apostle. The middle term, which he considers good if it joins forces with the spirit, is approved of by many also. But the spirit, the best of ourselves, from which springs as from a fountain all our happiness—the spirit, by which we are joined to God—they are so far from thinking it precious that they never even ask whether it exists or what is is, although Paul mentions it so often in his teaching. And so we get this utterly reversed estimate of things; what we should particularly honour passes without

---

[1] Aristotle, *Moralia*, I.   [2] 1 Thess. v, 23.

a word and what we should strive for with all our might is regarded with contempt. Hence gold is more valued than learning, ancient lineage more than virtue, the gifts of the body more than the endowments of the mind, ceremonies are put before true piety, the rules of men before the teaching of Christ, the mask is preferred to the truth, the shadow to the reality, the counterfeit to the genuine, the fleeting to the substantial, the momentary to the eternal.

The reversing of values brings about a reversed use of words. What is sublime they call humble; what is bitter they call sweet; the precious is called vile, and life, death. To give one or two instances in passing: can those people be said to *love* who ruin others by indulgence, or who have designs on their modesty and fair fame? when no enemy could do worse? They call it justice, when evil is conquered by evil and crime by crime, and when the injury received is paid back with high interest. It is supposed to be unfair to marriage to expect it to be untainted, as near as possible to virginity and as far as possible from the brothel. A man is called traitor and enemy of his prince, because he wishes that prince not to be free to act outside the law and against the right—because, in fact, he wants him to act like a true prince, and to be as far as possible from the portrait of the tyrant, the most hideous of wild beasts. The man who is called the supporter, the friend, the partisan of princes, is he who corrupts them by wrong education, instils into them worthless opinions, cheats them by flattery, makes them an object of popular hatred by his evil counsels, involves them in wars and crazy disturbances of the peace. They say it increases the dignity of a prince to have a touch of the tyrant—that is, a large share of the worst of evils. They call anyone who wishes to cut down enforced taxation an embezzler of public money. But since the chief attributes of the prince, by which he represents God, the only true king, are these three, goodness, wisdom, and power, is it really being a friend to the prince to rob him of his two most important possessions, goodness and wisdom, and leave him with only power, and that not only false, but not even his own? For power, unless it is allied to wisdom and goodness, is tyranny and not power, and, as it has been conferred by popular consent, so it can be taken away; but even if a prince loses his throne, if he possesses goodness and wisdom, they are his own, and go with him. It is a capital offence to desecrate the royal standard; but a reward is given to those who vitiate the mind of the prince, and turn him from a good one to a cruel one, make him crafty instead of wise and a tyrant instead of a ruler. One death is too mild a punishment for the attempt to poison the prince's cup; is a prize to be offered for corrupting and poisoning his mind with unwholesome ideas, as it were tainting the very fount and source of the common weal, to the detriment of the whole world? The office of a prince is called dominion, when in reality to fulfil the role of a prince is simply to administer what belongs to all. The marriage alliances of kings, and their treaties continually being renewed, are supposed to be the cement of Christian peace—when it is from these sources that nearly all wars and most disturbances in human affairs arise. It is called a just war, when princes act in collusion to exhaust and oppress the state; they call it peace, when they plot together for the same purpose. They say it is an extension of empire, when the name of one town or another is added to the domains of the prince, although it may be bought by pillaging the citizens and shedding much blood, by making so many women widows and so many children fatherless.

In the same way they call the priests, bishops and Popes 'the Church', when in reality they are only the servants of the Church. The Church is the whole Christian people, and Christ himself says it is too great to lie down before the bishops who serve it—they would have less obsequious treatment, but be more truly great, if they were to follow Christ in his life and actions as they are his successors in their office—if they were to do as he did, who, although he was prince and lord of all, took upon himself the part of a servant and not of a master. The whole force of the thunderbolt is hurled against those who defraud the priests' collecting-bag of a few coins—they are called enemies of the Church, and very nearly heretics. Now I am not on the side of the defrauder, let no one think it; but pray tell me, if there is any pleasure in hating the enemy of the Church, could there be any enemy more pernicious, more deadly than a wicked Pope? If there is any diminution of the landed property or income of the priests, a general protest arises that the Christian church is being oppressed. When the world is being incited to war—when the evil-living of the priests is the means of bringing so many souls to ruin—no one mourns for the sad fate of the Church, although this is when the Church is really being hurt. They say that the Church is being honoured and adorned, not when piety is growing among the people, when vices are diminishing and good behaviour increasing, when sacred learning is in full bloom, but when the altars glitter with jewels and gold; nay, even when the altars themselves are neglected, and the accumulation of property, troops of servants, luxury, mules and horses, expensive erection of houses or rather palaces, and all the rest of the racket of life, make the priests no better than satraps. And all this seems right and proper, so much so that in the very papal documents themselves we find this kind of clause: 'Since such-and-such a cardinal, keeping up an establishment of so many horses and so many officials, does great honour to the Church of God, we grant him the fourth part of the dignity of a bishop.' And for the ornament of the Church, the bishops, priests and clergy are ordered to wear silk and purple. O marvellous dignity of the Church! What is there left, when we have lost even the name of honour? There are those —I have no wish to mention them—who spend the wealth of the Church on wicked purposes, to the great offence of the people. When they have made a gain, we congratulate them and say the Church of Christ has been added to; whereas the Church has one kind of true wealth and one only—the advance of the Christian life. They call it blasphemy, if anyone speaks without due reverence of Christopher or George, or does not put every fable from every source on the level of the Gospel. But, to Paul, it is blasphemy whenever the evil ways of Christians bring shame upon the name of Christ before the eyes of the heathen. What are the enemies of Christ likely to say, when they see Christ in the Gospel calling men to despise riches, renounce the pursuit of pleasure and abandon pride, and they observe exactly the opposite going on among the chief of those who profess themselves Christians, but live so as to out-heathen the heathens in their passion for heaping up wealth, their love of pleasure, their sumptuous living, their savagery in war, and almost all other vices? The wise reader will understand what I am passing over in silence here, out of respect for the name of Christian, and what I am privately sighing for. How much they must laugh, don't you think, when they see that Christ in the Gospel did not want his followers to be marked out by their dress, or by ceremonies or by particular foods, but wished Christians to be known by this mark, that they should be united in their love for one another—and then they look round and see us so far from being united, that no breed of men were ever in such shameful and deadly turmoil. Prince makes war on prince, state fights with state, there is no agreement between one school and another, or one religion (as they say now) and another; brawls, factions, litigation abound among us. This is the real blasphemy, and the authors of it are those who provide its just cause. They call it heresy, to say or write anything which differs in any way from the petty propositions of the Masters of Theology, or even to disagree on matters of grammar; but it is not heresy, to proclaim the chief part of human felicity to lie in precisely the very thing which Christ always teaches us to set aside; it is not heresy, to encourage a mode of life quite unlike the teachings of the Gospel and the ordinances of the Apostles; or to run counter to the meaning of Christ, who sent his Apostles out to teach the Gospel armed with the sword of the Spirit, which alone makes it possible (earthly passions having been cut away) to do without the sword—to run counter to this, I say, by arming them with steel to defend themselves from persecution? (There is no doubt that under the name of the sword he would include the ballista, the bombard and the machine, and all the rest of the apparatus of war. In the same way the burdensomeness of the wallet in which they carried their money for everyday necessities, may be taken to apply to everything which makes provision for this life.) But he who teaches these things is counted among the great theologians.[1] It is an unforgivable sacrilege to take anything from a church; and is it to be held a light offence to plunder and defraud and grind down the poor and the widow, the living temple of God? Yet this is done everywhere by the princes and the nobles (sometimes by bishops and abbots). It is wicked profanity to pollute the sacred building by fighting or by seminal fluid, and yet we do not execrate the man who profanes that temple of the holy spirit, a pure and chaste maiden, who violates and corrupts her by means of endearments and gifts and promises and enticement? But the man who does this is popularly called a merry, fashionable fellow. I am not defending ill-doing, as I have said before, I am pointing out that the mass of the people have far more esteem for what they can see with their eyes, than for the things which are all the truer for being less easy to discern. You see the consecration of the stones of the temple, but, because you cannot see the dedication of the spirit, you think it unimportant. You fight for the preservation of its ornaments, but when it comes to protecting uprightness of life no one seizes that Gospel sword of which Christ said 'let him sell his garment and buy one'.[2] It is called the height of piety, to take up arms for the defence or the increasing of the authority and wealth of the priesthood, and throw sacred and profane together into the confusion of war. But while the priests' money, a paltry thing in itself, is being championed, what a tremendous desolation of all religious life is incurred by allowing war? For what evil is there which war does not bring about?

Perhaps here the reader's unspoken thought shouts at me, asking 'What are all these disgusting remarks leading up to? Do you want a prince to be like Plato makes the guardians of his republic? Do you want to rob the priests of their power, dignity, glory and riches, and recall them to the wallet and staff of the Apostles?' Careful with your

---

[1] This sentence was substituted in 1523 for the following: 'For thus far the words of Luke are distorted by that great Lyranus, who is to be set far above all the Jeromes, and yet he is counted among the great theologians.' The medieval theologian Nicolaus of Lyra (c. 1265–1349), to whom Erasmus alludes ironically here, was the author of two commentaries on the whole Bible, *Postilla litteralis* and *Postilla mystica*. (Brackets in the text have been added by the translator.)

[2] Luke XXII, 36.

words, please. I am not robbing them, but enriching them with greater possessions than these, I am not turning them out of their domain but calling them to better things. I ask you, which of us has the more splendid ideal of the greatness of a king, you or I? You want him to be able to do whatever he likes, to be a tyrant and not a prince; you glut him with pleasures, hand him over to luxury, make him the slave and captive of all his desires, you want him to be no wiser than the man in the street, you load him down with the things which even among the pagans it was fine to despise. I want him to be as near as possible to the likeness of God, whose image he represents, I want him to excel others in wisdom, the true glory of kings, and to be far from all low passions, the diseases of the soul, by which the stupid and common vulgar herd is carried away. I want him not to admire anything mean, to rise above wealth, in short to be to the state what the soul is to the body, what God is to the universe.

Which of us two estimates more truly the dignity of a bishop? You weigh him down with earthly riches, entangle him in sordid and vulgar cares, involve him with the storms of war. I want him, as the vicar of Christ and the guardian of the sacred spouse, to be free from all earthly contagion, and to resemble as closely as possible the one whose place and office he fills. The Stoics say that to be a good man is only possible if one is free from the maladies of the soul. By the maladies of the soul they mean the desires or affections. Much more then should Christians be free from these things, but especially the prince. And still more especially the prince and father of the Church, a prince belonging to heaven and ruling over the people of heaven. I want the priest to reign, but I consider mere earthly power too unimportant for this man of heaven to be burdened with it. I want to see the Pontiff ride in triumph, not in the bloodthirsty triumphs of a wicked Marius or a conscienceless Julius, so empty as to be the butt of the Satirists (if old Democritus were to see them I think he would die of laughing), but truly magnificent and Apostolic, such as Paul (a warrior himself and a much finer general than Alexander the Great) describes with a great flourish, as it were blowing his own trumpet:

In labours more abundant, in stripes above measure, in prisons more frequent, in deaths oft. Of the Jews five times received I forty stripes save one. Thrice was I beaten with rods, once was I stoned, thrice I suffered shipwreck, a night and a day have I been in the deep; in journeyings often, in perils of waters, in perils of robbers, in perils by mine own countrymen, in perils by the heathen, in perils in the city, in perils in the wilderness, in perils in the sea, in perils among false brethren; in weariness and painfulness, in watchings often, in hunger and thirst, in fastings often, in cold and nakedness. Besides those things that are without, that which cometh upon me daily, the care of all the churches. Who is weak, and I am not weak? Who is offended, and I burn not?[1]

And a little before this:

In all things approving ourselves the ministers of God, in much patience, in afflictions, in necessities, in distresses, in stripes, in imprisonments, in tumults, in labours, in watchings, in fastings; by pureness, by knowledge, by longsuffering, by kindness, by the Holy Ghost, by love unfeigned, by the word of truth, by the power of God, by the armour of righteousness on the right hand and on the left, by honour and dishonour, by evil report and good report; as deceivers, and yet true; as unknown, and yet well known; as dying, and behold, we live; as chastened, and not killed; as sorrowful, yet always rejoicing; as poor, yet making many rich; as having nothing, and yet possessing all things.[2]

Do you see the trophies of war, the victory, the Apostolic triumph? This is that famous glory, by which Paul sometimes swears, as by something sacred. These are the high deeds for which he believed there was laid up for him an immortal crown.[3] Those who claim to stand in the place and wield the authority of the Apostles, will not be reluctant to follow in the Apostles' footsteps. I wish the Popes to have the greatest riches—but let it be the pearl of the Gospel, the heavenly treasure, which abounds to them all the more, the more they lavish it on others; for there will be no danger of kindness perishing through kindness. I wish them to be fully armed, but with the arms of the Apostle: that is, with the shield of faith, the breastplate of righteousness, the sword of salvation, which is the word of God.[4] I wish them to be fierce warriors, but against the real enemies of the Church, simony, pride, lust, ambition, anger, irreligion. Christians must always be watching out for, and attacking, Turks such as these. It is in this sort of war that the bishop should be general and exhort his troops. I want the priests to be acknowledged among the first of the land, but not for their noisy domineering, rather for the excellence of their holy learning, for their outstanding virtues. I want them to be revered, but for their upright and ascetic lives, not only for their titles or dramatic garb. I want them to be feared, but as fathers, not as tyrants. I want them to be feared, but only by evil-doers, nay, I want them to be such as strike awe, not terror or hate, into the hearts of the wicked. Finally, I wish them abundant delights, but delights of a rarity and sweetness far beyond what the common herd can know.

Do you want to hear what are the true riches of a Pope? Listen next

[1] 2 Cor. XI, 23–9. [2] 2 Cor. VI, 4–10.
[3] 2 Tim. IV, 8. [4] Ephes. VI, 14–17.

to the prince of Popes: 'Silver and gold have I none, but such as I have give I thee: in the name of Jesus arise and walk.'[1] Do you want to hear the grandeur of the name of an Apostle—surpassing all titles, all arches[2] and statues? Listen to Paul, the truly illustrious: 'For we are to God a sweet savour of Christ in every place.'[3] Do you want to hear of power more than kingly? 'I can do all things,' he says, 'through Christ who strengtheneth me.'[4] Do you want to hear of glory? 'You are my joy and crown in the Lord.'[5] Do you want to hear the titles worthy of a bishop, the ornaments of a real pontiff? Paul points them for you, 'sober, blameless, prudent, given to hospitality, apt to teach; not given to wine, no striker, but patient, not a brawler, not greedy of filthy lucre, not a novice; moreover he must have a good report of them that are without, lest he fall into reproach and the snare of the devil.'[6] Look upon the ornaments which grace Aaron the priest of Moses, the riches which adorn him, the many-hued embroideries, the starry shining of varied gems about him, the gleam of gold. What all these signify you may find out from the interpretations of Origen and Jerome, and you will understand what the trappings are which should be furnished to bishops who are truly great.

Who should the pontiffs portray in their lives, if not those whom they portray on their seals, whose titles they bear, whose places they occupy? Which models are more suitable for imitation by the vicar of Christ—the Juliuses, Alexanders, Croesus, and Xerxes, nothing but robbers on the grand scale, or Christ himself, the only leader and emperor of the Church? Whom could the successors of the Apostles more properly strive to copy, than the prince of the Apostles? Christ openly declared that his kingdom was not of this world, and yet you think it right that Christ's successor should not only accept worldly power, but canvass for it, and leave no stone unturned, as they say, to get it? In this world there are two worlds, at variance with each other in every way: the one gross and material, the other celestial, having its thoughts centred even now, as far as may be, on that which is to come hereafter. In the first of these the chief place goes to him who is least endowed with true possessions, and most weighed down with false ones. The pagan king, for instance, surpasses everyone in lust, luxury, violence, pomp, pride, riches, and greed, and he comes first just because the major portion of this flood of sewage has come his way, and the least share of wisdom, self-control, moderation and justice, and the rest of the things which are truly valuable. In the second, on the other hand,

---

[1] Acts III, 6.　　　[2] *Fornices*: the 1515 edition has *formas*, also 1526.
[3] 2 Cor. II, 15.　　　[4] Phil. IV, 13.
[5] Phil. IV, 1.　　　[6] 1 Tim. III, 2–7.

the highest is the man who is least besmirched with those gross and vulgar gifts, and richest in the true wealth of heaven. Now why should you wish a Christian prince to be just what the philosophers, even pagan ones, condemned and scorned? Why should you consider his greatness to rest on precisely those things which it is finest to despise? Why should you load the Angel of God (for so is the bishop called in Holy Writ) with those things which would be unbecoming to an ordinary good man? Why should you estimate him according to the wealth which makes robbers rich, and tyrants terrifying?

A priest is something celestial, he is more than man. Nothing is worthy of his lofty station, except what is heavenly. Why do you dishonour his dignity with commonplace things? Why do you taint his purity with the squalor of the world? Why do you not let him wield his own kind of power? Why may he not be illustrious with his own kind of glory, revered for his own majesty, rich with his own wealth? This man was chosen for the highest ends from the divine body, which is the Church, by the divine spirit. Why do you force him to take part in the wild commotions of the despots? Paul prides himself on having been set apart: why do you plunge my churchman into the slime of the dregs of the people? Why drive him to be worried by moneylenders? Why drag this man of God into business scarcely fitting for men at all? Why measure the blessedness of Christian priests by those things which were a laughing-stock for Democritus and a cause for sorrow to Heraclitus, which Diogenes rejected as trivial, which Crates put aside as burdensome, which all the saints fled from as pestilential? Why evaluate the successor of St Peter on those very riches which Peter himself gloried in not possessing? Why think the Apostolic rulers should give an impression of greatness, by those very trappings which the Apostles themselves trampled underfoot, and thereby were great? Why call 'Peter's patrimony' a thing which Peter himself was proud not to have? Why think the vicars of Christ should be ensnared by riches, when Christ himself called them thorns? The true, the chief duty of such a man is to sow the seed of the Word of God, so why overwhelm him with wealth, which chokes the seed when it is sown? He is the expert, the judge, of equity; why do you want him to serve the mammon of unrighteousness? It is for him to dispense the holy sacraments, why do you make him the overseer of the vilest things? The Christian world looks to him for the nourishment of sound doctrine, it expects him to supply wholesome advice, fatherly consolation, a pattern of life. Why should a man destined and devoted to such high things be reduced to the treadmill of vulgar cares? This both robs the bishop of his own dignity and deprives the people of their bishop. Christ has his own kingdom, of such rare excellence that it should never be polluted by heathen rule, or rather tyranny; he has his own magnificence, his own riches, his own delights. Why do we mix up together things which are so conflicting? Earthly and heavenly, highest and lowest, heathen and Christian, profane and sacred—why do we confuse them all? So many and so great are the gifts of the Spirit, in the generous overflowing of its wealth—gifts of tongues, gifts of prophecy, gifts of healing, gifts of knowledge, gifts of wisdom, gifts of learning, the discerning of spirits, the gift of exhortation, the power to console.[1] These are sacred offerings, how can you put them on the same plane as the unhallowed gifts of the world? (Not to say put them out.)[2] Why try to combine Christ and Mammon, and Belial with the spirit of Christ? What has the mitre to do with the helmet, holy vestments with warlike armour, blessings with bombards, the merciful shepherd with the armed robbers—what has the priesthood to do with war? Is the same man to demolish towns with machines and hold the keys of the kingdom of heaven? Is it right that the maker of war should be the one who greets the world with the solemn word of peace? Can he have the face to teach the Christian populace that riches are to be despised, when money is the be-all and the end-all of his life? How can he have the impudence to teach what Christ taught both by precept and example, what the Apostles are always impressing on us—that we must offer no resistance to evil, but overcome evil with good, pay back an injury with a kindness, overwhelm an enemy with good deeds—when for the sake of possessing one little town or levying a tax on salt he throws the whole world into the storms and tumults of war? How can he be a leader in the kingdom of heaven, for so Christ calls his Church, who is entirely immersed in the kingdom of this world? But you are excessively pious, you want the Church to be adorned with this kind of riches too. I would agree, if the thing did not carry with it, for the sake of a little benefit, such a number of evils. Once you have granted imperial rule, you have granted at the same time the business of collecting money, the retinue of a tyrant, armed forces, spies, horses, mules, trumpets, war, carnage, triumphs, insurrections, treaties, battles, in short everything without which it is not possible to manage the affairs of empire. Even if the wish is there, when will there be the leisure to carry out the duties of an Apostle, for one who is torn asunder by so many thousand cares? While the lists of the levied troops are being made out, while treaties are being made or annulled, while force is applied to those who refuse to obey authority, and those who have revolutionary ideas are persuaded to remain loyal, while enemies are being crushed and citadels

---

[1] I Cor. XII, 4–10.   [2] Play on *conjungis* and *extinguis*.

fortified, while plans are being considered and secular embassies handled, while the captains are being received at banquets and friends promoted to honour, and those driven away who must give place to the more fortunate—and many other things, which are beyond remembering, and yet must be done! Does it seem to you to argue a real understanding of the high distinction of a Pope and cardinals, to think they should be dragged away to these squalid matters of business—from prayer, in which they speak with God, from holy contemplation, by which they live with the angels, from the verdant meadows of Holy Scripture, where they walk in bliss, from the Apostolic office of spreading the Gospel, in which they are most like Christ? Is it truly wishing them well to want to force them into this storm of affairs, these toilsome distresses, from so great a felicity and tranquillity of life, which they were enjoying? The fact is, not only that political power carries with it infinite hardships, but also it is much less successful in the hands of the priesthood than in those of laymen. And that for two reasons, partly because the rank and file of men are more willing to give this kind of obedience to laymen than to ecclesiastics, partly because the former, intending to leave the kingdom to their children, do their best to make it as flourishing as possible. The latter, on the other hand, since they come to power later in life and often as old men, and rule for themselves, not for their heirs, are more given to plunder than to embellish, precisely as if they were offered a prey rather than a province. Add to this that, when a secular ruler takes possession, he may have to fight once for his kingdom, and once for all those favoured by the prince are raised and enriched. When it is otherwise, the contention is always being renewed, and those thrown out of power whom the previous ruler had raised up; over and over again there are new men to be enriched at the expense of the people. It is not unimportant too, that a people will more easily bear the rule of one to whom it is accustomed, even if his rule is severe; and, if he should die, he yet seems to be living in his son and heir, and the populace fancies that it has not changed one prince for another, but has the same one renewed. Children are liable to resemble their parents in their ways, especially when they have been educated by them. But when sovereignty is vested in men dedicated to God, there is suddenly a complete change all round. Add to all this that the secular ruler comes to the management of power after much study, educated to it from his cradle. But in the other case it often happens that the highest position of all is allotted without warning, so that he who was by nature born to the oar, is lifted to sovereign power by the whim of fortune.[1]

[1] An allusion to Julius II.

Finally, it is hardly possible for one man to be equal to two difficult forms of administration, like Hercules with his two monsters. It is the most difficult of things to fulfil the duties of a good prince. And yet it is much finer, but also much more difficult, to act as a good priest. Pray, why both? Is it not inevitable that, when they take both offices upon themselves, they must discharge neither well? Hence it results, I think, that while we see cities ruled by temporal kings flourishing more and more—this is clear from their wealth, their buildings, their men— the towns ruled by priests are lifeless and falling to ruin. Whatever was the need to add one thing to another like this, when they are accompanied by so many disadvantages? Are you afraid that Christ will not be powerful enough through his own wealth, unless a lay tyrant contributes a little of his power? Do you think Christ is too unadorned unless an ungodly soldier makes him an allowance of gold, a Phrygian embroiderer, a few white horses, and a retinue, that is, spatters him with a little of his pomp? Does he seem to you not magnificent enough, unless he may use those insignia which that most ambitious Julius refused, for fear of envy? Do you judge him insignificant unless burdened with worldly kingship, which means tyranny if it is used selfishly and press of business if one uses it for the common good? Leave worldly things to the world; in a bishop, what is lowliest surpasses all the pride of empire. The more you add in the way of worldly goods, the less will Christ bestow of his own; the purer the man is from the former, the more will the latter be lavished upon him. You see now, I think, how everything comes out differently if you turn the Silenus inside out. Those people who seemed the heartiest supporters of the Christian prince—you can see now that they are the greatest traitors and enemies he can have. You would have said that some people were defending the dignity of the Pope, and you understand now that they besmirch him. Now I am not saying this because I think everything the priests happen to have should be taken away from them, whether power or wealth: for no religious man should favour civil strife: but I wish them to remember and be aware of their own greatness, so that they may either cast away altogether these common, not to say heathen, things, and leave them to the lowest of men, or else at least hold them contemptuously and, as Paul says, have them as if they did not have them at all. Finally, I want them to be so adorned with the riches of Christ, that everything which may come to them from the glory of this world may either be outshone by the light of better things, or seem sordid by comparison. And so it shall be, that what they possess, they may possess in joy, and all the more for being free from care; for when there is an increase they are not in fear lest anyone break through and steal, and if there is any falling-off they will not struggle so furiously to retain base and passing things. Finally, they will not be in the position of losing their true possessions while they exult over riches that are not for them. They will not lose the pearl of the Gospel as they strive for the sham jewels of the world. In saying this I am leaving out of account that these very things, which we think should be despised, are all the more likely to be added to those who despise them, and they will follow those who flee from them, much more creditably than if they are chased and snatched at. From whence did the Church get its wealth, unless from the contempt of wealth? from whence its glory, unless from putting glory aside? Laymen will be readier to give their worldly wealth away, if they see that it is rejected by those whom they believe to be wiser. Evil princes must perhaps sometimes be tolerated, some respect must be paid to the memory of those whose place they apparently occupy, something is due to their title. It would be as well not to try to find a remedy, because I dare say if the attempt were made without success the result would be even worse disaster. But human affairs are really in a bad way, if those whose life should be a kind of miracle are the sort of people who provoke cheers from the worst of men and signs and groans from the good, and whose entire prestige depends on the support of villains, or on the moderation of the ordinary people, or the inexperience of the artless, or the tolerance of the good; or should even be those who shelter behind public dissensions, who become great through nothing else than civil strife, whose good fortune is fed by the misfortune of the public.

If the priests had a true estimate of the matter, the truth is that the acquisition of secular wealth brings so much trouble with it that it would be better to refuse it even when voluntarily offered. They become slaves of the princes and the court, they are at the mercy of rebellion, they are involved in wars, in the midst of which they die; in short, even if we suppose that their servitude to the monarch is an honourable estate, what becomes of the fathers of the Christian people in the meantime? where are the shepherds? What sort of arrangement is it, that bishops and abbots should buy titles of that sort at a high price from the monarchs? An abbot seems to lack honour if he is not a count as well. It is an ornament to the priesthood to buy the title of duke. A fine coupling of words, to be sure—abbot and despot, bishop and fighting-man. But what is much more absurd is that in these capacities they act the part of strong men, but in the function which should really have been their own, they are mere shadows. They have hands and swords, with which they kill the body—and that is justice, if you like; but the same people have no tongue to heal the soul. The abbot has learnt how to draw up a line of battle, but he does not know how to lead people to religion. The bishop is well versed in methods of warfare with arms and bombards, but he is dumb when it comes to teaching, exhorting, consoling. He is well armed with javelins and missiles, but absolutely unarmed with Holy Scripture. And meanwhile they exact every farthing from their people which would be owed to devout abbots and good bishops; in fact often it is not the sum due, but any sum they like. The Lord will give his blessing to the people for their patience, which endures such men for the sake of peace; but I fear they will find God a severer judge than their people. What else does this general turmoil tell us, but that God is angry with us all? What else is left for us to do, but for us all, great and small alike, churchmen and laymen, with humble hearts, to fly for refuge to the mercy of God? How much wiser that would be, than for each to refuse to acknowledge his fault and blame it on the other, thus provoking still more the divine wrath, and making more deadly wounds by biting each other, instead of healing ourselves. The people murmur against the princes, the princes spare neither sacred nor secular, the populace insults the priesthood. It certainly often happens that God, displeased by the evil-doing of the people, sends them the rulers they deserve.

Nothing has been gained so far, from complaints, harshness, quarrels, and turmoil. There is one way left—let us all make a joint confession together, that the mercy of God may be ready for us all.

But where is my flow of words carrying me—professing to be a proverb-writer, I am turning into a preacher? To be sure, it was the drunken Alcibiades with his Sileni which drew us into this very sober discussion. However, I should not have too many regrets for having strayed if what did not pertain to relating proverbs turned out to pertain to amendment of life, and what made no contribution to learning did conduce to piety; and if what seemed subordinate or unrelated to the plan of this work, could be adapted to a plan for living.

III. WAR

Erasmus's protests against war are scattered through the *Adages*; he rarely misses an opportunity.

I. I. xxviii: *Sero sapiunt Phryges* (The Phrygians are wise too late). . . . Demades used to say, according to Plutarch, that the Athenians never decreed peace except in mourning; meaning by this that they were fonder of war than they should have been, and that it took a public calamity to make them think of peace. But how much more insane are we than the Athenians, for even after the lessons of so many years' suffering we do not hate war, nor do we even begin to think about peace, which ought to be perpetual between Christians.

II. II. xci: *In seditione vel Androclides belli ducem agit* (In a revolt even Androclides can be a general). . . . In a social upheaval the very lowest may sometimes be in command for a while. This can be turned to apply to evil princes, who have less importance in the state when things are quiet, and who for this reason sometimes take pains to stir up public agitation by the skill of a tyrant, so as to rob the people more easily at their pleasure. Or to some Theologians, unworthy of the name, who stir up strife and dissension among Christ's people, apparently so that they may make themselves famous —they prefer to owe their distinction to the woes of the general public, rather than to live in obscurity.

II. VI. xxiii: *Bellum haudquaquam lachrymosum* (War without tears). War without tears, where victory is won without blood and slaughter. Or where someone has succeeded in extricating himself from a dangerous affair without damage to himself; or where a fight is conducted with angry words but without any danger of coming to blows. Or where the contest is carried on in such a way that neither side sustains any harm, as in a literary controversy which leaves the loser more learned and the winner more friendly. [Examples.] But this means a war carried through by words and not by weapons. For that is indeed the only kind worth waging for wise men. Otherwise armed warfare is for wild beasts and paid soldiers [gladiators] whom I put below the wild animals. And yet no one would believe, if we did not see it with our own eyes, how much this sort of war pleases Christian princes. Fighting is done with machines such as were never imagined by pagan ferocity or barbarism. There is even a people, among the Germans, who count it their chief distinction to have slain as many mortals as possible with the sword—which is frightful enough in itself, but how much more horrible because they do it for pay, like a public executioner given a reward for butchery.

III. I. xvi: *Haud annuncias bellum* (You are not bringing news of war). This is usually said when someone brings joyful news to the town, because war is of all things the most disastrous; and yet today, at the rumour of war most mortals grow cheerful, especially that scoundrelly breed of mercenaries (Cares) who get their living from the miseries of the human race.

III. VII. xxix: *Testa collisa testae* (Pot hits pot). . . . When two conflict to the detriment of both. A conflict between kings waging war on each other is very like a collision between two pots. Sometimes they are both destroyed. Certainly neither will come out of it without grievous damage, but what seems to me most unjustly arranged by the fates is this: whereas it would be right for the hardships of war to come back on the heads of those who were the makers of war, and to whom conquest was important, the fact is that the greatest part of these calamities falls on those who are involved in war against their will, looking on it as an abomination; and for them, if the outcome of the war were the most prosperous imaginable, there would not be a pennyworth of profit.

IV. II. lxii: *Mala ultro adsunt* (Evils come of their own accord). ... The common people say this, not without reason: misfortune comes of its own accord, and all unsought. And yet everywhere, by our vices, we invite war, lawsuits, diseases, as if too little misfortune came without our seeking.

The two long essays on war are the best-known parts of the *Adages*: *Spartam nactus es, hanc orna* and *Bellum*, or *Dulce bellum inexpertis.*

The first is much the shortest, but has been much quoted owing to its personal tone and pathetic subject. The pupil of Erasmus mentioned here is Alexander Stewart (natural son of James IV of Scotland, and Archbishop of St Andrews at an early age), who was fifteen when they first met in December 1508.[1] The young man had been sent to Italy to study, and Erasmus became his teacher of literature, remaining with him at Padua and Siena until the middle of 1509; during these few months they had time for an expedition to Naples and Cumae. The young Scots nobleman had an energetic personality and made a deep impression on Erasmus. He was Chancellor of Scotland in 1510, and became co-founder of St Leonard's College at St Andrews in 1512. When he fell at Flodden he was just twenty. Among Erasmus's memories of him there is a story of an occasion when he imitated Erasmus's handwriting on the margins of a book so successfully as to deceive even Erasmus himself, afterwards confessing the joke.[2] It was he who gave his tutor the ring with the head of the god Terminus, which was a treasured possession to the end of Erasmus's life.

Judging by the examples he had before him, Erasmus treats war as mainly a matter of territorial conquest. It is noticeable that although he finds several instances of the use of this proverb in antiquity, he does not give its origin.

The most famous essay in the *Adages, Dulce bellum inexpertis* or *Bellum* as it was called, has had a lively history of its own. Printed separately by Froben in 1517, it ran through a number of Latin editions (the *Bibliotheca Erasmiana* enumerates twenty-one, all but two in the sixteenth century, and five reprints where it appears in conjunction with another work). A German translation was printed twice in the sixteenth century, another German version in the seventeenth. There was also an English translation quite early, printed in London, 1533–34.[3] But the main current of English translations belongs to another story: in the late eighteenth and early nineteenth centuries a determined

[1] For details see Allen, 604, 2 n.; the story of the forgery in Allen, VII, p. 386, and x, p. 312. Also de Nolhac, *Erasme en Italie*, pp. 53–4, 60–3.

[2] This was in spite of a strong tendency to short-sightedness, which is mentioned in a letter recommending careful choice of spectacles (Allen, 1833).

[3] Reprinted by J. W. Mackail, *Erasmus against War* (Boston, 1907).

effort was made to utilise the *Bellum* in an organised move towards pacifism. A translation made by Vicesimus Knox under the title of *Antipolemus:*[1] *or the plea of reason, religion, and humanity against war* was published in London in 1794, and a shorter version of this was reprinted a dozen times during the first half of the nineteenth century (the last in 1853) in New York and Dublin as well as in London. It was adopted as a tract by the Society for the Promotion of Permanent and Universal Peace, and also by the Society of Friends.

This English translation gave rise to a French one, printed eight times, in London, Paris and Nîmes. It even reappeared in 1855 in Welsh. But the Dutch translations of the seventeenth century all appear to stem from one which was printed as part of the celebrations when the bronze statue of Erasmus was erected at Rotterdam (the first of these is dated 1622).

Finally, the *Dulce bellum inexpertis* was given a critical edition, with a new translation into French, in 1953.[2] The present translation follows the text of the Leyden *Opera* but is indebted to this recent critical edition for help at many points.

Another well-known essay on the subject, the *Querela Pacis*, was composed by Erasmus in 1517 at the request of John Le Sauvage, Chancellor of Burgundy.[3] This was a command performance and more formal in tone. The *Dulce bellum inexpertis* can be taken to represent Erasmus's personal views, and should be linked with Colet's preaching against war in 1513 and the measured viewpoint of More's *Utopia*.

(g) *Spartam nactus es, hanc orna*[4]

This proverb tells us that whatever province we happen to have made our own, we must fit ourselves to it, and suit our behaviour to its dignity. Cicero, to Atticus:[5] 'All that is left to me now is, "You have drawn Sparta; make the best of it!" But, by Hercules, I cannot. I understand Philoxenes, who preferred to go back to prison.' And again, in book 1: 'For that reason, that Sparta which you say has fallen to my lot I will not only never desert, but, even if I am deserted by her, I shall still stand by my ancient creed.'[6] What Cicero is referring to is an

---

[1] Erasmus wrote a work of this name during his visit to Italy in 1506–8, but this has not survived.

[2] *Dulce bellum inexpertis*, texte édité et traduit par Yvonne Rémy et René Dunil-Marquebreucq (Bruxelles, 1953), henceforward called *Bellum*.

[3] See Allen, 603.

[4] 'You have obtained Sparta, adorn it' (or, 'administer it'), II. v. i; LB. 551 E.

[5] Book IV, epistle 6.

[6] Cicero, *Ad Atticum*, I, 20, trans. E. S. Shuckburgh, 1899.

anapaestic line, from some tragedy, *Spartam nactus es, hanc exorna*. The Scholiast of Theocritus indicates an allusion to this proverb in *The Wayfarer*:

> Here vie with me, here graze your oxen;
> Treading your own land, desert not the oaks.[1]

The proverb can thus be used in various ways; for instance, when we recommend someone to keep up the part he had elected to play, with proper dignity. You are a bishop, behave like a bishop, and not like a satrap. You are a husband, take heed to the responsibilities of a husband. You are a courtier, behave like a courtier. You are a judge, act neither like a friend nor an enemy, but like a judge. A principality is yours, fulfil the office of a prince. You are a private citizen, conduct yourself like one. Aristophanes uses it in a similar way; for it is written in the comedy called *Thesmophoriazusae*:

> A poet, sir, must needs adapt his ways
> To the high thoughts which animate his soul.[2]

Or else when we enjoin someone to be content with his lot whatever may befall. Just as an experienced pilot shows himself to be a good skipper in any storm, so the wise man bears himself wisely in any turn of fortune. You have ample means, handle them wisely; you have not, make use of the advantages of poverty. You possess learning, use it to live a good life. You are without it, don't fret—piety is sufficient to obtain salvation. Plutarch says in his treatise 'On Tranquillity of Mind', that everybody should be satisfied with his lot: 'Your portion is Sparta, adorn her!'[3] In the same book he says that this saying comes from Solon. There is a reference in Euripides:

> Sparta is yours, govern it;
> Our own lot is Mycenae.[4]

These seem to be the words of Agamemnon to Menelaus. Something like this is the Platonic phrase, 'What is to hand, use well', or 'be content with'. Now, the majority of people pay more attention to increasing possessions than to managing them well, unlike what Socrates so rightly says in the *Theaetetus* of Plato: 'For it is better to do a little well, than a great deal as it should not be done.'[5] This saying should be engraved everywhere in the halls of princes, *You have*

---

[1] Theocritus, v, 59–60.
[2] Aristophanes, *Thesmophoriazusae*, 149–50, trans. B. Bickley Rogers (1924).
[3] Plutarch, *On Tranquillity of Mind*, XIII.
[4] Euripides, fragment 723.   [5] Plato, *Theaetetus*, 187 e.

obtained Sparta, adorn it; you will hardly find one of them who really thinks out what it is to play the part of a prince, or who is satisfied with his own dominion and does not try to extend his frontiers. The duty of a prince is to make provision in every kind of way for the needs of the state, to preserve public liberty, to foster peace, to cut out crime with the least possible hurt to his own people, to take care that he has reverend and upright magistrates. So, when he is completely unconcerned with these things, and spends his time in dicing, dancing, wenching, playing music, hunting, making bargains, in short turning his whole attention to other things, then this proverb must be dinned into him: *You have obtained Sparta, adorn it.* Again, when he neglects the realm which is his own and spends his time abroad, coveting the dominions of others; when he drags his people into the most hazardous situations, completely exhausts them and risks himself and the well-being of all on the gamble of war—and all so that he may add one little town or another to his territories—then is the time to bring forward this adage, *You have obtained Sparta.* There is nothing finer in a prince than to beautify whatever belongs to the land which fortune gave him, by his wisdom, goodness and industry. You happen to have a small town— copy Epaminondas, exert yourself to make that dull little town famous and wealthy. You happen to have a wild and unmanageable people: do your best to tame it gradually and render it obedient to law. You may have a realm which is not very splendid; do not worry your neighbours, but improve what you have without doing harm to others. The desire to possess a strange country hardly ever turns out well. Some nations are far apart in outlook and speech, like the Germans and the Spaniards; some are isolated by nature herself, as islands are by the sea, and the Italians both by the sea and the massive chain of the Alps. In some cases frontiers are settled by chance. If each does his best to embellish his own possessions, then all will be flourishing everywhere. And among friends, Christian friends too, all will be in common. Now, it happens only too often that while we are trying to weaken another's belongings we ruin our own entirely; and even if we succeed, it is at a huge cost— of our citizens' blood, of expense, of danger, of sweat, of bereavement, of innumerable ills—that we buy some empty title, and the smoke of a great name. Xerxes, Cyrus, Alexander the Great, would both have lived longer and achieved truer glory, if they had preferred to manage their states aright instead of harrying foreign states by force of arms. Charles, Duke of Burgundy, the great-grandfather of the present one, if he had turned that powerful intellect of his, and his greatness of soul, to enriching his own possessions rather than conquering others, he would not have met a miserable death in war, and could have ranked among the most highly praised of princes. A large part of our realm was at that time in the grip of a deadly plague. By a dissension that was utterly stupid, certainly, but of the most destructive kind, two parties divided everything between them, one taking its name from a hook and the other from a fish.[1] City was fighting with city, village with village, house with house; even those who shared one bed were divided by party strife; brother was set against brother, the bonds of nature broken. Everywhere robbery, quarrelling, slaughter and pillage were rife. And meanwhile that good prince, just as if all this were not in the least important, was laying siege to others' ramparts far away.

Charles, King of France, the eighth of the name, travelled all through Italy and came back to his own country; but with such damage and danger to himself and his people, that he was sorry for that success. There are some who declare that he might have lived to old age, if he had left Italy to the Italians. What shall I say of Philip, the father of the present Charles?[2] He went to Spain, not to try the fortune of war, but on invitation, to take possession of part of the kingdom, when everything was at peace. And yet how this lucky expedition was wept over by his own country, crushed under an intolerable burden of taxation? He himself was several times in peril of his life. He lost Francis of Busleiden, Archbishop of Besançon, a man matchless in every way.[3] And even though he came back, he had not finished with those disasters. Once more he left his country, was tossed about by a wild storm and thrown on to the coast of England, which was not very favourable at that time to our people. What happened to him there, what he had to undergo, what promises he made, on what conditions he was allowed to leave, had better be left without comment. He served necessity, I acknowledge and admit, but why was it necessary for him to get into that necessity? And he was not warned by these adversities to go back to his own country. He had to revisit Spain, where he died still young, a man born to the highest destiny, if only he himself had not grudged his own good fortune. This single death was a double disaster—the country was bereft of an excellent prince and Maximilian of an only son.

What shall I say of the Most Christian King of France Louis XII? He made an expedition against Venice, apparently impregnable at that time, and by the one campaign he restored so many towns to the Pope, Julius (II), so many to the Emperor Maximilian, and kept so many himself. He came home, with all his business, as it seemed, successfully concluded. But what a flood of evils this let loose for the French! They had supplied Julius with so many glorious triumphs at the cost of their

---

[1] *piscis asellus*, the donkey-fish, no doubt an allusion to a party badge.
[2] Philip I of Spain, father of Charles V.   [3] See Allen, 157, 59 n.

own blood, only to be thrown out of Italy by his doing with a greater loss of blood. Was this not enough, and to be branded with the marks of shame into the bargain? If Julius had not been carried away by death, we should have seen that realm, the most prosperous in the world, totally overthrown.

What shall I say about his serene majesty, King James of Scotland? He was a man who would have enjoyed unclouded happiness together with unclouded esteem, if he had always contained himself within his own frontiers. His personal beauty was such that even from far off you could see he was a king. He had wonderful powers of mind, an incredible fund of universal knowledge, invincible courage, truly royal loftiness of soul, consummate courtesy, the freest openhandedness. In a word there is no quality which befits a king, in which he was not so pre-eminent that he won praise even from his enemies. The wife who had fallen to his lot was Margaret, the sister of his majesty King Henry VIII of England; in beauty, in prudence and love for her husband, she was such that he could have asked no better wife from the gods. As for the kingdom of Scotland, which is said to be behind many others in wealth, in famous inhabitants and sumptuous living, he had given it such lustre by his virtues and so enlarged and embellished it, that he would have deserved the praise of being a most excellent king, if he had confined himself to this field of action for his glory. But, alas, it is never a happy thing for the country when the king leaves it, and rarely is it lucky for the prince himself. Prompted by over-zealous friendship for the King of France, and hoping to divert the King of England from his campaign against the French by threatening trouble (at home) and recalling him to the defence of his own island, he (the King of Scots) crossed the frontiers of his kingdom and opened war on the English. Need I say what followed? He died bravely indeed, but his death was a disaster, not so much to himself as to his kingdom. He perished in the prime of life. For many a year Scotland might have enjoyed such a prince, Margaret such a husband, his son (for he had a son by her) such a father, and he himself have enjoyed all these things and his own prestige, if he had not grudged himself life.

Killed with this bravest of fathers, was a son worthy of him—Alexander,[1] Archbishop of St Andrews, a young man, indeed only twenty; in whom you would have found no quality lacking for perfect manhood. He was exceedingly handsome, tall and stately as a hero, with a mind which was even-tempered but keen in the acquisition of all

[1] In 1515 he is called *Gulielmus*. This was changed to Alexander in 1520. Was William one of his additional baptismal names? For Erasmus's liking for the name William, see Allen, 534, where he lists eleven Williams among his friends.

kinds of knowledge. [I know this] for I lived with him once in the town of Siena; he was having lessons from me at that time in rhetoric and Greek. Great heavens, what a mind that was, swift, felicitous, ready to follow up anything, and how much it could grasp at once! At the same time he was studying law, but not taking much pleasure in it because of the mixture of barbarous terms and the boring prolixity of the commentators. He used to listen to the theory of oratory, and write out a speech and declaim it, thus exercising both tongue and pen. He was learning Greek, and every day at a certain time handed back the exercise he had been given. In the afternoon he would study music, playing the monochord, the recorder or the lute. Sometimes he would sing. Even mealtimes were put to use for study: the chaplain would always read aloud some serious book, for instance the Decretals, or St Jerome, or Ambrose; and the voice of the reader would never be interrupted, except when one of the learned men in the midst of whom Alexander was sitting made an observation, or when he himself asked a question, not entirely understanding what was being read. After dinner there might be stories told, but short ones, and with a literary flavour. In this way there was no part of life without its contribution to study, except what was given to divine service, and to sleep. For if there could have been any time left over—and really there was hardly enough time for all this varied programme of study—if by chance there were any extra time he spent it on reading history. For he was particularly attracted to that kind of knowledge.

As a result of all this, when he was a mere youth barely out of his eighteenth year he had gone so far in his literary studies that you would have rightly marvelled at it in any grown man. And it did not happen with him, as it sometimes does in others, that literary brilliance meant laxity in morals. He was modest in his behaviour, but in such a way as to reveal a marvellous discretion. His mind was lofty and far removed from sordid desires; but he was not either severe or haughty. There was nothing he did not feel, and he often concealed his feelings; and he could never be stirred to anger. Such was the gentleness of his nature and the moderation of his mind. He used to be very fond of jokes, but intelligent ones with no sting in them—flavoured with the wit of white Mercury, not black Momus. If any quarrel broke out among the servants in the house, it was wonderful to see the skilfulness and simplicity with which he settled it. Lastly, he had the deepest religious feeling without a trace of superstition. In short, no one was ever more worthy to be the son of a king, and of that king. Would that his filial piety, which was admirable, could have been fortunate too. He went with his father to the war; he could not fail his father in his need.

Tell me, what had you to do with Mars, the stupidest of all the poets' gods, you who were consecrated to the Muses, nay, to Christ? Your youth, your beauty, your gentle nature, your honest mind—what had they to do with the flourish of trumpets, the bombards, the sword? Why should a scholar be in the front line, or a bishop under arms? You were influenced, it seems, by exceeding filial devotion and, while you were strongly showing your love for your father, you fell miserably slain by his side. So many endowments of nature, so many good qualities, so many high hopes were swallowed up by one battle-charge. Something of mine was lost there too. Namely, the pains I took in teaching you, for whatever in you came from my workmanship was mine.

But what a fund of happiness was there, if only some evil genius had not compelled the king to overstep the boundaries of his kingdom and try the fortune of war with a most warlike foe in a foreign field. Would that he had chosen to finish what he had so finely begun, that is, to beautify the Sparta which was his. The proper field, and the finest, for the high deeds of princes is within the frontiers of their own realm. Among the bees, the others fly here and there, but the king alone, as he lacks a sting, also has wings much smaller in proportion to his body, so that he is less fitted for flight. The ancients painted Venus standing on a tortoise-shell; indicating thus that the mother of the family should never leave the house, because her whole function was contained within the walls of home. But it would have been much more to the point to exhort princes by this symbol, for, if one of them does wrong, it is to the detriment not of one family but of the whole world. Is there so little business to do at home, that it must be sought abroad? Everywhere there is the filthy sludge of crime, so many acts of sacrilege, of robbery and violence, so much injury done and affronts given, so much bribery of officials, so many laws either formulated by tyrants or twisted to serve tyranny, without mentioning the smaller things such as the neglected streets of the towns, the dilapidated churches, the uncared-for banks of rivers. To find a remedy to all this with the least expense of life to your subjects, so that the state may feel the cure without the cost, is not this to fill the office of a great prince, a function worthy of immortal praise? If you want to extend the domains of your glory outside the limits of your own kingdom, let your neighbours have proof of your greatness by your good deeds, not by your bad ones. You burn the farms, trample down the crops, destroy the towns, drive away the flocks, kill the men, and then at last you call yourself great. A fine contest, if you had been competing with a robber. Hesiod wrote that a bad neighbour was a great evil, and a good one a tremenous advantage. Let your neighbours see how true this is: let your greatness arouse their wonder as your goodness arouses their love.

But we have spent long enough on our grief, and on the memory of pupil. It remains to turn once more to our list of proverbs.

(h) Dulce bellum inexpertis[1]

Among the choicest proverbs, and widely used in literature, is the adage: λυκὺς ἀπείρῳ πόλεμος, that is, war is sweet to those who have not tried it. Vegetius uses it thus, in his book on the Art of War, III, chapter xiv,[2] 'Do not be too confident, if a new recruit hankers after war, for it is to the inexperienced that fighting is sweet.' There is a quotation from Pindar:[3] 'War is sweet to those who have not tried it, but anyone who knows what it is is horrified beyond measure if he should meet it.'

There are some things in the affairs of men, fraught with dangers and evils of which one can have no idea until one has put them to the test.

> How sweet, untried, the favour of the great!
> But he who knows it, fears it.[4]

It seems a fine and splendid thing to walk among the nobles at court, to be occupied with the business of kings, but old men who know all about the matter from experience are glad enough to deny themselves this pleasure. It seems delightful to be in love with girls, but only to those who have not yet felt what bitter there is in the sweet.[5] In the same way this idea can be applied to any enterprise carrying with it great risks and many evils, such as no one would undertake unless he were young and without experience. Indeed Aristotle[6] in his *Rhetoric* says this is the reason why youth tends to be bold and age to be diffident, because the former is given confidence by inexperience, and the latter acquires diffidence and hesitancy from familiar knowledge of many ills. If there is anything in mortal affairs which should be approached with hesitancy, or rather which ought to be avoided in every possible way, guarded against and shunned, that thing is war; there is nothing more wicked, more disastrous, more widely destructive, more deeply tenacious, more loathsome, in a word more unworthy of man, not to say of a Christian. Yet, strange to say, everywhere at the present time war is being entered upon lightly, for any kind of reason, and waged with

---

[1] IV. I. i; LB. 951 A.
[2] Chapter xiii, not xiv (see *Bellum*, p. 16).
[3] Stobaeus, *Flor.* 50, 3.
[4] Horace, *Epistles*, I, 18, 86–7.
[5] Pun on *amori* and *amari*.
[6] Aristotle, *Rhetoric*, οἱ νέοι; II. 12. 9, οἱ πρεσβύτεροι, II. 13. 7.

cruelty and barbarousness, not only by the heathen but by Christians, not only by lay people but by priests and bishops, not only by the young and inexperienced, but by the old who know it well; not so much by the common people and the naturally fickle mob, but rather by princes, whose function should be to restrain with wisdom and reason the rash impulses of the foolish rabble. Nor are there lacking lawyers and theologians who add fuel to the fire of these misdeeds and, as they say, sprinkle them with cold water.[1] And the result of all this is that war is now such an accepted thing that people are astonished to find anyone who does not like it; and such a respectable thing that it is wicked (I nearly said heretical) to disapprove of the thing of all things which is most criminal and most lamentable. How much more reasonable it would be to turn one's astonishment to wondering what evil genius, what a plague, what madness, what Fury first put into the mind of man a thing which had been hitherto reserved for beasts—that a peaceful creature, whom nature made for peace and loving-kindness (the only one, indeed, whom she intended for the safety of all), should rush with such savage insanity, with such mad commotion, to mutual slaughter. This is a thing which will supply even more food for wonder to anyone who has turned his mind away from accepted opinions to discern the real meaning and nature of things, and who considers for a little with the eye of the philosopher, on the one hand the image of man, on the other the picture of war.

First of all, if one considers the outward appearance of the human body, does it not become clear at once that nature, or rather God, created this being not for war, but for friendship, not for destruction, but for preservation, not for aggressiveness but for kindness? For she endowed every one of the other living creatures with its own weapons. She armed the charging bull with horns, the raging lion with claws. She fixed murderous fangs to the boar, and protected the elephants not only with their hide and their size, but with a trunk as well. She armoured the crocodile on all sides with scales, the dolphins with fins for weapons, the porcupines she defended with quills, the ray with a sting. To the cocks she fixed a spur. Some she fortified with a shell, others with a hide or a scaly covering. There are some whose safety she provided for by giving them swiftness, like doves. Again there are some to whom she gave poison as a weapon. To these things she added a fearsome brutish appearance, savage eyes, and a harsh voice. She implanted some inborn enmities. Only man was produced naked, weak, tender, unarmed, with very soft flesh and a smooth skin. Among his

---

[1] See I. x. li. Erasmus connects this saying with racehorses who were sprinkled with water to make them fiery, or with water used in forges.

members nothing would seem to have been intended for fighting and violence; rather even I might say that the other creatures, almost as soon as they are born, are self-reliant and able to protect themselves, but only man makes his appearance in such a condition that he must depend for a long time on the help of others. He cannot speak, nor walk, nor find his food, he only wails for help; so that from this one may conjecture that this animal alone was born for friendship, which is initiated and cemented by mutual aid. Accordingly nature wished man to owe the gift of life not so much to himself as to loving-kindness, so that he might understand that he was dedicated to goodness and brotherly love. And so the appearance she gave him was not fearsome and terrifying, as with the others, but mild and gentle, bearing the signs of love and goodness. She gave him friendly eyes, revealing the soul. She gave him embracing arms. She gave him the significance of the kiss, a union by which soul meets with soul. On him alone she bestowed laughter, the sign of merriment; on him alone, tears, the mark of mercy and pity. A voice she gave him too, not fierce and threatening as with the beasts, but friendly and caressing.

Not content with all this, nature gave to him alone the use of speech and reason, the thing above all which would serve to create and preserve goodwill, so that nothing should be managed by force among men. She implanted in him the hatred of solitude, the love of companionship. She planted deep in his heart the seed of goodwill. She arranged that what is most salutary should also be most sweet; for what is pleasanter than a friend? And again what is more necessary? And so even if it were perfectly possible to live a comfortable life without relationships with others, nothing would seem merry without a companion, unless one were to throw off human nature altogether and sink to the level of a wild beast. She added also the love of learning and the pursuit of knowledge; and this, just as it is instrumental in drawing the mind of man away from all savagery, has the greatest power of knitting up friendships. Indeed, neither family connections nor blood relationship bind souls together in a closer or firmer bond of friendship than does a shared enthusiasm for noble studies.

In addition to this, she distributed among mankind endowments of mind and body, with wonderful variety, so that each could find in another something to love and encourage for its excellence, or to seek out and cherish for its usefulness and necessity. Finally, she implanted in man a spark of the mind of God, so that, without having any reward in view, he might take a disinterested delight in being of service to all. For that is the property and nature of God, to shower his benefits for the good of the whole world. Otherwise, what is that rare pleasure which we feel in our souls, when we know that we have been the means of someone's salvation? And it is for this reason that one man is dear to another, because of the strong link of a great benefit bestowed. And so God has placed man in this world as a kind of image of himself, so that like an earthly deity he might provide for the well-being of all. Even the brute beasts feel this, as we see not only gentle animals but also panthers, lions and fiercer beasts than these, when in great danger, fly to man for help. He is the final refuge for all creatures, the most hallowed sanctuary for the whole world, the anchor which none refuses to call sacred.[1]

Thus we have sketched, in outline, the portrait of man. Now if you like, we will put up on the other hand, for comparison, the picture of war. Imagine now that you see before you the barbarous cohorts whose very faces and shouts strike terror to the heart:[2] the iron-clad troops drawn up in battle array, the terrifying clash and flash of arms, the hateful noise and bustle of a great multitude, the threatening looks, harsh bugles, startling peal of trumpets, thunder of the bombards (no less frightening than real thunder, but more harmful); a mad uproar, the furious shock of battle, and then wholesale butchery, the cruel fate of the killers and the killed, the slaughtered lying in heaps, the fields running with gore, the rivers dyed with human blood. It sometimes happens that brother falls on brother, kinsman on kinsman, friend on friend, while the general madness rages, and plunges his sword into the vitals of one who never gave him cause for offence, even by a word. A tragedy like that contains such a mass of woes that a human heart can hardly bear to describe it. Not to mention other evils, common and trivial in comparison: the trampled crops, the burnt-out farms, the villages set on fire, the cattle driven away, the girls raped, and the old men carried off captive, the churches sacked, robbery, pillage, violence and confusion everywhere. And I am leaving out the things which result from any war, however successful and right it may be: the grinding of the peasantry, the over-taxing of the landowners, so many old men left desolate, for whom the slaughter of their sons means a sadder death than if the enemy had taken away both life and the consciousness of sorrow, so many old grandmothers left destitute, more cruelly killed that way than by the sword, so many women widowed and children orphaned, so many homes made houses of mourning, so

---

[1] *Sacra ancora*, I. I. xxiv.

[2] A passage in a letter to Ammonius, 1 September (1513), gives a similar enumeration (Allen, 273). Erasmus is referring to the graphic description of life in the field, given in Ammonius's letters from the English camp in France, whither he had accompanied Henry VIII. This may give a clue to the date of the writing of *Bellum*: like the previous adage, in autumn 1513.

many rich men reduced to beggary. As for the damage to morals, what need is there to speak of that, when everyone knows that the universal demoralisation of life is the result of war? It breeds the contempt of duty, indifference to law, readiness to dare any kind of crime. It is the source from which wells up this flood of robbers, church-breakers, and cut-throats. And the most serious thing of all is that this deadly pestilence cannot be contained within its own limits, but once it has begun in one corner it floods like a contagious disease into the surrounding regions, and even sweeps the more distant ones with it into the general uproar and turmoil, either for reasons of trade or because of an alliance or a treaty. In fact war is born from war, and a make-believe war leads to a real one, and from a tiny war a huge one grows; and it is not unusual for the same thing to happen in this case as we are told of in the fables about the Lernaean monster.

It is for these reasons, I think, that the poets of old time (who saw with great discernment into the nature of things, and shadowed it forth by the aptest symbols too) recounted that war was a product of the infernal regions, by the agency of the Furies, and that not every Fury was equipped for that business—the most pestilential one was picked out,

> who has a thousand names,
> A thousand hurtful arts.[1]

Armed with innumerable snakes, she winds her hellish horn; Bellona[2] cracks her furious whip; wicked Rage, breaking all bonds, flies up with bloody face, hideous to see. The grammarians did not fail to see all this too, since some of them say that war is called *bellum* by antiphrasis, because in war there is nothing either good or beautiful (*bellum*); war, in fact, is called war as the Furies are called the Eumenides. Others prefer to think that the word *bellum* is derived from *bellua*, a beast, because it is the action of beasts, not men, to come together to destroy each other. But to me it seems more than savage, more than brutish, to resort to armed conflict. In the first place, most of the wild animals live in peace and good understanding with their own kind, they go in herds, and support each other with mutual help. Not all wild creatures are given to fighting (for there are some quite harmless ones, like hares and fallow deer) but only the really savage ones like lions, wolves, and tigers. And even these do not make war on each other as we do; dog does not eat dog, fierce lions do not fight each other, there is peace between snake and snake, venomous creatures agree together. But there is no wild beast more harmful to man than man. And then, when they do fight, they fight with their own weapons, but we use instruments

---

[1] Virgil, *Aeneid*, VII, 337–8.   [2] Goddess of War.

invented against nature by the art of demons, to arm men for the destruction of men. If the animals turn fierce, it is not for any casual reason, but because hunger drives them to madness, or they know they are being hunted, or they are afraid for their young. But we men, O God in heaven, what tragic conflicts we stir up for what frivolous reasons! For the emptiest of claims on property, out of mere childish spite, because of the interception of a woman,[1] or for reasons much sillier than these. And then among wild animals it is single combat, and very short, and however bloody the battle, as soon as one or other is wounded, they break it up. Who ever heard of a hundred thousand animals rushing together to butcher each other, which men do everywhere? One may add that just as some wild creatures have a natural repugnance from others of a different kind, so there are some with whom they have a real and solid friendship. But between man and man, each with any, there is perpetual warfare, and no treaty stands firm among any mortal men. So true it is that anything that diverges from its own true nature degenerates into a species far worse than if its vices had been engendered by nature herself. Do you wish to know what a savage and loathsome thing war is, and how unfit for man? Have you ever seen a lion fighting a bear? What distended jaws, what roaring, what growling, what ferocity, what mangling! It strikes horror in the spectator, even from a safe distance. But how much more hateful and savage is the spectacle of man at blows with man, furnished with such arms and such weapons? I ask you, who would credit these to be men, unless the evil were so taken for granted as to have dulled the sense of wonder? Eyes flash, faces grow pale, the very step betrays fury, the voice is harsh and grating, there are shouts of madness, all the man is made of iron—there is the clang of arms, the thunder of bombards. It would be kinder if man devoured man for food, if he drank his blood; and indeed it has come to this in some cases, when hate prompted a deed which might have found some excuse in need or necessity. But now the same thing is done in a crueller way, with poisoned darts and hellish contraptions. Nowhere is there any trace of humanity.

Do you think Nature herself would recognise her own creation? And if anyone were to point it out to her, would she not utter a curse on this wicked crime in words like these: 'What an extraordinary sight I see before me! What depths of hell have hatched this monstrosity for us? There are those who call me a harsh stepmother, because I engendered a few venomous creatures among all the grand total of

[1] A vague reference to the matrimonial plans of the Emperor Maximilian, whose plan to marry his daughter to Charles VIII was foiled by that monarch's marrying Anne of Brittany, Maximilian's proposed bride.

created things, although even they were to contribute to the comfort of man; or because I made a few animals not gentle enough, although there is no wild creature so savage that it cannot be tamed by skill and kindness—the art of man can make lions grow gentle and serpents docile, and bears obedient. What stepmother, and worse, has given us this new wild beast, a plague to the whole world? I brought forth one animal entirely for beneficence—peaceful, friendly, a ready helper. What has happened to make him degenerate into a wild beast like this? I see nothing left in him of the man I made. What evil genius has spoilt my work? What witch has conjured his human mind out, and a brute's mind in? What Circe has changed his native shape? I would order the unhappy creature to look at himself in a mirror—but what can the eyes see, when the mind is missing? Still, look at yourself if you can, raging fighter, if by any means you can come to your senses. Where did you get that threatening crest on your head? that glittering helmet? those horns of iron? those winged elbow-cops? that scaly cuirass? those brazen teeth? that plate armour? those death-dealing darts? that more than savage voice? that more than bestial face? that thunder and lightning, more terrifying and more deadly than the thunderbolt of Jove? I made you a creature near divine. What came into your head to make you change into a brute so monstrous that no brute will count as a brute in future when compared with man?' These and many other similar things she would say, I think—Nature, the mighty maker.

This then is the way in which man is fashioned, as we have just shown, and this is what war is like, as we have only too often experienced; and it is with no small wonderment that we may ask what god, what malady, or what chance first put it into the human heart to plunge a deadly weapon into human vitals. It must have been a gradual process which led to such a remarkable state of insanity.

No one falls all at once to depths of shame[1] as the satiric poet says. The greatest evils have always found their way into the life of men under the semblance of good. Long ago, then, when rude primitive men lived in the woods, naked, without ramparts, roofless, it sometimes happened that they were attacked by wild beasts. And so it was on them that man first made war, and the one who had defended the human race from the onslaught of the wild animals was held to be a man of mettle, and taken for leader. Indeed it seemed entirely right that the stabbers should be stabbed, the butchers butchered, especially when they were attacking us without provocation. Since these exploits won high praise—for that was how Hercules was made a god—spirited youth began to hunt the animals far and wide, and to show off their

---

[1] Juvenal, *Sat.* II, 83.

skins as a trophy. Then, not content with having killed them, the hunters wrapped themselves in their skins against the winter's cold. These were the first murders and the first spoils. After this they went further and dared to do a thing which Pythagoras deemed thoroughly wicked,[1] and which might seem monstrous to us, were it not for custom, which has such power everywhere that among some races it was considered dutiful to throw an aged parent into a pit after battering him to death, and so take away life from the one who gave it; or it was thought pious to feed on the flesh of one's intimate friends, and fine to prostitute a virgin in the temple of Venus; and many other things more absurd than these, which would appear shocking to everyone if they were described.[2] So true it is that nothing is too wicked or too cruel to win approval, if it has the sanction of habit. What then was the deed they dared to do? They were not afraid to feed on the carcasses of slain animals, to tear with their teeth the dead flesh, to drink the blood and suck the juices, and, as Ovid says, 'to stuff their entrails with other entrails.'[3] That deed, horrible as it might seem to more gentle minds, was sanctioned by use and convenience. The very look of the carcasses became a pleasure. The flesh was buried in coffers, and preserved with spices; an epitaph was written, 'Here lies a boar, here is a bear's grave.' Cadaverous pleasures! They went still further. From the harmful beasts they proceeded to the harmless ones. They made a general attack on sheep, 'beast without trickery or guile',[4] they attacked the hare, who had committed no other crime than to be eatable. They did not hold their hands from the domestic ox, which had kept the ungrateful family for so long by its labours; they spared no species of bird or fish, and the rule of gluttony reached such a point that no animal was ever safe from the cruelty of man. Habit made it possible for them not to see the savagery of this treatment of all forms of life, as long as there was no slaughter of man.

But vice is like the sea: we have the power to shut it out altogether, but, once we have let it in, there are few of us who can impose a limit; both are forces which roll on by their own impulsion and are not controlled by our will. Once these beginnings had given them practice in killing, men were incited by anger to turn their attacks on men, either with sticks and stones or fisticuffs. So far they fought with arms like these, I imagine, and they had already learnt from the slaughter of flocks and herds that man too could be killed with very little trouble. But this kind of barbarity was confined for a long time to single com-

[1] Diogenes Laertius, VIII, 24.
[2] Plutarch, *De Carnium Usu*, and Herodotus mention these customs.
[3] Ovid, *Metamorphoses*, XV, 88.   [4] Ovid, *Metamorphoses*, XV, 120.

bat. The war was brought to an end by the defeat of one antagonist; sometimes both fell, but then both were unfit to live. One may add that there was often some semblance of right in withstanding an enemy; it began to be a matter of praise to have destroyed some violent and dangerous man, such as they say Cacus and Busiris were,[1] and to have rid the world of such monsters. Exploits of this kind are among Hercules' titles to praise. Then people began to band themselves together, according to kinship, neighbourhood, or friendly alliance. And what is now called brigandage was then called war. It was waged with stones and burnt stakes. A stream in the way, or a rock, or some similar obstruction put an end to the battle. But meanwhile, as ferocity increases by being exercised, anger rises, ambition grows hotter, ingenuity provides weapons for the use of fury. They invent arms to defend themselves with, and they invent missiles to destroy the enemy. Now it was everywhere, and in greater numbers, and under arms, that they began to make war on each other. This was clearly madness, but it was not without honour. They called it 'bellum', and decided it was valour if anyone risked his own life to defend his children, his wife, his flocks, his dwelling from the attacks of the enemy. And so, little by little, military science developed with civilisation, and city began to declare war on city, region on region, kingdom on kingdom. Yet there still remained, in a thing so cruel in itself, a few traces of the humanity of earlier times; they sent priests to demand satisfaction,[2] they called the gods to witness, they skirmished with words before coming to blows. The battle was fought with ordinary weapons, and with courage, not trickery. It was a sin to attack before the signal was given; fighting must cease when the general had sounded the retreat. In short, it was more a contest of bravery and honour than a lust for killing. Nor did they take up arms except against foreigners, whom they called for this reason 'hostile' (*hostes*, the enemy, as it were *hospites*, strangers). So empires were built, and never did any nation achieve empire without great shedding of human blood. From then onwards there have been continual changes and chances of war, as one thrusts the other from the seat of empire and seizes it himself. After all this, as the supreme power had come into the hands of the worst rogues, anybody and everybody was attacked at will, and it began to be not the evildoers but the wealthy who were in most danger from the perils of war; the whole aim of fighting was not glory now but base profit, or something

[1] Cacus, a brigand, and Busiris, king of Egypt, both killed by Hercules.
[2] The *Fetiales* were a college of priests, under the Republic, who had special duties in connection with war (cf. II. IX. lxi, on the custom of the Augur, crowned, leading the line of battle, though himself immune from attack).

even more discreditable than that. I have no doubt that Pythagoras, wisest of men, foresaw all this when he made his philosophical observation urging the inexperienced multitude to abstain from slaughtering the flocks. He saw what would happen—that those who accustomed themselves to shed the innocent blood of an animal which had done them no harm, would not hesitate to abolish a man, when they were moved by anger or provoked by injury. What is war, indeed, but murder shared by many, and brigandage, all the more immoral from being wider spread? But this view is jeered at, and called scholastic ravings, by the thick-headed lords of our day, who seem to themselves to be gods, though they are not even human except in appearance.

From these beginnings, however, such a point of lunacy has been reached, as we see, that it fills the whole of life. We are continually at war, race against race, kingdom against kingdom, city against city, prince against prince, people against people, and (the heathen themselves admit this to be wicked) relation against relation, kinsman against kinsman, brother against brother, son against father; finally, a thing which in my opinion is worse than these, Christians fight against men; reluctantly I must add, and this is the very worst of all, Christians fight Christians. And, O blindness of the human mind! no one is astonished, no one is horrified. There are those who applaud this thing, greet it with cheers and call it holy when it is worse than hellish, and urge on the princes already crazed with fury, adding as they say 'oil to the flames'.[1] One, from the sacred pulpit, promises pardon for all the sins committed by those who fight under the banners of his prince. Another cries: 'Your invincible Highness, only remain in your present favourable state of mind towards religion and God will fight on your side.' Another promises certain victory, perverting the words of the prophets by applying them to wickedness, quoting such things as: 'Thou shalt not be afraid of any terror by night, nor for the arrow that flieth by day, nor for the demon of noon,' and, 'A thousand shall fall beside thee, and ten thousand at thy right hand,' and, 'Thou shalt go upon the asp and the basilisk, the lion and the dragon shalt thou tread under thy feet.'[2] In short, the whole of this mystical psalm was twisted to apply to profane things, to this or that prince. There was no lack of prophets like these on both sides, and no lack of people to applaud such prophets. We heard warlike sermons of this sort from monks, theologians, bishops. All go to war, the decrepit, the priest, the monk, and we mix up Christ with a thing so diabolical! Two armies march against each other each carrying the standard of the Cross, which in itself might

[1] See I. II. ix.   [2] Psalm xc (xci in A.V.), 5–6, 7, 13.

teach them how Christians should conquer. Under that heavenly banner, symbolising the perfect and ineffable union of all Christians, there is a rush to butcher each other, and we make Christ the witness and authority for so criminal a thing!

For where is the kingdom of the devil if not in war? Why do we drag Christ into it, when he would be less out of place in a house of ill fame than in a war? The Apostle Paul is indignant that any quarrel should arise between Christians which needs the presence of the judge to settle the dispute.[1] What if he could see us, warring the world over, and for such trivial causes, more savagely than any heathen, and more cruelly than any barbarians? What would he say if he saw this done with the authority, the exhortation, the incitement of those who represent the Pope—the peacemaker, the binder together of all things— and by those who greet the people with the word of peace?

I am not deaf to what those professional fighters, who reap their harvest from the ills of mankind, keep shouting at me: 'We entered on war unwillingly, forced to it by the misdeeds of others! We demand our rights!' Whatever evils war brings, must be put to the account of those who find reasons for war. But they must be quiet for a little while, and we shall confute their special pleading in due course, and remove the make-up which we use to cover up our disease.

Just as we have placed man side by side with war, that is, the most pacific of creatures with the most utterly monstrous of things, now let us draw a comparison between war and peace, contrasting the most wicked and pitiable of things with what is best and happiest; and it will then be perfectly obvious that it is sheer madness to strive for war with so much effort, such expense, such danger, such misfortunes, when concord could be bought at much less cost.

First of all, what is there, in the whole of existence, better and sweeter than friendship? Absolutely nothing. But what is peace, except friendship among many? Just as war is nothing else but a private quarrel extended to others. The characteristic of good things is that the wider their range, the greater the advantages they bring. Therefore, since affection between one individual and another is a pleasant and valuable thing, how great must be the happiness when one kingdom or one nation is knit with another in bonds of friendship? On the other hand, the nature of evil things is such that the wider they spread, the more they deserve their name. If it is wicked for one man to draw sword on another, how much more disastrous and immoral it is for thousands of men to do the same! Concord allows small things to grow, but in discord even great things come to grief. Peace is the mother and

[1] 1 Cor. VI, 1.

nurse of all that is good. War takes all that is joyous and beautiful and speedily smashes it, quenches it, wipes it out at one blow, and pours out a sludge[1] of evil over the lives of men. In time of peace, it is just as if spring-time were shedding its sunshine over human affairs; fields are tilled, gardens grow green, flocks graze in contentment, buildings go up on country estates and in the towns, what is dilapidated is repaired, edifices are adorned and extended, wealth increases, there is opportunity for enjoyment, the laws are in full strength, statecraft flourishes, religious fervour grows, justice holds sway, humanity is influential, arts and crafts are carried on with enthusiasm, the poor earn more and the opulence of the rich is more splendid. All good learning thrives, the young are educated, the old enjoy tranquillity and leisure, girls are happily married,

> young mothers are praised
> For children like their fathers,[2]

good men prosper, bad men are less bad. But as soon as the wild storm of war breaks out, great heaven! what a tidal wave of misfortune rushes in, flooding and overwhelming everything! Flocks are driven away, crops trampled underfoot, peasants slaughtered, farms burnt, flourishing cities which took centuries to build are overturned by a single squall. So much easier is it to do harm than good! The citizens' wealth falls into the hands of accursed brigands and mercenaries. Homes mourn, everywhere there is fear, sorrow, wailing and lamentation. The skill of the craftsmen is at a standstill, the poor must either go fasting or have recourse to immoral earnings. The rich are reduced either to mourning for their lost possessions or to fear for what they have left—in either case they are to be pitied. There are no weddings for the maidens, except in sadness and sorrow; deserted wives sit in barren homes; the laws are silent, humanity is jeered at, there is no place for justice, religion is held up to scorn, there is no difference between sacred and profane. The young are riddled with all kinds of vices, the old weep, and curse their length of days. Study and learning are without honour. In short, we meet more evils in war than any words can express, still less any words of mine.

It might perhaps be endurable, if wars only made us miserable and not wicked and malevolent too; if peace only made us happier and not better. But anyone who seeks for war is wicked. Too many already, alas! are the woes which continually afflict wretched mankind, exhausting and consuming it, whether it will or no. About two thousand years

---

[1] *Lerna* = a lake used as a sewer, near Mycenae (see I. III. xxvii).
[2] Horace, *Odes*, IV, 5, 23.

ago, the doctors listed three hundred names of diseases[1] apart from those which are always starting up new, and apart from old age itself, the malady with no cure. We read of whole cities overthrown by earthquake in one place, or set on fire by lightning in another, or whole regions swallowed up by landslides, or citadels undermined and collapsing, not to mention the vast number of people who meet their death by accidents so ordinary as to be taken for granted—tidal waves, floods, avalanches, toppling buildings, poisoning, falls, accidents due to wild beasts, food or drink or sleep. One person chokes on a hair while drinking milk, another on a grape-seed, another on a fish-bone stuck in his throat. There are those who have died for sudden joy (and for great sorrow, but this is less extraordinary). Then there are fatal epidemics, which rage quite often everywhere. There is no part of the world where human life, so transitory in itself, is not in danger. In fact it is a prey to so many evils that it was not without reason that Homer declared man to be the most wretched of living creatures.[2] But these troubles cannot easily be evaded and they are not brought upon us by our own fault, and so they only make us unfortunate, not criminal. Why on earth should people who are exposed to such innumerable calamities want to go looking for trouble, as if they had none already? And looking not for just any trouble, but the most terrible of all, so catastrophic that it beats all the rest, so fertile that it embraces everything else, so deadly that it makes people as wicked as they are unhappy, most miserable and yet not to be pitied (except for those who want war least and suffer from it most). Add to all this, that the advantages of peace are widely distributed and most people have a share in them. In war, if anything turns out fortunately (though, heavens above, could there be any good fortune here?) it affects only a few, and they the unworthy ones. The salvation of one is the ruin of another; the riches of one are the spoils from another; if one triumphs the other mourns, so that ill-luck may be grievous, but good luck is bloodstained and inhuman. What most often happens is that both sides weep over what is called a Cadmean victory. And I wonder whether there has ever been a war with so happy an outcome that a wise victor would not be sorry to have entered upon it. Therefore, since peace is of all things the best and the most joyful, and war conversely the most miserable and the most iniquitous, can we consider these people to be in their right minds who have the power to achieve peace with little effort and yet prefer to prepare for war at the cost of the greatest difficulties?

[1] Allusion to the *Corpus Hippocraticum* of the fifth and fourth centuries B.C. (see *Bellum*, p. 46). [2] *Iliad*, XVII, 446–7.

At the outset, what an unpleasant thing is that first rumour of war, and then what resentment the prince must incur when he mulcts his subjects by frequent levies of taxation! What a business it is to raise extra troops and keep them together, to enlist foreign regiments of mercenaries! What an expense and trouble to fit out navies, to construct and repair fortresses and camps, to furnish tents, to arrange for the manufacture and moving about of machinery, weapons, missiles, baggage, transports, commissariat! What infinite labour is involved in constructing banks, excavating ditches, digging trenches, arranging hours of watch, posting sentinels, going through manœuvres! I am leaving out alarms and perils (for what is not to be feared in war?). Who could possibly reckon up all the hardships which these military idiots undergo in their camps (and they ought to have worse, just for having elected to undergo them!)—victuals which would have turned the stomach of the Cyprian bull;[1] sleeping quarters which would be scorned by a dung-beetle; snatches of sleep which they cannot take when they like. A tent which lets in the wind all round, or no tent at all. They must endure an outdoor life, sleep on the ground, stand in their arms, bear hunger, cold, heat, dust, rain; they must obey their commanders, take beatings with rods—there is no bondage more humiliating than a soldier's life. As well as all this they must march to death at the fatal signal, either to kill mercilessly or fall miserably. All these evils are undergone for the sake of arriving at the unhappiest state of all! So as to afflict others, we afflict ourselves first with all these endless miseries!

If we would only take a reckoning and calculate in sober earnest the cost of war and the cost of peace, we should soon understand that peace can be obtained at a cost of ten times less care, effort, hardship, danger, expense and bloodshed than what we spend on war. You lead a huge crowd of men into danger for the sake of taking a fortified town; but with the aid of these men, and with no danger, you could have built a far finer town. But you want to do damage to the enemy—this in itself is inhumane. Just consider a moment whether you can harm him without harming your own people first! To run into certain trouble, while the outcome of war remains uncertain, seems the act of a madman.

Admitting that it has happened to the heathen to be brought to this lunacy by stupidity, or by anger, or ambition, or avarice, or barbarity, or else—I should rather imagine—by the Furies from Hell, how did we get it into our heads that Christian should draw a bloody sword on Christian? If one brother kills another, it is called fratricide. But a

[1] 'The Cyprian bulls were regarded as specially disgusting: they lived on human excrement (Pliny believes that they looked to it for a remedy for the colic)' (*Bellum*, p. 50).

Christian is nearer allied to another Christian than any brother can be, unless the bonds of nature are closer than those of Christ! What an absurd thing it is, that there should be almost continuous warfare between those who are of the household of one Church, who are members of the same body and glory in the same Head, that is Christ; who have one father in heaven, who are quickened by the same Spirit, initiated into the same mysteries, redeemed by the same blood, regenerated by the same baptism, nourished by the same sacraments, fighting under the same commander, eating the same bread, sharing the same cup; having a common enemy in the Devil, and finally called together to the same inheritance! Where could one find so many vows of perfect concord, such innumerable lessons of peace? One commandment Christ called his own—the commandment of love. What could be more opposed to this than war? He greets his friends with the blessed salutation of peace. He gave his disciples nothing but peace, only peace he left with them.[1] In those holy prayers of his he prays his Father above all that 'they may all be one' (that is, Christians), as he and his Father are one.[2] In this you hear something which goes further than peace, further than friendship or concord.

The prefiguration of Christ was Solomon, whose name was 'peacemaker' in Hebrew; he chose Solomon to build the Temple. David, otherwise distinguished by many excellent virtues, was cut off from the building of the Temple because he was a man of blood.[3] And yet he, David, made war by the commandment of God, but it was against the wicked, and in an age which had not yet been taught, by him who came to complete the Mosaic law, that we must love our enemies. When Christ was born, the angels sang not of wars or triumphs, but of peace. Before his birth, the poet of prophesy had sung of him: his place was made in peace.[4]

Examine the whole of his teaching: you will find nothing anywhere which does not breathe the spirit of peace, which does not savour of love. And since he knew that peace could not exist except among people who sincerely despised the things for which this world contends, he commanded us to learn of him, and be meek.[5] He called them blessed who think nothing of riches and their daughter Pride, for he calls them the poor in spirit; blessed are those too who spurn the pleasures of this world, whom he calls those that mourn; those who allow themselves to be turned out of their possessions, knowing that here we are in exile, and that for the devout the true country, the true treasure, is in heaven. Blessed, he said, are those who are good to all and yet are evil spoken

[1] John XIV, 27.   [2] John XVI, 21.
[3] I Chron. XXII, 8.   [4] Ps. LXXV, 3. in the Vulgate.   [5] Matt. XI, 29.

of and despitefully used, but do not retaliate.[1] He said, 'Resist not evil.'[2] In short, just as the whole of his teaching spelt tolerance and love, so his entire life was a lesson in compassion. That was how he reigned, he fought, he conquered, he triumphed. The Apostles taught exactly the same, they who had imbibed the Spirit of Christ in its pristine purity, and were still drunken with that glorious wine.

What else rings through all Paul's letters, but peace, gentleness, and love? What does John say, over and over again, but 'love one another'? And Peter? What else do all true Christian writers say? How comes it that there is such a commotion of wars among the sons of peace? Is it a mere fable, when Christ says 'I am the vine, ye are the branches'?[3] Who ever saw branch fight with branch? The expression Paul used more than once,[4] is it meaningless—that the Church is nothing if not one body with many members, joined to one head, which is Christ? Who ever saw the eye fight with the hand, or the belly with the foot? In this universe, composed of such different elements, there is a harmony. In the body of a living creature, there is peace between one member and another; each part has its own gifts, and uses them not for itself but for all the others. If anything happens to one, the whole body comes to its help. Are we to suppose that the natural bond uniting the parts of a perishable body is more powerful than the bond of the spirit in the mystic and immortal body?

Do we use in vain the prayer which Christ taught us, 'Thy will be done, on earth as it is in heaven'?[5] In the City of God there is supreme concord. And Christ wished his Church to be simply this: a people of heaven, living on earth as nearly as may be on the model of the celestial city, hastening towards it, drawing strength from it.

Let us suppose now that some strange visitor, either from those cities on the moon inhabited by Empedocles, or from one of those innumerable worlds imagined by Democritus, has arrived at this world of ours, eager to find out what goes on here.[6] Suppose that he has gained detailed information, and heard that there is a certain animal, curiously made up of a body which it has in common with the beasts, and a soul which reflects the mind of God; and that this being is so

[1] Matt. v, 11, 12; Luke vi, 27–8.   [2] Matt. v, 39.
[3] John xv, 5.   [4] Eph. iv, 16, v, 23; Rom. xii, 5.   [5] Matt. vi, 10.
[6] The editors of *Bellum* trace this allusion to Democritus to a passage of Diogenes Laertius, and to Cicero, *De Natura Deorum*, i, 26, 73. The mention of Empedocles seems to derive from an impression rather than from any definite allusion (see *Bellum*, p. 56). This might be taken as an example of the way in which the *Adages* sometimes strikes a modern note by chance. These 'other worlds' were for Erasmus simply the reverie of the Greek philosophers; but they were just becoming an objective reality for mankind.

noble that, though he lives in exile here, yet he holds sway over all other
living beings since owing to his celestial origin he is always striving
towards heavenly and immortal things; and that God cared for him so
much that, seeing that he could not reach what he longed for either by
natural powers or philosophic reasoning, he sent his only son to bring
him a new kind of teaching. Suppose then that this visitor, after learning all about the life and precepts of Christ, wishes to look out from an
observatory and see what he has been told about. When he has seen
the other animals behaving well, each in his own kind, following the
laws of nature and only asking for what nature dictates, and one animal
trafficking, bargaining, quarrelling, warring, would he not think that
any animal except man was the 'man' of whom he had heard? Suppose
his guide explained to him then which was man, and he tried to discern
the whereabouts of that famous Christian flock which, by following the
teaching of that wonderful heavenly Master, offers a faithful copy of the
city of the angels—would he not locate the Christians anywhere but in
those regions where he saw such opulence and luxury, such lustfulness
and pomp, such tyranny, ambition, trickery, envy, anger, dissension, such
brawls, fights, wars, and tumults, in fact a sump of all those things Christ
condemns, worse than is to be found among any Turks or Saracens?

Where did it come from, this plague that creeps through the people
of Christ? Probably it was little by little that this evil, like most others,
found acceptance with the heedless. Every bad thing either finds its way
into human life by imperceptible degrees, or else insinuates itself under
the pretext of good. What crept in first was erudition, the ideal instru-
ment, apparently, for confuting the heretics, armed as they were with
the writings of the philosophers, poets, and orators. At the beginning
these things were not learnt by Christians, but any who had made their
acquaintance before having knowledge of Christ turned what he already
possessed to pious uses. Eloquence too, at first disguised rather than
spurned, was finally openly approved. Then, on the pretext of combat-
ing heresy, a conceited taste for controversy crept in, which was the
cause of no little evil to the Church. Finally, things came to the point
where the whole of Aristotle was accepted as an integral part of
theology, and accepted in such a way that his authority was almost as
sacred as that of Christ. For if Christ had said anything which is not
easily fitted to our way of life, it is permitted to interpret it differently;
but anyone who dares to oppose the oracular pronouncements of
Aristotle is immediately hooted off the stage. From him we have
learnt that human felicity cannot be complete without worldly
goods—physical or financial. From him we have learnt that a state
cannot flourish where all things are held in common. We try to

combine all his doctrines with the teaching of Christ, which is like mixing water and fire.[1]

We have also taken over some things from Roman law, for the sake of its evident justice, and to make everything fit together we have twisted the Gospel teaching to it, as much as possible. But this code of laws permits us to meet force with force, to strive each for his own rights; it sanctions bargaining, allows usury—within limits; it regards war as praiseworthy, if it is just. 'Just' is defined as what has been ordered by the prince, even if he be a child or a fool. In fact the whole of Christ's teaching has been so contaminated by the writings of the dialecticians, sophists, mathematicians, orators, poets, philosophers and lawyers of the pagan world that a great part of one's life must be spent before one can turn to reading the Scriptures, and the result is that when one does get to them one is so corrupted by all these worldly ideas that the precepts of Christ either seem thoroughly shocking, or are distorted in accordance with the doctrines of these other authorities. And there is so little disapproval of this state of things, that it is regarded as sacrilege for anyone to speak about Christian scriptures without having crammed himself 'up to the ears' as they say[2] with nonsense out of Aristotle, or rather out of the sophists. As if the teaching of Christ were not truly something that could be shared by all, or had any kind of connection with the wisdom of the philosophers.

We came in for much honour after this, spontaneously offered, and then we began to exact it as our due. That seemed quite right and proper. Then we received money, but as alms to be distributed among the poor; then for our own use. Why not, since we had learnt that charity begins at home? There were plenty of excuses for this fault: it is a duty to consider the interests of children, it is right to prepare for the coming of old age. Why should we refuse riches, say they, if they are gained honestly? By these stages it has gradually come to the point where the richest man is considered the best, and never was wealth in such honour among the heathen as it is now among Christians. For what is there, either sacred or profane, which is not under the thumb of wealth? It seemed as if a certain amount of power should go with these honours. And people were not lacking who were willing to concede it. This also became an accepted thing, gradually and cautiously. The title

[1] iv. iii. xciv. The editors of *Bellum* point out that in the above passage Erasmus is judging the influence of Aristotle from the distortion of his views by the Schoolmen. This is in accordance with the passage quoted on p. 73, and many others, e.g. iv. iv. xcvii. But these remarks do not constitute a proof that he did not know Aristotle in any other form! That would indeed be extraordinary. The Aldine Aristotle had been in circulation since 1495–8. (See *Bellum*, p. 60.)

[2] See ii. iii. xxvii. Metaphor from a two-handled amphora.

was enough, the holders readily left its duties to others. In the end, bit by bit, we have arrived at a point where a bishop does not feel like a bishop unless he has some modicum of worldly power, and an abbot thinks he lacks honour if he cannot sometimes do what tyrants do. Finally, brazen-faced, we threw aside all sense of shame and broke down all the barriers of self-restraint. Whatever the heathen knew in the way of avarice, ambition, luxury, arrogance, despotism, we imitate, equal and surpass.

Not to mention less important things, did the heathen ever make war on each other as continuously or as savagely as Christians among themselves? What storms and surges of war have we not seen in these last few years, what treaties broken, what carnage? What nation has not been in conflict with what other nation? And then we execrate the Turk, as if there could be any spectacle more agreeable to the Turks than what we ourselves provide for them daily by our massacres of each other. Xerxes was mad, when he led his vast multitude to invade Greece. Would you consider a person sane who wrote threatening letters to Mount Athos to tell it to get out of his way—who ordered a beating to be given to the Hellespont because it was not accommodating when he wanted to sail across it? Alexander the Great was mad. Who will deny it? That precious demigod wished for several worlds to conquer—so great was the fever for glory which possessed his boyish soul.[1] And yet these men, whom Seneca had no hesitation in calling insane robbers,[2] warred more humanely than we do, warred with more honest good faith, not with machines and technique like ours, or for such frivolous causes as we Christians.

If you turn over the pages of pagan history, how many cases you find of leaders who avoided war with admirable tactics, who preferred to attack the enemy by good offices rather than attack him by force of arms.[3] Some would even rather give up their supremacy than try their fate in the field. As for us, there is nothing that we pseudochristians do not snatch at as a reason for war. The pagan warriors, before they took to arms, took to parley. Among the Romans, after everything had been tried, a *fetialis*[4] was sent with the *paterpatratus*, certain ceremonies were performed; they were trying to find reasons for delay, in fact, so as to temper the rage for fighting. And when all this had been done, it was not permitted to close with the enemy until the signal had been given, and it was given in such a way that the ranks did not know when it

[1] Herodotus, VII, 20, 35; Plutarch, *De Cohibenda Ira*; Quintus Curtius, *Life of Alexander the Great*.
[2] Seneca, *De Ira*, III, 14–22. [3] Play on *devincire* and *devincere*.
[4] See above. The *paterpatratus* was the chief of the *fetiales*.

would be. Even after the signal, anyone who was living in the camp without having taken the military oath was not allowed to challenge or strike the enemy. Thus the elder Cato sent word to his son idling in camp to come back to Rome, or else, if he wished to remain with the army, to ask the commander's leave to join battle with the enemy.[1] Just as the signal for attack did not give the right to fight except to those who had taken the oath, so when the retreat was sounded it took away from everyone the power of killing; this was so much the rule that Cyrus praised a certain soldier who was standing with sword raised to kill an enemy when he heard the retreat sounded, and at once released his opponent. These arrangements had the result that no one thought he had the right to kill a man unless necessity compelled him to do so.

Nowadays, among Christians, a man is considered valiant if chancing to meet in a wood one of the opposite side—not carrying arms but money, not wanting to fight but to run away from fighting—he has killed him, stripped him when killed, and buried him when stripped. Those are called soldiers, who rush of their own accord to the fight in the hope of a small profit, and fight on either side, like gladiators, though they may be brothers against brothers, and both belong to the jurisdiction of the same prince. And these men come home from battles like these, and tell tales of their exploits like soldiers; they are not punished as robbers and traitors to their country and deserters from their prince. We recoil with horror from an executioner, because he cuts the throats of condemned criminals, although he is paid by order of the law to do it; but men who have left their parents, wives and children to rush off to war uncompelled, not for honest wages but asking to be hired for some infamous butchery—when these men go home they are almost more in general favour than if they had never gone away. Out of their misdeeds they think they have won some distinction. The stealthy removal of a garment makes a man infamous,[2] but the man who has gone for a soldier, and been a soldier, and come back from soldiering with the spoils of so many innocent people, is counted among honest citizens. Among the soldiers, the one who has conducted himself with the most savagery is the one who is thought worthy to be captain in the next war. Thus, if one considers the old rules of military service, one can see that among Christians it is not military service at all but brigandage.

If you compare Christian monarchs with pagan ones, how weak our cause seems to be! They had no ambition but glory. They took pleas-

[1] Plutarch, *Quaestiones Romanae*, xxxix.
[2] The editors of *Bellum* (p. 66 n.) interpret this as meaning not a common theft but the abandonment of his uniform by a deserter.

ure in increasing the prosperity of the provinces they had subdued in war; where people were barbarous, without letters or laws, living like wild animals, they taught them the arts of civilisation; they populated the uncultivated regions by building towns; they improved unsafe places by constructing bridges, quays, embankments, and by a thousand other amenities they made man's life easier, so that it became a fortunate thing to be conquered. How many things are related of them, wisely said or soberly done, even in the midst of war! The things which are done in wars between Christians are too obscene and appalling to be mentioned here. The fact is that we only copy the worst of the ancient world—or rather we outdo it.

But it would be worth while to listen to the reasons we give to justify this great insanity of ours. 'If it were always a sin to make war', they say, 'God would not have commanded the Jews to war against their enemies.' True, but we must add that the Jews hardly ever warred against each other, but only against the foreigner and the wicked. We Christians fight with Christians. For them, the cause of conflict was a difference of religion, worshipping of strange gods; we are led to the same by childish anger, or greed for money, or thirst for glory, and often by the hope of dirty winnings. They fought by divine command, but it is the force of passion which puts the sword in our hand. Anyway, if the example of the Jews is so attractive, why do we not practise circumcision? or make animal sacrifices? or abstain from pig's flesh? why do we not marry several wives? Since we cry shame on these customs, why is it that we want to follow their example solely in making war? Why, in a word, do we here follow 'the letter which killeth'?[1] War was permitted to the Jews but, like divorce, 'for the hardness of their hearts'.[2] But since Christ gave the command to put up the sword[3] it is not fitting for Christians to fight, except in that noblest of all battles against the most hideous enemies of the Church—against love of money, against anger, against ambition, against the fear of death. These are our Philistines, our Nebuchadnezzars, our Moabites, and our Ammonites, and with these we must make no truce, we must persistently be at war, until the enemy is completely wiped out and peace is established. Until we subdue these, there can be no true peace either with oneself or with others. This is the only war which results in true peace. He who has won the victory in this, can have no desire to engage in war with any mortal man. I am not influenced at all by the

[1] 2 Cor. III, 6. [2] Matt. XIX, 8.
[3] Matt. XXVI, 52; John XVIII, 11. It is worth noticing as an example of Erasmus's careful corrections that, where all editions since 1523 have *non decet*, 'it is not fitting', the 1515 edition had *nefas est*, 'it is a sin'.

fact that the 'two swords'[1] are interpreted by some as meaning the civil
and ecclesiastical powers, both of which are claimed for the successors
of St Peter; since Christ suffered Peter to err in this, for the purpose of
leaving no doubt in anyone's mind that, when he was ordered to put up
the sword, it meant that war was now forbidden, even though it had
seemed to be allowable before. 'But Peter fought', they say. He fought,
but still as a Jew, who had not yet received a truly Christian spirit.
He fought—not for his own rights or his own property as we do, not
even for his own life, but for the life of his Master. He did fight—but
it was not long before he denied his Lord. If the example of his fighting
attracts us, then the example of his denial should too. And though he
made his mistake through honest affection, still he earned a reproof.
Moreover, if Christ approves this method of defending him—an interpretation which is foolishly adopted by some—why do his whole life
and teaching speak of nothing but tolerance? Why did he throw his
disciples to the tyrants armed only with staff and wallet? If that sword
which Christ ordered them to buy after selling everything else[2]
signifies a temperate self-defence against persecution (as some interpret
it, not only ignorantly but impiously) why did the martyrs never use it?
Here those rabbinical distinctions are brought forward: 'it is lawful for
a paid soldier to fight, in the same way as it is lawful for a butcher to
prepare meat according to his skill; the one has learnt to cut up beasts,
the other men. It is allowable for citizens to fight, but in a just war.'
('Just' indeed—this means any war declared in any way against anybody by any prince.) 'Priests and monks are not allowed to brandish
a sword, but they can be present and take command.' 'It is a sin to fight
in a spirit of vengeance, but not if it is for love of justice.' Who does
not think his own cause just? 'Christ sent out his disciples without
defence, but, while he was still with them, they had no need of defence.
When the time came for him to go away, he commanded them to take
their wallets and their swords, the wallet against lack of food, the
sword against their enemies. And then those words, "Take no thought
for the morrow", "do good to them that hate you", and so on, were
only valid till the time of his departure.[3] When Paul or Peter says the
same things, these are counsels and not precepts.' It is with this kind of
shining truth that we feed the desires of princes, and so we hand out to
them the means of flattering themselves. One would think there was a
danger of the world's having a rest from war, some day—and so we
defend war out of the words of Christ; and as if we were afraid that

---

[1] Luke XXII, 38. This interpretation dates from the ninth century and was held
through all the Middle Ages (see *Bellum*, p. 70).
[2] Luke XXII, 36.   [3] Matt. VI, 25–34; Luke XII, 5; 22–31; Matt. VI, 44.

greed might get tired of piling up riches, we make Christ our authority
for amassing wealth, twisting his words until it seems as if he had commanded, not tolerated, those very things which he had previously forbidden. The world had its own laws before there was any Gospel, it
administered punishment, it went to war, it piled up stores in the
money-box and the larder. The Lord did not come merely to tell us
what was permissible—how far we were allowed to fall below perfection—but to show us the goal we must strive towards with all our
might. One is suspected of heresy, if one earnestly tries to dissuade
men from war; but those who water down the Gospel teaching with
interpretations like these, and offer princes the opportunity to flatter
their own desires, *they* are orthodox, and great doctors of divinity! A
doctor who is truly Christian never approves of war; perhaps sometimes he may think it permissible, but with reluctance and sorrow.

They say, however, 'the law of nature dictates it, it has legal sanction, it is accepted by custom, that we should repel force by force, and
each defend our own life, and our money too, when it is "the breath
of our body" as Hesiod says.'[1] Very well. But grace, the grace of the
Gospel, is more efficacious than all this, and lays down that we must
not curse those who curse us, but repay evil with good, that if someone
takes away part of our possessions we must give him the whole, that
we must also pray for those who seek to kill us. 'All that applies to the
Apostles', they say; but it applies still more to the whole people of
Christ, to the body, as we said before, which must be a complete whole,
even if one member excels another in endowments. The people to
whom the teaching of Christ may not apply are those who do not hope
to reach their reward with Christ. Let those struggle for money and
lands and sovereignty who mock at Christ's words 'Blessed are the
poor in spirit',[2] but these are the truly rich who wish for nothing in this
world in the way of wealth or honours. Those who place the greatest
happiness in riches fight to save their own life, but without understanding that this is death rather than life, and that immortality is prepared
for the faithful.

They raise the objection that some Popes have both instigated and
abetted war. They produce writings of the fathers in which war is
apparently mentioned with approval. There are certainly some of
these,[3] but they date from the later times, when the fervour of the
Gospel was weakening, and they are very few, while there are innumerable writings of authors of unquestioned sanctity which argue against
war. Why should these few come into our minds rather than all the

---

[1] Hesiod, *Works and Days*, 688.   [2] Matt. v, 3.
[3] Those of St Augustine, for instance.

rest? Why do we turn our eyes away from Christ to men, and prefer to follow doubtful examples rather than the infallible authority? The Popes were men, first of all. And then it might well be that they were badly advised, or not attentive enough, or lacking in prudence or piety.[1] However even these, you will find, did not approve of the kind of war which we are constantly waging. I could prove this by the clearest arguments, if I did not want to avoid being held up by this digression. St Bernard praised warriors, but in such terms as to condemn all our soldiering. However, why should I be more impressed by the writings of Bernard or the arguments of Thomas[2] than by the teaching of Christ, which forbids us entirely to resist evil, at any rate by the popular methods?

'But,' they say, 'it is permissible to sentence a criminal to punishment; therefore it is permissible to take vengeance on a state by war.' What is there to say in answer to this? So much, that one can hardly begin. I will only point out the difference between the two cases; that the felon has been convicted in the courts before he is punished by the law, but in war each side is prosecuting the other; in the first case the suffering falls only on the person who did wrong, and the example is before everyone, but in the second case the greatest part of the suffering falls on those who have least deserved it, namely on the peasants, old people, wives, orphans, young girls. Moreover, if there is any advantage to be gained from this worst of all experiences, it is entirely drawn off by a few thieving scoundrels—it goes to pay the mercenaries, the out-and-out profiteers, perhaps a few leaders by whose instigation the war was stirred up (for this very reason) and who are never so well off as when the state is on the rocks. In the case of the felon, the reason for not sparing one is that all should be the safer; but, in war, it is for the sake of taking vengeance on a few, or perhaps even one person, that we inflict such cruel suffering on so many thousands of innocent people. It would be better for the fault of a few to go unpunished than to demand an uncertain retribution from one or another, and meanwhile throw both our own people and those whom we call our enemies—our neighbours, who have done us no harm—into certain danger. Better leave the wound alone, if no surgery can be done without grave harm to the whole body. If anyone cries that it is unjust that the sinner should go unpunished, I answer that it is much more unjust to bring desperate calamity on so many thousands of innocent people who have not deserved it.

[1] Up to 1526, this ran: 'they were either stupid or bad.'
[2] St Bernard, Sermo II, *Ad Milites*; St Thomas Aquinas, *Summa*, II a II ae. See *Bellum*, p. 76.

However, in these days we notice that almost every war arises from some claim or other, and from the selfish treaties of princes; for the sake of asserting the right of dominion over one small town, they gravely imperil their whole realm. And then they either sell or give away the very thing they have laid claim to with so much bloodshed. Someone may say, 'Do you want princes not to assert their rights?' I know it is not for such as myself to argue boldly about the affairs of princes, and, even if it were safe to do so, it would take longer than we have time for here. I will only say this: if a claim to possession is to be reckoned sufficient reason for going to war, then in such a disturbed state of human affairs, so full of change, there is no one who does not possess such a claim. What people has not, at one time or another, been driven out of its lands or driven others out? How many migrations have there been from one place to another? How often has there been a transfer of sovereignty, either by chance or by treaty? I suppose the Paduans might try to recover the site of Troy, because Antenor[1] was a Trojan of old; or the Romans expect to own Africa and Spain, because these were once provinces of Rome. In addition we call rule what is really administration. No one can have the same rights over men, free by nature, as over herds of cattle. This very right which you hold, was given you by popular consent. Unless I am mistaken, the hand which gave can take it away. And look what petty affairs are in question: the matter under debate is not whether this or that state is to obey a good prince or be enslaved by a tyrant, but whether it is to be counted as belonging to Ferdinand or Sigismund, or pay tax to Philip or Louis.[2] This is that important right for which the whole world is to be entangled with war and slaughter.

But let us suppose that this 'right' is really worth something, that there is really no difference between a privately owned field and a state, nor between cattle bought with your money and men, not only free men but Christians—still it would be only acting like a prudent man to consider whether it is worth so much that you should pursue it to the immense detriment of your own people. If you cannot show that you have the mind of a prince, at least act like a man of business. For him, expense is not to be considered, if he sees that the only way of avoiding it would cost much more, and he takes it as a gain, if what he chances to lose he loses without much loss. In the state's emergency, you might follow an example from private life about which they tell a rather amusing story. There was a disagreement between two kinsmen about an inheritance. As neither would give in to the other, it looked as though the affair would have to go to court and the quarrel be ended

---

[1] Virgil, *Aeneid*, I, 242–9.   [2] Imaginary rulers.

by the decision of the judge. Counsel had been approached, the action was prepared, the affair was in the hands of the lawyers. When the judges had been addressed and the case formally opened, pleading began—in fact, war was declared. At this point one of the contestants came to his senses just in time. He went to see his opponent privately and spoke to him as follows: 'To start with, it is really not very decent that those whom nature has joined by blood should be parted by money. And then, the workings of the law are always uncertain in their results, no less so than war. It is in our power to begin this, but not to end it. The whole case is about a matter of a hundred gold pieces. We shall spend twice that, if we go to law, on clerks, investigators, barristers, solicitors, judges, and the judges' friends. We shall have to be polite to them, flatter them, and make them presents; not to speak of the worry of canvassing, the trouble of running here and there. Even if I win hands down, it seems to me more loss than gain. Why don't we have an understanding between ourselves, not with these knaves, and share out between us what we should have to pay out uselessly to them? You give up half yours, and I will give up half mine. In this way we shall be the richer for our friendship, which we were going otherwise to lose, and we shall escape a great deal of trouble. If you refuse to give up anything, I will leave the whole business for you to arrange. I would rather this money went to a friend than to those insatiable blood-suckers. It will be a great gain to me to have preserved my fair fame, kept a friend, and avoided such a mass of troubles.' His adversary was convinced by the truth of this and by his relative's sense of humour. They settled the thing between them, to the wrath of the lawyers and judges, those crows whose gaping beaks they had foiled. Take a lesson from their good sense, when you are dealing with a much more dangerous thing. Do not think only of what you wish to gain, but think too of what you will lose to gain it—the sacrifice of so much that is good, the danger and disasters you will incur. If you find, by balancing one set of advantages and disadvantages with another, that an unjust peace is far preferable to a just war, why do you want to try the fortune of Mars? Who except a lunatic would fish with a golden hook? If it is clear that the cost would far exceed the gain, even if everything were to go well for you, would it not be better to give up a little of your rights, rather than buy a small advantage with such innumerable ills? I would rather anyone had the title to possession, rather than have it proved mine by the shedding of so much Christian blood. There is one man, whoever he may be, who has been in possession for many years, has got used to the reins of government, is acknowledged by his subjects, and fulfils the duties of a prince, and then another is to arise who rakes up a claim out of chronicles or faded charters[1] and turns a well-established state of affairs upside down? Especially when we see that in human affairs nothing stays the same for long, but ebbs and flows like the tide, at the whim of fortune. What is the use of asserting one's claim so noisily to something which will soon, by some chance or another, belong to someone else anyway?

Finally, if Christians cannot bring themselves to despise these trivialities, what need is there to fly to arms at once? The world has so many earnest and learned bishops, so many venerable abbots, so many aged peers with the wisdom of long experience, so many councils, so many conclaves set up by our ancestors, not without reason. Why do we not use their arbitration to settle these childish disputes between princes?[2] But there is more credit given to those who bring forward the pretext of the defence of the Church, as if the people were not really the Church, or as if the whole dignity of the Church rested on the wealth of the clergy, or as if the Church had originated, grown and established itself by war and carnage, instead of by those who shed their own blood, and lived in tolerance and forgetfulness of their own life!

To me it does not even seem recommendable that we should now be preparing war against the Turks. The Christian religion is in a bad way, if its safety depends on this sort of defence. Nor is it consistent to make good Christians under these auspices. What is taken by the sword is lost by the sword.[3] Are you anxious to win the Turks for Christ? Let us not display our wealth, our armies, our strength. Let them see in us not only the name, but the unmistakable marks of a Christian: a blameless life, the wish to do good even to our enemies, a tolerance which will withstand all injuries, contempt of money, heedlessness of glory, life held lightly; let them hear that heavenly doctrine which is in accordance with this kind of life. These are the best arms with which to defeat the Turks. Now, only too often, we use evil to combat evil. I will say further, and I wish it were more daring than true, if you take away the name and sign of the Cross, we are just like Turks fighting Turks. If religion has been established by armed force, strengthened by the sword, increased by wars, let us defend it by the same means. If everything has been done by different methods from these, why do we take refuge in pagan ways, as if we had lost confidence in the protection of Christ? They say, why should we not cut the throats of those who cut ours? Do you feel let down, if others are

---

[1] Or: obliterated inscriptions.
[2] This idea of arbitration by a council or parliament was a return to the past for Erasmus, but has a very modern ring (see *Bellum*, p. 84 n.).
[3] Matt. xxvi, 52.

more criminal than you? Why do you not rob the person who robs you? Or swear at the man who swears at you? Or hate the one who hates you? Do you think it is a Christian deed to kill even the wicked—at least we think them so, but they are men for whose salvation Christ died—and so make a sacrifice to the Devil which he finds most welcome—give double pleasure to the enemy, because a man has been killed, and a Christian has done the killing? In most cases, those who wish to appear truly Christian attempt to do the greatest possible harm to the Turks, and what is beyond their power they seek to bring down in curses on their enemies' heads; a thing in which on its own showing one might detect a lack of Christianity. In the same way, some who wish to be considered superlatively orthodox call down violent maledictions on those whom they call heretics—though they themselves might perhaps be more deserving of the name. Anyone who makes a claim to orthodoxy should do his best by mild reasoning to bring back the erring to his right mind. We spit on the Turks, and for that we think ourselves fine Christians, when perhaps we are more detestable before God than the Turks themselves. If the early messengers of the Gospel had been of the same mind towards us as we are to the Turks, where should we be now—we who are Christians because of their forbearance? Up and at the Turks!—turn the ungodly to godliness if you can; if you cannot, wish for it, and I will acknowledge the Christian spirit.

There are so many mendicant Orders in the world, who wish to be thought the pillars of the Church! Out of all these thousands what proportion is there who hold their life lightly for the sake of propagating the religion of Christ? But there is no hope of it, they say. Hope there would be, indeed, if the Dominicans and Franciscans copied the ways of their founders, who were conspicuously, I think, men who held their lives in contempt; I do not need to cite the example of the Apostles. Even miracles would not be lacking for us, if it were necessary for the glory of Christ. At present, those who pride themselves on being the vicars and successors of Peter, the prince of the Church, and the other Apostles, put all their faith in human support. Strict adherents of the true religion they are indeed—they live in wealthy cities given over to luxury, where they are corrupted themselves more quickly than they reform others, and where there are plenty of pastors to teach the people, and priests to sing God's praise. They dwell in princes' courts—what they do there, I will not mention at present. I only hope they are not more out of place than 'a dog in the bath'. They are on the look out for wills, they chase after money, they are obsequious to the tyranny of princes; and, so as not to appear to be doing nothing, they censure passages of books as erroneous, suspect, scandalous, irreverent, heretical and schismatic. For they prefer to dominate, to the detriment of the Christian people, rather than to extend the kingdom of Christ at any risk to themselves.

Those whom we call Turks are to a great extent half-Christian, and probably nearer true Christianity than most of our own people. How many are there among us who believe neither in the resurrection of the body nor in the survival of the soul? And meanwhile it is through them that an attack is made on the so-called heretics who doubt whether the Pope has jurisdiction over the souls tormented by the fires of Purgatory.[1] Let us cast out the beam from our own eye, and then we can cast out the mote from our brother's eye.[2] The end and aim of the faith of the Gospel is conduct worthy of Christ. Why do we insist on those things which have nothing to do with morality, and neglect the things which are like pillars of the structure—once you take them away, the whole edifice will crumble at once? Finally, who will believe us, when we take as our device the Cross of Christ and the name of the Gospel, if our whole life obviously speaks of nothing but the world? It must be added that Christ, in whom nothing was imperfect, yet did not extinguish the smoking flax nor break the bruised reed, according to the prophecy,[3] but cherished and bore with the imperfect until it could grow better. We are getting ready to annihilate all Asia and Africa with the sword, though most of the population there are either Christians or half-Christians. Why do we not rather acknowledge them, give them encouragement and gently try to reform them? If we have designs of political expansion, if we are hankering after their wealth, why do we cover up such a wordly thing with the name of Christ? While we attack them with human means alone, why do we bring the entire part of the world which remains to us into certain peril? What a small corner of the world is left to us! What a multitude of barbarians we are challenging, few as we are! Someone will say: 'If God be for us, who can be against us?'[4] And he will have the right to say it, if he trusts solely in God. But what does our Commander Jesus Christ say to those who rely on other means in their striving? 'They who take the sword shall perish by the sword.'[5] If we wish to conquer for Christ, let us gird on the sword of the word of the Gospel, let us put on the helmet of salvation and take the shield of faith, and the rest of the truly Apostolic panoply.[6] Then it will come about that, when we are conquered, we are conquerors

[1] Allusion to the traffic in Indulgences (see *Bellum*, p. 89 n., and Renaudet, *Etudes érasmiennes*, p. 167 and p. 153, n. 2).
[2] Matt. VII, 5. [3] Matt. XII, 20; Isa. XLII, 3.
[4] Rom. VIII, 31. [5] Matt. XXVI, 52. [6] Eph. VI, 14–17.

all the more. Even supposing the outcome of the war was favourable to us, who ever saw anyone made truly Christian by the sword, by slaughter, fire and pillage? There would be less harm in being frankly Jew or Turk than a Christian hypocrite. 'But we must protect ourselves from their onslaught!' Why then do we call down their onslaught on our heads by our dissensions? They will not easily attack us, that is certain, if we are in agreement, and they will be sooner converted to the faith by our good offices, if we seek to preserve them rather than wipe them out. I would rather have an honest Turk than a fake Christian. Our business is to sow the seed of the Gospel, Christ will give the increase. The harvest is plentiful, if the labourers are not lacking. And yet, for the sake of turning some of the Turks into bad and make-believe Christians, how many among the good Christians are made bad, or the bad worse? What else can be the result of such a tumult of wars? I am loth to suspect here what only too often, alas! has turned out to be the truth: that the rumour of war with the Turks has been trumped up with the purpose of mulcting the Christian population, so that being burdened and crushed in all possible ways it might be all the more servile towards the tyranny of both kinds of princes (ecclesiastical and secular).

I am not saying that I would absolutely condemn an expedition against the Turks, if they had attacked us first, and so long as we conducted the war which we claim to wage in the name of Christ, with Christian minds and with Christ's own weapons. Let them feel they are being invited to be saved, not attacked for booty. If language fails us, let us go to meet them with something else—conduct worthy of the Gospel. The manner of life will have a mighty eloquence. Let us take to them a plain and truly Apostolic profession of faith, not so overloaded with human learning. Let us demand from them, more than anything else, the things we have been taught to value by the Holy Scriptures and the writings of the Apostles. It will be easier to reach agreement on a few things, and concord will be more easily maintained if on most questions each is free to understand things in his own way, so long as it is without contention.[1] All this will be more fully discussed when I publish the book entitled *Antipolemus*, which I wrote when living in Rome, for Pope Julius II, at the time when he was deliberating whether to make war on Venice. This is a fact to be deplored, rather than denied.

If one examines the matter with close attention, one will find that almost all wars between Christians have arisen from either stupidity or wickedness. Some young men, with no experience of life,

[1] It is impossible to read these words without thinking of the *Utopia*.

inflamed by the bad example of our forbears told in the histories that
fools have compiled from foolish documents, and then encouraged by
flatterers and stimulated by lawyers and theologians, with the consent
and connivance of bishops, and even at their desire—these young men,
I say, go into war out of rashness rather than badness; and then they
learn, to the suffering of the whole world, that war is a thing to be
avoided by every possible means. Some are urged into war by a secret
hate, others by ambition, others by the fierceness of their character.
Our *Iliad* contains nothing, indeed, but the heated folly of stupid kings
and peoples.[1]

There are those who go to war for no other reason than because it is
a way of confirming their tyranny over their own subjects. For in times
of peace the authority of the council, the dignity of the magistrates, and
the force of the laws stand in the way, to a certain extent, of the prince's
doing just what he likes. But, once war has been declared, then all the
affairs of the State are at the mercy of the appetites of a few. Up go the
ones who are in the prince's favour, down go the ones with whom he is
angry. Any amount of money is exacted. Why say more? It is only then
that they feel they are really kings. Meanwhile the generals act in collusion to pick the unfortunate population to the bone. When people are
in this frame of mind, do you think they will be slow to seize any opportunity which presents itself of making war?

Then we cloak our disease with respectable titles. I am really
hankering after the riches of the Turks, and I cover it up with the
defence of religion; I am obeying my private hatred, and I use as an
excuse the rights of the Church. I am the slave of ambition, I am moved
by anger, I am carried away by my fierce and undisciplined character,
and I allege as my reasons for action a broken treaty, a violated alliance,
some omission in betrothal arrangements, or something else of the
kind. It is amazing how rulers fail to achieve the very thing they are
striving after, and, while they are stupidly seeking to avoid this or that
misfortune, fall into another, or even much deeper into the original one.
For truly, if they are led by the hope of glory, it is more splendid by far
to preserve than to destroy, much finer to build a city than demolish
it. Then, even supposing the war to have the most successful outcome
possible, how very small a share of the glory redounds to the prince!
A great part of it is claimed by the people, whose money paid for the
whole thing, a greater goes to the foreign mercenaries, as often happens,
and to the paid soldiers, some of it to the leaders, and most of all to
fortune, which is always of the greatest importance in war, as in every
other business. If it is lofty pride which urges you to go to war, do

[1] Horace, *Epistles*, I, ii.

consider, I beg, how mistaken you are about your own interests when
you reason like that. You are unwilling to yield to one person, a
neighbouring prince for instance, perhaps your kinsman, who possibly
once did you a kindness; think how much more humiliating it is to be a
suppliant, to beg for help from barbarians, and, what is worse, from
men polluted with every kind of crime, if one can give brutes of that
kind the name of men; while you must coax and flatter and wheedle the
blackguards, murderers and robbers—for they are the people through
whom war is waged. And, while you are trying to look like a fire-eater
to your equal, you are forced to be submissive to the very dregs of
humanity. While you are getting ready to thrust some neighbour out of
his territory, you have to admit a riffraff of dirty scoundrels into your
own. You have no faith in your kinsman, and you trust yourself to an
armed multitude! Would not peace have made you a great deal safer?

If you are lured by the hope of gain, make some calculations. War
might attract you, until you saw that you were liable to immeasurable
expenditure for the sake of a return not only much smaller, but quite
uncertain. But you were consulting the interests of the State? The truth
is that there is no way leads more quickly and utterly to the ruin of the
commonwealth than war. Even before you begin, you have already
done more harm to your country than you would do good by being
victorious. You exhaust the citizens' resources, you fill the homes with
mourning and the whole country with robbers, thieves and lechers.
These are the leavings of war. And though before you were at liberty
to enjoy the whole of Gaul, you are now excluded by your own act
from many provinces.[1] If you really love your people, why do not
these thoughts come into your mind: 'Why should I expose this fine
flower of youth to every misfortune? Why am I going to make so
many women widows, so many children fatherless? Why am I prepared to vindicate with the blood of my people a vague title, a doubtful
right?' When war was undertaken on the pretext of defending the
Church, we have seen the clergy so crushed by frequent tithes that no
enemy could have treated them with greater enmity. And so, when we
are foolishly trying to avoid one pitfall, we tumble straight into another
by our own doing. Because we cannot endure a slight insult, we condemn ourselves to the greatest humiliations. While we are ashamed to
comply with the wishes of a prince, we have to ask favours of the
lowest of the low. While we are rashly striving for freedom, we enmesh
ourselves in the closest servitude. While we are chasing after a little
gain, we are earning immense losses for ourselves and our people. A
prudent man would reckon up all this in his mind; a Christian, if he

[1] Addressed to Francis I, or with a look back at the activities of his predecessor?

were truly Christian, would take every means to avoid, avert and stave off a thing so hellish, so foreign to the life and teaching of Christ.

If there is no way of avoiding it, because of the general wickedness, when you have left no way untried and no stone unturned in your efforts for peace, then the thing to do will be to take care that only bad people are involved in so bad a thing, and to bring it to a conclusion with the minimum of bloodshed. For, if we bend our efforts to being in very truth what we are reputed to be, that is, if we neither admire nor desire anything that is of this world, if our one aim is to take flight from this life as unburdened as we may, if we strive with all our might towards heavenly things, if we place our whole happiness in Christ alone, if we believe that everything truly good, truly splendid, truly joyful, exists only in him; if we are convinced that no one can harm the faithful, if we consider how empty and ephemeral the playthings of human life are, if we ponder deeply on how difficult a thing it is for man to be turned into a god, as it were, and to be so purged here and now, by almost tireless meditation, from the contagion of the world, that once the body is laid aside he may pass to the company of the angels; in short, if we show we possess the three qualities without which no one can deserve the name of Christian: innocence, that is to be pure from vice; charity, to do good to all as far as we may; and patience, to tolerate evildoers and where possible overwhelm the evil with good—tell me, if we do this, what war could possibly arise between us over trifles?

If Christ is a figment, why do we not frankly reject him? Why do we glory in his name? If he is really the way, the truth and the life[1] why is there such a great contrast between our way of living and this example? If we acknowledge Christ as our authority, Christ who is Love, and who taught nothing, handed down nothing that is not love and peace, come, let us follow him, not only in name, not by wearing his badge, but in our actions, in our lives. Let us embrace the cause of peace, so that Christ in return may acknowledge us for his own. It is for this end that Popes, princes and states should take counsel together. There has been enough shedding of Christian blood. We have exhibited enough sideshows[2] to the enemies of the name of Christ. If the populace is turbulent, as it often is, it must be restrained by the princes, who should be to the State what the eye is to the body, or reason to the soul. Or again, if the princes stir up trouble, it is for the Popes to settle the disturbance with their prudence and their authority. May we at long last, satiated with wars, be touched by the yearning for peace. Calamity itself leads us to this; the world, weary of wrong, prays for it; Christ beckons us to it; we are exhorted to it by Pope Leo, the tenth of the

[1] John XIV, 6.   [2] *Voluptates*: 'spectacles, shows to amuse the people' (Cicero).

name, who fills the place on earth of the true peacemaker, the Solomon, Jesus Christ; Leo, as little ready to do harm as a lamb, but a raging lion when it comes to opposing all that is against piety; whose every wish, every counsel, every effort is directed towards making those who are joined by a common faith be united in common concord. He is striving to make the Church flourish, not by wealth or power, by its own particular gifts. A noble task indeed, and worthy of such a hero, sprung from the illustrious Medici, by whose statecraft it came about that the famous city of the Florentines had such a flowering in long years of peace; their house was always the home of all good learning. The Pope himself, endowed with a gentle and serene character, was initiated from the cradle, as they say,[1] into the study of the humanities and the gentler Muses, and he brought to the pontificate a life and reputation quite unsullied, and untouched even in that freest of all cities, Rome, by the slightest suspicion of slander. He did not seek to be Pope himself; such a thing was far from his expectations, when he was called by name as by a divine voice to bring succour to a world wearied by the long convulsions of war. Julius[2] can have his glory; he can keep his victories, he can keep his splendid triumphs. Whether such things are fitting for a Christian pontiff, it is not for such as myself to pronounce. I will only say this: that glory of his, however great, was accompanied by the ruin and misery of a vast number of people. A far greater, truer glory will accrue to our Leo from the return of peace to the world, than Julius could derive from so many wars valiantly embarked upon or successfully carried through.

But we shall seem to be delaying unduly over this digression, to those readers who are more interested in hearing about proverbs than about war and peace.

IV. OTHER SUBJECTS

(i) *Virum improbum vel mus mordeat*[3]

Κἂν μῦς δάκοι ἄνδρα πονηρόν; that is, a bad man may be bitten, if only by a mouse. (A hemistich from an heroic poem.) The meaning is, that the wicked do not escape vengeance; somehow they have to

[1] I. VII. lii.   [2] The previous Pope, Julius II.
[3] I. VIII. xcvi; LB. 332 B. It is suggested by P. S. Allen that the doctor mentioned here might be the Dutchman Bont, who was an acquaintance of Erasmus in Cambridge (see Allen, 225, 275). Erasmus writes: 'There is a doctor here of our nation who does marvellous things by means of a quintessence, making old men young again and bringing the dead to life. There is some hope that I may grow young again, if I taste his quintessence—and, if that happens, I shall not be sorry to have come here!' Dr Bont and his young daughter both died of the plague in 1513.

pay the penalty of their misdeeds. It can also be applied to those who pick a quarrel over some frivolous subject, and pretend to be the injured party, so as not to have to give anything away. Something like this happened not long ago in England, to a doctor who was a compatriot of mine and a close friend. Let me tell the story here, in passing. A certain citizen of London, very well off, and considered extremely respectable, had been cured by the skill of this doctor, not without danger to himself. For the man was ill of a particularly infectious fever. And, as it happens when people are in danger, the doctor had been promised mountains of gold if he would be willing to stand by his patient in his hour of need; and the man had entreated him in the name of the friendship between them. Why say more? He persuaded the doctor, who was young, and a Dutchman. He went to him. There was nothing he did not do. The man was saved.

When the doctor shyly mentioned a fee, that trickster wriggled out of it, saying that payment would certainly be made but that the keys of his money box were in the hands of his wife. 'And you know what women are', said he. 'I should not like her to know that I had paid so much.' A few days later the doctor met the man in the street; he was glowing with health and bore no sign of his illness. The doctor accosted him and reminded him that the fee had not been paid. The fellow declared roundly that the money had been paid at his order by his wife. The doctor denied this. Now see what an excuse for getting angry that good man had found: as the doctor spoke to him in Latin in the second person singular, he pretended to be deeply insulted. 'Heavens,' he cried, 'do you, a Dutchman, say "thou" to an Englishman?' And at once, as if he had gone out of his mind, shaking his head with rage and uttering dire threats, he went away. That was how that honest citizen got out of his responsibilities—he deserved to catch the plague again.

I laughed at this story, but not without sympathy for my friend, so unjustly deceived, and amazement at such ingratitude. There is gratitude from lions who have been helped when in danger; snakes will remember a good turn. Here was a man who repaid another man, his good friend too, for a service—and what a service, which nothing could ever repay—with a mean trick. But I have not told this tale to bring discredit on the man's nationality, only through indignation at what was done. It would be unjust to judge all Englishmen by the example of a single rogue like this.

(j) Ollas ostentare[1]

Χύτρας ἐπιδείκνυσθαι, to make a show of kitchen pots. This is to bring forward something which is ridiculous and squalid, but also of great importance. Plutarch, in his book *On Hearing*,[2] criticises the Sophists, whose custom was to embellish undignified subjects with a glaze of words, in singing the praises of vomiting, fever, Busiris, and so on: and so on: he says that they are *showing off kitchen pots*. It is not a bad idea, however, to play sometimes on this kind of subject, for the sake of exercising or relaxing one's mind, given that the joke is an intelligent one[3] and the pleasure not unmixed with profit. Seeing that

> A true word spoken in jest
> What hinders?

In fact, truth finds a way into the minds of men more agreeably, and with less danger of giving offence, by favour of these pleasantries; Aulus Gellius does not hesitate to put those absurd fables of Aesop before the famous doctrines of the Stoics, stern and fallen from Heaven as they are. Plutarch himself was joking in his *Gryllus*, amusingly enough, but in such a way that you can see it is a philosopher joking and not a buffoon. I joked too, some years ago, in my *Praise of Folly*, on which I spent no more than a week's work, and without the help of any books, because my luggage had not arrived. Such as it is, I find the book has won the full approval of open-minded people, who know something about good literature. They say that as well as the fun of the jest there are many things in it which do more for the improvement of morals than the *Ethics* and *Politics* of Aristotle—after all, he was a pagan, and spoke of these things in a more than pagan way. And yet I hear that some have taken offence, but only a few, and those of the kind who like nothing unless it is barbarous and silly and foreign to all the Muses. They themselves read Juvenal (otherwise they bitterly hate the poets) so as to fill their sermons with abuse against the vices of princes, priests, merchants, and especially women, often painting such pictures of them that it comes to giving lessons in obscenity. As for me, although it would not have been unsuitable to the matter in hand, and there was a wide field of opportunity, I satirised no one by name, and without disturbing that Camarina[4] of vices and crimes, I dwell

---

[1] II. II. xl; LB. 460 D.   [2] Plutarch, *On Listening to Lectures*, 44 f.   [3] *eruditius*.
[4] Erasmus gives an explanation taken from Servius. 'Camarina' was the name of a marsh near the town of that name, which bred pestilence. The townsfolk enquired of an oracle whether it should be drained, but the oracle forbade this. However, they did drain it, and thus provided solid ground for invasion by their enemies.

briefly on points that are funny rather than vile. 'But', they say, 'you criticise bishops, you criticise theologians, you criticise princes.' I answer first, that these critics are ignoring the fact that I do it gently, not offensively. Then they have forgotten that rule which St Jerome is always impressing on us: where there is a general discussion about vice, there can be no insult to any individual, and no one person is given a black mark and told he is wicked, but all are admonished to avoid wickedness. Or perhaps they mean to assert that all princes are wise, all theologians distinguished, all bishops and pontiffs like Paul and Martin, all priests and monks like Antony and Jerome? And then, they are not giving full weight to something which is very important in a dialogue, the fitness of the speech to the speaker; and they imagine it is Erasmus speaking, not Folly. It is just as if one were to write a dialogue between a pagan and a Christian, and be told it was sacrilegious to make the pagan say anything against Christian doctrine. Finally, since even tyrants will take anything from their jesters, and laugh, and think it unmannerly to be offended by any pleasantries, it seems extraordinary that these people (it doesn't matter who they are) cannot bear to hear anything from the very lips of Folly—as if anything that was said about vice must immediately apply to themselves. But this is more than enough on that subject. We must get back to our kitchen pots.

4

FROM LATER EDITIONS

(a) Ut fici oculis incumbunt (1517)[1]

Ὥσπερ τὰ σῦκα ἐπὶ τοὺς ὀφθαλμοὺς ἔφυ, i.e. as figs (sties) are native to the eyes. This is said of those who urge on and push forward some piece of business. The metaphor is taken from sties, that is from that defect which clings to the eyes and cannot be removed without harming the eye itself. Aristophanes says in the *Frogs*: 'Like a sty sticking to the eyes, so was he.'[2] It may be applied not unsuitably to those people who cannot be removed without great disaster, although they are an intolerable burden to others. If only there were not, and had never been, princes and princes' grandees of this kind! Insatiable in their greed, most corrupt in their appetites, most malignant in their cruelty, in-human in their despotism—real enemies of the public weal, and high-way robbers—armed for the destruction of the community not only with the usual weapons of force and wealth, but with new arts which no Dionysius or Phalaris ever discovered—and yet they are so glued to the nation, they so dominate it and clamp themselves on it, that they can neither be endured nor torn away. So much so, that there is no council, no magistracy, no sacred rite, no part of the commonwealth into which they do not throw out active roots, like a disease spreading through all the veins of the body. If only men would understand—but how can they, since they have perception and wisdom only for doing harm?—that there is one safeguard left to save the world from ship-wreck, and that is that the tyranny of those in power should be kept in bounds by a proper agreement and mutual understanding between citizens and between states. It is a matter of first importance to destroy this tyranny. In time of peace they feel that they are less free to act, because affairs are conducted according to law and policy, not by fraud or by force of arms. For that reason they do everything they can to prevent the people enjoying peace. They see that the happiness of the country depends particularly on having a prince who is upright, wise, and watchful, a real prince, in fact. And so the guardians of the prince take quite extraordinary trouble to see that he never becomes a man. The great lords—those who fatten on public misfortune—do their best to make him effeminate with a life of pleasure, and take care that he

[1] 'As sties stick to the eyes', II. VIII. lxv.; LB. 653 F.
[2] Aristophanes, *Frogs*, 1247.

144

knows nothing which a prince really ought to know. Villages go up in flames, lands are laid waste, churches are ravaged, innocent citizens are murdered, everything is overturned, while the prince idly plays at dice, amuses himself with dancing and players, hunts, drinks, makes love. O extinct line of Brutus! O thunderbolt of Jove, either blunted or blind! There is certainly no doubt that these corrupters of princes will pay the penalty of their crimes to God, but too late for us. Meanwhile we must endure them, lest anarchy—on the whole a worse evil—take the place of tyranny. The experience of public events has often proved —and the recent peasants' revolt in Germany shows us—that the harshness of princes is to some degree more tolerable than the confusion of anarchy. In the same way, lightning terrifies everybody but only strikes down a few, whereas a tidal wave spares no one, but floods in, jumbling and rolling together everything in its way.

What a worthless aristocracy is to the state, perhaps some are to the Church—a proportion of the members of those Orders which are popularly called Mendicant. I am not accusing the good among them, nor attacking the Order itself—I am referring to the bad ones, always the biggest number. These people have so spread themselves throughout the body of the state, that nothing is ever done without them. They preside at assemblies, although this is the first duty of the bishops; they hold tyrannous sway in the schools, a duty which is next in importance. The Sacraments of the Church are administered by them, and it is through them that we become priests. It is they who pass judgement about professions of faith, with a severity exceeding that of the censor: 'this man is a Christian, that one a half-Christian, this one a heretic, that one a heretic and a half.' Into their bosoms the populace pours the hidden deeds of life, and the most secret thoughts of the heart; but this is not enough for them, there is no treaty contracted between princes in which they do not bear a part. No marriage takes place without them. In contests in the theatre, in public lotteries, they act the part of judge, so shameless are they. Lastly, one may not die without them. There is no princely hall into which they have not insinuated themselves. If the princes intend to perpetrate some shameless deed, it is through these people that they carry it out. If the Roman pontiffs have designs which are not quite according to the early Apostolic holiness, these are the intermediaries they prefer to use. For instance, if there is some war, some public disturbance, some levying of taxes, some particularly flagrant delay of justice, they are there, acting the chief parts in the play. And all the time they are imposing on the simple populace with a display of sanctity. Compared to them, priests are no priests at all; bishops, if they are to be believed, are asleep on both ears.

Poor forsaken populace, instead of having a single race of shepherds it is torn to pieces by two kinds of wolves, since the bishops on the one hand rule like tyrants, and, on the other, there are these people who are not shepherds at all but robbers of another sort!

Again I must point out that I am not censuring the good, nor the Order itself. For those who are incorrupt among them deplore just what I deplore. And yet the bees may at length eject from the hive the drones, as having no sting, and treat them as thieves. These drones have worse stings than any hornet, and neither kings nor Popes can destroy them without a catastrophe to the Christian religion, so firmly have they entrenched their contingents and filled the whole world with their strongholds and their multitudes, and every day they set up new hives; and on this pretext, forsooth, that the devout Rule of the earlier monasteries, which was the foundation on which those houses were built, had failed; as if indeed their own incorruptibility were not to fail soon after, if incorruptibility there ever were. And so it happens, that the world is burdened with crowds of idle and worthless monks, that the princes are cheated of their people, the bishops of their flocks, the people of their shepherd, and the purity and freedom of the Christian religion sink bit by bit into Judaistic formalism. Just as it is difficult to say whether concord or dissension between bad princes is worst for the common weal, because if they fight they do it much to the detriment of the people and if they agree it is to conspire for the general ruin—in the same way one cannot say which it is to be hoped for (or rather I should say which is to be loathed the most), an agreement between these people or a dissension. Either thing results in harm to the public at large.

I think the word *ficos* is used here to mean a hard swelling rising on the side of the eyes; a thing which is most troublesome and yet cannot be removed without danger, because it is so near to the eye, a part which will not bear much touching or interference. Suidas mentions this proverb.

(*b*) *Esernius cum Pacidiano* (*1517*)[1]

[This story stands alone in the *Adages* as a satirical attack on a person mentioned by name. Erasmus says it is included as light relief; it was a piece of contemporary journalism, as the dispute in question occurred at Easter, 1517, and Erasmus wrote his account of it as an extension to the proverb for the edition of the *Chiliades* published by Froben in November 1517. Although Erasmus was no longer resident in England, he had spent some time in London in April of that year, for the purpose of receiving his dispensation from the Pope at the hands of his friend Ammonius at Westminster (9 April), and so he was present during the events he describes.

[1] II. v. xcviii; LB. 580 F.

Henry Standish (d. 1535) was a Franciscan, a D.D., Warden of the Franciscans in London by 1515, later Provincial of the Order, and appointed Bishop of St Asaph in 1518. He was a favourite of Henry VIII, and often preached before him. In December 1515 he opposed Convocation about the punishment of clerics by lay tribunals, supporting the king's view, and it is to this that Erasmus alludes in his character-sketch. Erasmus had disliked him from the first and had already had several brushes with him, 'as preaching against Colet for a "poet", 1512–13' (Allen, 608, 14 n.) and as objecting to the new edition of Jerome (cf. Allen, 337, 678 n.). More had warned Erasmus in October 1516 that trouble was brewing for him among a hostile group in London led by an eminent Franciscan (Allen, 481). No doubt this had something to do with the tone of the following passage.

For all this see Allen, 608, 14 n., and for Erasmus's confident relations with Wolsey at this time see Allen, 577.]

The same idea [as in the preceding adage, *Bithus contra Bacchium*] is to be found in this passage from Lucilius, 'Esernius, a good match for Pacidianus.'[1] These were two gladiators, equal in all respects, and far and away superior to all the rest. Cicero in his book on 'The Best Kind of Orator'[2] says: 'I, however, am introducing a noble pair of gladiators (if I may be allowed to compare the smallest things with the greatest). Aeschines, like the Esernius of whom Lucilius speaks, is no base character, but learned and keen-witted, and he is matched by this Pacidianus, by far the best of men since men ever existed.'

A show of this kind was put on recently for us, to everyone's delight, in London among the English, by two theologians. One of them was the great Standish, κορυφαῖος (leader) as the cloistered friars call it in that island, of the Franciscans, an amazingly wordy man, an enthusiastic Scotist, an intrepid soul; and such a strapping fellow, too, with such powers of physical endurance, that he might have been a soldier of the Old Guard[3] or a gladiator himself if he had not been a theologian. The other was an Italian, of the Order which is popularly called Servite Brothers, because, as I understand (even if they are blacker than beetles), they serve the Virgin Mary alone, and have nothing to do with Christ or with any other of the Saints. This was one perhaps not inferior to the other in scholarship, but he was no match for him in those powers which make a gladiator, or so it seems to me. This man had beaten a retreat to England during Lent, as his custom was, and wanted to prove that the attention he had been giving to theological studies in Paris for

[1] *Remains of Old Latin* (ed. E. H. Warmington, Loeb classics), III, p. 56.
[2] Cicero, *De Optimo Genere Oratorum*, XVII.
[3] *triarius miles*. The *triarii* were the veteran Roman soldiers who formed the third rank from the front when the legion was drawn up in order of battle (see I. I. xxiii).

several years had not been wasted, so he began to put forward a number of conclusions, as they are called, for disputation among the learned. Most of them referred to the merchant class, except for the first, which seemed to be intended as an insult to St Francis. This was more or less the gist of it: 'The Friars Minor [Franciscans] commit a sin if they accept money, either in person or through others, and consequently those who give them money commit a sin too, since anyone who provides the occasion to sin is himself guilty of sin.'

For a foreigner to dare to do such a thing, there must be a reason— and it was this. The said Servite was living here among the Augustinians, who call themselves Hermits, speaking by contraries, I imagine. In London these people make a good profit out of the merchants, especially the Italians, and consequently the Friars hate them. Standish, therefore, to divert this source of profit to his own people, admonished the public in a sermon to be very, very careful whom they made their confessions to—for only two Orders were given the right by the Pope to hear confessions from all and sundry, that is to say, the Franciscans and the Jacobins.

This was obviously a call to all the other Orders to go hungry. They got together and suborned the Servite to avenge them for such a drastic injury by bringing out his theses, since he was ignorant of the English language and could not speak to the populace. And so the conclusions which I mentioned at the beginning were placarded up on all the churches and at street-corners. The rumour of this filtered out gradually, as these things do, and reached the Standishian ears; and that devout and high-minded man was filled with righteous indignation. He muttered dire threats, and the whole thing seemed to be tending towards a great tragedy, had not some *deus ex machina*[1] intervened. For the sensible man was beginning to see that the thing would turn into a case of 'Saguntinian hunger'[2] if a proposition of that kind was heard in public. And among those people the man who has the largest pile of coin is regarded as the holiest. Why say more? The Servite was obliged to go and see Standish, to make his excuses and smooth the man down. He went, but unwillingly. For several people had terrified the stranger by telling him what a virulent man Standish was, how noisy and violently irascible; and they said that he was thought a great deal of by the general rabble, such as boatmen, ostlers, shoemakers, cobblers and fullers, and gentry of that sort; and that he had such force of character that he had strongly opposed the cause of clerical immunity, single-

---

[1] Appearance of a god providing the dénouement of a tragedy.
[2] See I. IX. lxvii, *Saguntina fames*. The story of the siege of Saguntum is told from Livy, Valerius Maximus, and Cicero.

handed, against the entire Church in England, and by so doing had earned the enmity of all the priests and bishops and a good part of the public, the part which was favourable to the clergy.

Well, the Servite came face to face with him; and as he (the Servite) had studied Rhetoric as well as Theology, he set about his effort at conciliation by these opening words: 'Excellent Father,' quoth he, 'I have not come here at all willingly, because I have heard from several sources that you have an uncontrollable temper, and, according to some people, you fly into mad rages.' And having thus far most skilfully secured a favourable hearing, he sketched the matter in a few words. 'Nevertheless,' he said, 'since those Fathers begged me so earnestly to do it, I am here, ready to listen if you have anything to say.'

The other immediately burst into violent abuse. He said the 'conclusion' was scandalous, it offended pious ears, it smacked of heresy, it was irreverent to the Seraphic Order of St Francis, and the Servite would soon have to pay the penalty, unless he recanted it. The Servite, as became a man of mettle, replied that he had proposed it for disputation, not for recantation. Standish was enraged beyond measure by such an impious remark; he ordered the man to busy himself for a moment, and rushed into the house. The Servite, taking no notice of the great man's orders even on this point, began to go away. But, as he went, Standish came with all his cowled supporters (he has a great many, no less sturdy and bold than the king's) and followed him, swept him off his feet as if he were some robber, and started dragging him inside again. Then the Servite, all alone and very frightened, did what people do in desperate situations, and cried out 'Jesus, Jesus', over and over again with all his might. Jesus was never among the Franciscans; but the poor man was being dragged away, and the name of Jesus attracted the attention of some builders' labourers who ran up with their stones and tools and snatched the man out of the hands of the gang.

Here ends the first act of the play.

The next act was conducted with loud abuse from both sides, the leader of each party screaming at his adherents. The Servite was even said to have hung up a votive tablet to Jesus the Saviour, with a picture of the scene in colour and an epigram written beneath. The story got about very soon among the public, and reached the ears of the cardinal,[1] who is ruler and judge in that country. He is a man of merry wit, and the performance seemed to have its funny side; he ordered both parties to appear before him. Standish made strong accusations. The Servite put up an energetic defence. The cardinal decided that as the proposition was scholastic in type and suitable for disputation, they should

[1] Wolsey.

dispute it on the Thursday after Easter in St Paul's Church, which is the most famous church in that island.

Neither side refused battle. The generals armed themselves, the soldiers got ready; the conclusions were posted up on all the doors, on posts, and at cross-roads, people came from far and wide to see the performance. Their views as to the favourite differed, but all were equally agog. Not to make a long story of it, the day of battle came; both learned and unlearned postponed everything else. Then, lo and behold, efforts made in certain quarters brought it about that an interdict of the king was issued through the cardinal, forbidding any action to be taken. At this Standish made a bid for arrogating the credit to himself, by sending out some of his people and spreading a rumour among the public that the Servite had fallen at his feet in supplication and begged that the disputation should not be held. Most people were on the point of believing this, since the other was a stranger and knew no English, had it not been that some god or other put an idea into the Servite's head. Climbing up into the pulpit, he addressed the crowd as follows: 'Learned doctors, and all you other worshipful men, today there was to have been a disputation, but his Eminence the Cardinal has ordered it to be cancelled, for very good reasons. I say this to prevent you waiting in vain.' When the Friars saw that such a prize of glory was being snatched out of their hands, they rose up against the man and would have torn him to pieces in the midst of the church, had not the cardinal, with some forethought, provided him with some people known to his own household as a guard. So the only thing the Friars could do was to shake their heads at him from a distance and make many threats, and go off once more to accuse him before the cardinal with a great uproar. 'He dared to disregard the king's command,' they said, 'by standing up like that to testify before the people that he was ready to defend so impious a conslusion.'

Both parties were ordered to appear. Standish brought, as well as his own supporters, a young boy in a friar's habit, already versed in Scotism. (It is so important to start educating the young in good time!) As he was going through the various ante-rooms to the cardinal's private apartments, he showed this boy to the nobles of the court (for he was well known to many of them, more so than liked). He declared that this remarkable boy would finish off the Servite and wipe the floor with him. 'The object of my coming,' said Standish, 'is to pit this boy against that fellow.' But the cardinal said it was not proper to set a boy against a graduate, as they are called. For the Servite was a Bachelor of Theology, though whether he was in the running or had arrived, whether he had taken his degree or was just going to take it, I am not sure. So a certain Franciscan was found to oppose him, but an Italian, to meet an Italian—as one crow flies at another's eyes. Some learned scholars and gentlemen stood around, all ears.

Then the Friar, with outstretched arm, began:

'You say that the Friars sin, if they handle money?'

'I do.'

'Do you deny that the Pope can give us permission to do this?'

'I do not deny it.'

'He did give us permission.'

'I believe so.'

'Then it is permissible.'

'I don't disagree.'

'But then your conclusion is a lie.'

The Servite eluded this shot this way:

'My conclusion was a pronouncement about the Friars Minor. It is not permissible for them; but for you, who are not Friars Minor, it is permissible.'

'But', said the other, 'the Papal Bull calls us Friars Minor.'

'It calls you so,' said the Servite, 'but it adds, *conventuales*. The cloistered Friars are Friars Minor only as a dead man is still a man.'

This silenced the Friar, for he was not expecting that solution, and the cardinal, admiring the subtlety of the argument, smiled good-humouredly. Standish saw the first round had not gone very well, so he stepped into the arena himself, with a threatening scowl and extended arm, and cried: 'I say you are excommunicate.' The other denied it, and Standish went on: 'We have a Pontifical Bull which excommunicates all those who dare to say that it is a sin for the cloistered Friars in England to accept money; and you have seen the Bull, and you go on saying it, therefore you are excommunicate.'

The noose would now have been round the Servite's neck, had he not wriggled out of it by saying that the Bull spoke of the cloistered Friars, who were not Friars at all, and his conclusion spoke of the Friars as plain Friars. The cardinal, who was doing all this for amusement rather than in sober earnest, dismissed both of them in such a way that it was not at all clear who was the better man. The Servite went back to Paris, to stage a triumph there. The Standishites on the other hand boasted among themselves that the Servite had been defeated by a boy, and brought to the point where he could not mutter a word. The conclusion remains to be disputed in the theological schools of Oxford and Cambridge.

This bit of play-acting gave me so much fun that I wanted to share the pleasure with you, gentle reader, to give you a little light relief from the tediousness of your reading.

(c) *Ne bos quidem pereat* (*1526*)[1]

We have already been told, in several proverbs, how much benefit is conferred by a good neighbour, and how much inconvenience results from having a bad one. But it is as well to repeat over and over again those things which make for happiness, so as to impress them deeper on our minds. This saying is not only concerned with setting up a house or an estate, but with almost the whole of life; so that what Porcius Cato[2] stated about the necessity of having an obliging neighbour relates not only to farming people but to every one of us. Indeed, if anyone who has reached an advanced age looks back on the whole course of his life, he will find that the greatest part of his weal and woe arises from good or evil neighbours. Columella quotes the poem of Hesiod as proverbial:

Nor would an ox die, if the wicked neighbour were not there.[3]

But the loss of an ox is a light matter compared to those ills which are caught from evil companions, from false friends, from wife and household if they are not loyal. Some think that the opinion of Cato is to be rejected because it does not lie in ourselves to choose our neighbour, as death or some other cause often brings about a change. There is no denying that, but still Cato gave good advice, when he said that the farmer should do what he could to secure a good neighbour—and not only good but well-intentioned. For he might be good without being accommodating towards you. There are two things which contribute especially towards achieving this: industry in tilling one's fields, and polite treatment of one's neighbour. Often enough we have a bad neighbour because we behave like bad neighbours ourselves. Columella judiciously writes, that it is a wise man who meets the ups and downs of chance with fortitude, but it is a madman who creates his own misfortune. And this is what a man does who spends his money on acquiring a worthless neighbour, when he might have heard from his cradle upwards—if he came of free parentage, that is,

Not an ox would perish if the bad neighbour were not there.

Not only of an ox can this be said, but of all the things that belong to our daily lives; in fact many people have preferred to be without

[1] 'Not even an ox might perish', IV. v. i; LB. 1049 A.
[2] Quotation from Columella, quoting Cato (when he should be quoting Varro)?
[3] Hesiod, *Works and Days*, 348. Quoted by Columella, I. III. 5.

their household gods and fly from their own homes, because of the hostility of their neighbours; unless we are to find some reason other than this for whole races abandoning their homeland and seeking another world, I mean for instance the Achaeans and the Iberians, the Albanians too, and the Sicilians, and in our early beginnings the Pelasgi,[1] the Aborigines,[2] and the Arcadians. But, leaving aside calamities affecting whole races, there have been private individuals (so legend tells us) who were detestable neighbours, both in lands of Greece and our western world itself,[3] unless the notorious Autolycus[4] could have been endurable to anyone as a next-door neighbour, or the dweller on the Aventine, Cacus,[5] given any cause for rejoicing to his neighbours on the Palatine. I prefer to pick out instances from the past rather than from the present, so as not to name my own neighbour, who allows no sizeable tree of our district to stand, no nursery garden to remain unspoilt, nor any stake supporting a vine, nor even allows flocks to graze carefree. In my view M. Porcius was certainly right in saying that one should avoid such a nuisance, and in advising anyone starting up as a farmer not to take it on of his own accord.

Up to this point Columella has supported Cato with a certain oratorical eloquence, and taught us what a nuisance a bad neighbour can be. Cato, however, was not thinking only of the neighbour's character, but also of his prosperity: 'Observe', says he, 'how flourishing the neighbours look. In a good district there must be signs of thriving. Sometimes a flourishing look argues the goodness of the ground, but where the soil is less fertile it is a sign of the diligence of the cultivator.' Just as a hard-working neighbour encourages attention to good farming, so spendthrift habits and idleness corrupt a nearby household. An over-powerful neighbour bears hard on the poor man near at hand, and neighbours who are very badly off are always pilfering, either by begging or by theft. With bad-tempered or unprincipled neighbours there is always a quarrel going on, over boundaries, or damage, or rights-of-way for walking or driving, or rain dripping from the gutters, or over the view from the windows or the windows themselves. If chance has given us a neighbour like that, and there is no possibility of exchange, it only remains to make a good one out of a bad one, for the sake of our own comfort—or at least to see that he is not made more difficult by provocation. For the worst thing of all would be for us to turn an obliging neighbour into a disobliging one by

[1] Early inhabitants of Greece.　　　　[2] Original inhabitants of Italy.
[3] Hesperia, a name given by the Greeks to both Italy and Spain.
[4] One of the Argonauts, a famous thief.
[5] The three-headed robber killed by Hercules.

our own behaviour. This is what Cato means when he says, 'Be good to your neighbours.' And lest you should think it enough to abstain from injuring them yourself, he adds, 'do not allow your household to behave badly.' Then he explains what advantage can be gained from good neighbours: 'If the neighbourhood views you with favour,' he says, 'you will sell your produce more easily, you will have less difficulty in hiring your services or in taking on farm-hands. If you build, they will help to provide you with men, mules, materials. If at any time you are in need of protection they will readily defend you.' In old days anyone who put up an estate for sale would instruct the auctioneer as to what the land had to recommend it—how good the climate was, how favourable the situation, how fertile the soil, how well-built the premises. But, when Themistocles, that keen-witted man, wanted to sell his farm, he ordered something else to be added to this list of merits—*that he had a good neighbour*. At first this was a subject of jests and laughter among the crowd, but soon they understood that it was the highest recommendation the land could have. It is of the utmost importance for the whole comfort of life, what sort of neighbour one chooses to have, or how one treats the neighbour one finds.

A prince who wishes to obtain possession of a realm which he cannot defend without the greatest effort and the most drastic expense to his ancestral domains, is creating bad neighbours for himself. On the other hand, if he associates with himself wise and sure counsellors, and magistrates who are upright and love their country, he wins good neighbours. Nor is it of little importance which other nations he binds to himself by alliance. One who takes a wife with a disagreeable character or insolent relations, for the sake of a dowry or social advancement, is making bad neighbours for himself. To enter into a pact of friendship with rogues is going to look for bad neighbours. To be led by desire for importance to throw oneself into a college or monastery where the inmates are vicious or merely superstitious, is to arrange to have bad neighbours. The first precaution must be to choose well, the second to amend, and the third to run away from what cannot be amended. Although even flight must be adopted with caution; or else flying from a fault leads one into a vice, if clumsily done, and it often happens that from hatred of one evil we fall headlong into a different and greater evil.

It is rare to repent of friendship, if one has chosen one's friend with judgement. And often it happens through our own fault that a friendship is broken, because we do not use our good friends well, or because we do not know how to bear with our more difficult ones or how to improve them. It is just as grave a mistake not to know how to extricate oneself when one has fallen into bad company, or to stick to those whom one secretly hates, or to break off friendship violently instead of letting it peter out.

This sort of thing happens to people like me, when we select, and try to keep, patrons and benefactors for our studies. We neglect those who are offered, or we greet with open arms those who are least adapted to us, or, if a suitable one happens to fall to our lot, we do not try to foster his good-will towards us by doing him services in return. I certainly made bad mistakes of the first sort when I was young. Truly, if I had responded then to the favours of the great people who were beginning to be interested in me, I should have got somewhere in the literary line, but an immoderate love of liberty made me spend a long time wrestling with faithless friends and stubborn poverty. And that would never have ended, had it not been for the great William Warham, Archbishop of Canterbury, a man to be reverenced not so much for the importance of his office and title as for his virtues, really outstanding and worthy of a great prelate. He enticed me, shy as I was, into the net of his friendship. I had only just discovered what a large-hearted man he was, when I went off to Italy. As I dawdled there, with no idea at all of coming back to Britain, he invited me back of his own accord with the offer of a benefice. This passed unheeded too.[1] But, when another wind blew me back to England, he bound me to him, not so much by his kindness, though that was and is a great characteristic of his, but by the charm and pleasantness of his ways and the remarkable steadfastness of his affection—such a rare thing in important men; so that willy-nilly I gave him my hand. That was the bait that lured me into his power. And so, much to my own benefit, I was caught, in fact acquiring him as a Maecenas is my one claim to be called lucky—but I should have been much luckier if it had happened sooner. Whether he regrets having such a beneficiary, I do not know, but certainly I have never yet succeeded in returning his kindness in any way satisfactory to myself, nor do I see how I ever could. And so I must ask all who are led by the love of religion and good letters, if they have begun to find any profit, anything they do not regret, in my writings, to render thanks to this holy bishop instead of to me, and to pay him back adequately if they can. For it will be paying him back, if they do not allow his memory to fade among the generations to come, since it is to his kindness that they owe anything they may have got out of my books—supposing they have got any value out of them at all.

Everywhere people are complaining and lamenting that there are no

[1] Erasmus did, however, dedicate to Warham his translation of Euripides.

Maecenases to promote study. But Maecenas did not adopt Virgil or Horace straight away, and he was no Maecenas to Mevius or Bavius.[1] A young man should first manage to produce an excellent specimen of his work, as a proof that what is conferred on him will not be wasted. He must not think all that is needed is to use any means whatever to extract a gift, or rather a bit of loot. Beneficence is not the reward of importunate begging, but of people who are getting steadily better both in literary work and moral character. The land encourages the farmer to sow a richer seed, if what was entrusted to it makes a fair return with a good interest. It is not a good thing to leave one's patron at once after wearing him out, as if one were going to pick up acorns under a second oak when everything had been shaken down from the first. It is best to devote yourself to one, or perhaps two, patrons as if you were going to rely on them for ever. How many cases we see now, of people whose immoral lives bring odium on literary studies and shame and ill-will on their patrons! It is no small part of the duties of gratitude to celebrate the name of a patron, but you must be careful how you praise, and whom. Vain flattery makes people distrust even the panegyrists who are speaking the truth, and the result is not that the reader thinks better of the person praised but worse of the person praising. Extravagant eulogies produce envy rather than glory. As to those who applaud things which the wise and good think wrong, their praise is nothing but blame. When you write an Encomium, let your facts be true, and then see that these true facts are treated so as to seem probable. None of the hyperbolae of some poets, by which they turn a man at will into a god! Rather paint those virtues which attract favour and good-will, virtues like piety, integrity, modesty, humility, kindness, simplicity and courtesy of manners. Nothing is more prone to envy than the human mind, nothing more spiteful than the judgements of men. Hence, if it is necessary to touch on those attributes which the public so admire that they envy the possessors of them, that is a matter to be treated carefully, if you don't want the subject of your praise to be the object of sorcery.

No one envies the rich man who treats his possessions—obtained of course either by the favour of fortune or by honest earnings—as if he were the distributor of them rather than the owner. Nor does everyone envy the powerful man who uses his power for the good of the state, outstanding by his rank but retiring in his humility, winning even the poor by his courtesy. No one envies the handsome, if they add modesty and chastity to the gift of nature. No one envies the hale and long-

---

[1] Maevius and Bavius were two bad poets of the Augustan age, who attacked the reputation of other writers and are satirised by Virgil in the third Eclogue.

lived, if they enjoy health and long life to the benefit of everyone else. Anyone who has not the brains nor the skill to treat these subjects as they deserve should abstain, rather than be like a bad artist who spoils a beautiful subject by his fumbling. Alexander was perhaps rather peevish when he refused to be painted by any hand but that of Apelles. Still, no beautiful person would care to be painted by Fulvius and Rutuba.[1] See that what you bring under the public eye is such that it holds the promise of being remembered by posterity. Finally, praise must be so handled that it does not appear to be a duty expected by the person you are praising, for no one is less wishful to be praised, or can less endure it, than those who deserve it most; but let it be clear that it is due to virtue itself (which trails its own glory behind it whether it will or no), and to the hope of inspiring others with the same zeal. In this way the praise will be valuable to the person who really deserves it, and there will be no danger of envy, or suspicion of adulation. When you are praising the dead, however, you may call upon a richer vein of eloquence, because then ill-will is softened and there is less reason to suspect flattery.

Up to now I have been showing how men of letters can recommend themselves to their patrons. I will say a few words now about the methods they may use to enable them to bring their studies themselves into general favour. For in many places the study of languages and what they call good letters is the butt of great ill-will. This is partly the fault of the older generation, who think they are losing some of their authority if the young acquire any of the new learning; they are content with what they learnt as children, and will not allow anything else to be taught, nor can they bear to learn, either because they are too stubborn or because they are ashamed. But the fault lies partly with those who brought in this new-old teaching. There are some unbearably insolent people in this group—as soon as they have learnt twelve words of Latin and five of Greek they imagine themselves to be Demosthenes or Cicero; they gabble away in their silly booklets, sometimes pretty spiteful too, they have an extraordinarily arrogant way of rejecting all liberal studies, and they pour scurrilous abuse on those who make these studies their business. There are even some who make use of good letters for the worst ends, for seditious evil-speaking, for disturbing, dislocating and overturning the peace and tranquillity of Christendom. Yet in the past those who were learned in these studies would use their eloquence to settle the disputes of princes, to wage war on the promoters of heresy, to celebrate the memory of the saints; they would sing the praises of Christ in verse and prose, they would exhort all to

[1] Gladiators, mentioned by Horace, *Satires*, II, 7, 96.

despise the things of this world and to love the things of heaven. Such were Basil, Nazianzenus, Ambrose, Prudentius, Lactantius—with them the knowledge of languages and classical literature aroused no envy or ill-will, because it was devoted to pious ends. It often happens that the way men live is attributed to their studies; and thus there are not a few in these days who have a detestation of the Gospel, because of the immoral lives of some who use the name of the Gospel to recommend themselves. If only those who profess this kind of learning were like Paul, abstaining from every appearance of evil that the Gospel might be glorified,[1] becoming all things to all men so that all might profit,[2] if only they would seek to commend their profession by their purity of life and their courtesy and restraint in speech, the benefits would be far greater and the odium much less. On the other hand, if the older men were ready to accept (with civility and fairness) what are really not new-comers and strangers, but guests of old days returning to claim their right of citizenship, they would find the addition of these things was far from useless, and lets in new light not negligible at all. As it is, they wage irreconcilable war on old friends, as if they were enemies. They call 'new' things that are the oldest of all, and they call 'old' what is really new. Among the doctors of the early Church the knowledge of the Scriptures[3] was combined with skill in languages and in secular literature.[4] We see the same thing among the early philosophers, in Medicine, in Law. What mistakes in grammar did Aristotle or Hippocrates make? Were Plato and Galen not eloquent? The legal lights of the past—what skill they had in both languages![5] How dignified and pure was their style in Roman speech! This is proved by those very fragments which bragging Justinian thrusts upon us in lieu of whole volumes, though even they are interspersed all through with monstrous textual errors. It is something new, when boys have to learn grammar, to stuff them with *modus significandi*, and read them crazy lists of words which teach nothing but to speak faultily. It is something new to accept a youth as a student in Philosophy, Law, Medicine or Theology, who can understand nothing in the ancient authors owing to his ignorance of the language they speak. It is something new, to exclude from the Holy of Holies of Theology anyone who has not sweated for years over Averroës and Aristotle. It is something new to stuff young men who are reading for a degree in Philosophy with Sophistical nonsense and fabricated problems, mere brain-teasers. It is something new in the public teaching of the Schools, for the answers

---

[1] 1 Thess. v, 22; 2 Thess. III, 1.   [2] 1 Cor. IX, 22.
[3] *sacra volumina*: the Old Testament.   [4] *Literae humaniores*.
[5] Latin and Greek.

to differ according to the methods of Thomists or Scotists, Nominalists or Realists. It is something new to exclude any arguments which are brought from the sources of Holy Scripture, and only accept those which are taken from Aristotle, from the Decretals, from the determinations of the Schoolmen, from the glosses of the professors of papal law, or from precedents (inane for the most part) distorted from Roman law. If we are to be offended by what is new, these are the really new things. If we approve of what is old, the oldest things of all are what are being brought forward now. Unless, maybe, 'new' means coming from the century of Origen, and 'old' means what started up three hundred years ago and has gone from bad to worse ever since.

But there are some people who are more unjust still. They are not afraid to jabber in private and in public, and even in their preaching, about this kind of literature being the source of all heresies, not noticing that this blasphemy falls on Jerome, Ambrose, and Augustine, and many others—doctors who are the glory of the Church. They stuff this kind of silly rubbish into the ears of young people at Confession. 'Beware of the Greeks, you'll turn into a heretic! Keep away from Hebrew, you might get like the Jews! Throw away Cicero, in case you are damned with him!' What solemn admonitions! They don't think what will happen—that the boys will blab it all out everywhere, to the amusement of sensible people. They instil the same thing into the ears of parents, for the express purpose of getting children committed to their charge for teaching. It is easy to impose on womenfolk and ordinary simple people with a pretence of sanctity. Really you might as well hand over the sheep to the wolf, as hand over the children to 'bellies' like these. What do I hear? The Waldensians, the poor folk of Lyon, Wyclif—they are all versed in languages and good letters? So I suppose Jerome was a heretic, since he was particularly distinguished in languages and all kinds of literature? If someone who knew only French were to write heretical opinions in that language, should we advise everybody against learning French? Lately they have begun to push the idea in the courts of princes that all this uproar, both Lutheranism and the peasants' revolt, have originated from language-study and classical literature. Courts have their Midases and their Thrasos, and the greatest princes are the more exposed to such plots, the more frank and candid they are, and the more passionately they follow their inclinations. If anyone who knows Greek and Latin is in danger of heresy, because Luther is not unacquainted with these tongues, why is it not just as good to say that such a person is quite safe, because John, Bishop of Rochester[1] and Jerome Aleander, Arch-

[1] John Fisher.

bishop of Brindisi, are champions of the tottering church—the latter a fine scholar in all languages, the former taking up the study of the three tongues with uncommon enthusiasm on the verge of old age?

They add another slander. Perhaps when a young man has come to Confession they hear something tinged with lasciviousness (the particular malady of that age). They ask what authors the young men read. When they hear it is Virgil and Lucian, they impute to study the vice that comes from youth or weakness of character, as if indeed they did not hear much worse things from those who have never had any truck with literature at all. The study of literature certainly does not free a man from all the vices, but it does shield the susceptible age from many of them. There is nothing so holy that it cannot be turned into an occasion for sin by the man who is naturally vicious. If the idea is to do away with everything which can lend itself to infamous conduct, why is such praise bestowed on enforced celibacy? Do they think no one knows what a quagmire of evils results from it? But what good can come of it all in the end, if while the supporters of learning are tearing each other to pieces all honourable studies collapse in ruins, as we see has already happened in some places? Yet without these studies the life of men is not that of men but of wild beasts.

The only course left to us now, therefore, is this: that the study of languages and of good letters, coming back to take their place amongst us and springing up again from the roots, as it were, should courteously and peaceably work their way into the company of those disciplines which have held sway for so many centuries in the universities, and, without disparaging anyone's particular study, should be of use to the studies of all. Let them pay some deference to professional dignity, make some allowances for long-established habit which has become second nature, and in many cases for a time of life not easily amenable to change. Those who seem incurable they may leave to their own devices, for fear of stirring up greater tragedies. Those who are tractable, they may allure by timely and pleasant suggestions. Let them warn, and help, and correct, as a conscientious maidservant warns, and helps, and corrects her mistress. Theology is by rights the queen of all the sciences, but she will have more honour and more learning if she receives such useful waiting-women with proper kindliness into her household. Philosophy is a glorious thing, but she too will gain in dignity if she acknowledges her old friends. Jurisprudence is a noble lady, and truly it is no little adornment to her to have such elegant ladies-in-waiting. Medicine is an excellent thing, but without the knowledge of languages and of the writings of the ancients it is almost blind. If they share their good things with each other in this way, each will become richer and more splendid. But I would wish rulers to be warned not to lend their ears to slanderers of the kind I have mentioned, but rather to consider how much profit and honour will accrue to their own affairs from studies of this sort, and how much has been gained by them in the past. Finally, greater happiness will attend the lot of all, both public and private, if each behaves as a good neighbour to the other. To come back to the proverb, it agrees with one which has been mentioned elsewhere: *Some trouble comes of a bad neighbour*, which Demosthenes makes use of in his speech against Callicteas: 'There is nothing, O Athenians, more harmful than to acquire a wicked neighbour, not content with what is his own.'

REMINISCENCES

The last edition of the *Adages* to receive a large bulk of additions was that of 1533. This contains all the matter of preceding editions together with 488 new proverbs, a new preface, and some pungent remarks appended to earlier adages; and it also increases an element which was always there, but less in evidence: personal reminiscence, not ironical now but expressing simply the pleasure of looking back.

It was to England that Erasmus's mind turned as he prepared the new edition. The *Adages* had always had a close connection with England, symbolised by the dedication to Lord Mountjoy. In the 1528 edition another dedication had been added to the first, and the name of Charles Blount—Mountjoy's eldest son—was joined to that of his father.[1] The new edition of 1533 had both a new preface[2] and a new dedicatory letter to young Charles[3] which contained a moving farewell to one of the kindest friends, William Warham, Archbishop of Canterbury. Warham had died on 22 August 1532.

I wrote this groaning and lamenting, and altogether in a miserable mood, because I had heard for certain of the death of that great man, that matchless man William Warham, Archbishop of Canterbury—or rather I should say, that he had moved out of this life's shadows into true and everlasting life. I am mourning for my loss, not his. For he was truly to me 'the anchor of my life'.[4] There was a pact between us that we should be together in death, he had promised that we should share a common grave, and I was sure that he would live longer than I should, although he was fourteen years older. Certainly it was not either age or disease which took him from us, but an accident, fatal not to him but to learning, to religion, to the kingdom and the Church, such was the man's piety, his prudence in counsel, his kind readiness to help everyone. Now that soul fit for heaven is reaping in Christ's presence a rich harvest, for the good seed which he sowed here. But I linger here still, half alive, not having kept faith with him—but, unless my presentiments are very far out, I shall soon keep my promise. It was a pact which might have seemed a friendly jest, but the event shows that it was a true agreement, so much has his death depressed my spirits, and nothing can raise them again—even time, which usually brings a cure for the sharpest grief, only makes this wound more and more painful. Why say more? I feel I am being called away. It will be joyful to die together with such a patron, the like of whom I shall never see again—if only it means that by the mercy of Christ I shall live with

[1] Allen, 2023.   [2] Allen, 2733.
[3] Allen, 2726.   [4] See I. 1. xxiv.

him there. He was a bright planet of the Church, and now shines brighter in heaven; may it be given to me, like a tiny star, to go to join my sun . . .

Working on the *Adages* had brought vivid memories, of the arch-bishop's library and his enthusiastic encouragement, and that kindly deeply lined face which Holbein drew. But perhaps Erasmus came to think that Warham's death was timely, when he learnt of the fate of Fisher and More.

It was in a mood of reminiscence, then, that he carried on his work on the adages. Not that his old fire was quite extinct: one may find an acid reference to a liar, with a spotty complexion[1] (perhaps Ulrich von Hutten and his *scabies*), or to people who, 'born in some obscure village, attach to themselves the name of some famous town',[2] or a grumble about the profit motive:

It would be a good thing if doctors did not bargain about fees, but would accept what the patient gave them on his recovery. For it is the same as Aristotle says there[3] about certain sophists who refused to take disciples except on agreed terms, and then after receiving the money failed to carry out the agreement. We see this done by untrustworthy doctors and surgeons, and often they are found to be impostors, who stipulate a huge fee, and do not move a finger unless the whole sum, or a large part of it, is paid over at once.

(IV. VIII. xxxvi.)

The clergy who must be paid to administer the Sacraments,[4] the monks who divide up amongst themselves the inheritance common to all,[5] the cardinals who only buy their office at the last moment so as to have the title inscribed on their tomb[6] or who use their magnificence to cloak their vices,[7] are still his quarry. And there are the modern succes-sors of the ancient joke about *operarii*, labourers who carry out a scheme without themselves knowing what it is about: apt for the preachers of the Word who cannot read it.[8] The ass in Apuleius knew the kind of people who went round pretending to be the bearers of sacred objects, and imposed on the simple; just as there are those who hawk relics of St Antony, Cornelius (the centurion) or John the Baptist, more for their own gain than for piety's sake.[9]

Similarly, the new adages are as full of learning as the old, and con-tain interesting parallels between the classics and the Bible.[10]

The striking thing about the latest adages is, however, their nearness to contemporary life and their use of varied memories. Classical terms are illustrated by homely Dutch similes. We have seen that *you could*

---

[1] IV. VI. vi.   [2] IV. I. ii.   [3] In the *Nicomachean Ethics*, book 9.
[4] IV. VIII. xlviii.   [5] V. II. xvi.   [6] IV. IX. vi.   [7] V. I. xliv.
[8] V. II. xi.   [9] IV. VIII. lv.   [10] IV. X. lxxiv, V. II. xvii.

light a lantern at his anger has its Dutch equivalent *you could have cooked an egg on his forehead.*[1] The classical *amphithetum* is either a jar which will stand on any side, or a vessel so large that it had to be lifted by two hands, 'the Dutch sailors call it *busa*.'[2] The ancients too knew the use of sabots, 'hollow shoes' fit for those who had to walk in the mud.[3] In Holland the common people have a saying that can be found in Pindar: 'You are lucky enough; do you want to be God?'[4] There are notes about national customs. The Greeks had a word, ἀδελφίζειν, to 'brother' somebody, and today among the Italians it is very common to say coaxingly, 'little brother . . .'[5] An amusing note about trousers (*one who is wearing trousers for the first time shows them off to everybody*)[6] recalls the young patricians of Venice, 'who if they happened to be on a journey would delight in wearing the French shirt without a coat over it, a thing which they would never have done at home'. More seriously, he traces legal customs from ancient times: the Westphalians have an order of judges called *Certi*, who are sworn to silence and in this resemble the Areopagites of Athens,[7] and English law preserves a trace of Roman finickiness: 'A marked trace of this superstition remains to this day among the English, who reject a legal document entirely if a single letter is dropped from a surname.'[8]

He looked back to old journeys. 'Gathering shells'[9] reminded him of the visit to the grotto at Cumae, with its walls decorated in a varied pattern of shells like mosaic work; popularly supposed to be the cave of the Sybil, it was more likely a haunt of robbers and pirates, he says. And another phrase took him back to student days in Paris, and he saw again the long procession of clergy winding down from the abbey which crowned the hill and carrying the shrine of Sainte Geneviève to Notre Dame, to aid the people's prayers to be delivered from the floods of the Seine. In 1497 he had apparently taken this, quite simply, at its face value. In 1533 he takes for granted equally simply that the same human motive was behind this demonstration and the parallel religious functions of antiquity.[10]

There are some anecdotes told for the pleasure of telling a story, without any sting. One regrets that there are not more of these pleasant vignettes.

IV. VII. lx: *In crastinum seria* [Leave serious matters for tomorrow]. In our own day, too, it is uncivil to talk of serious matters at a party. When I was a boy in Holland I heard a story not unlike this proverb. A man was sitting at

[1] IV. X. lxxviii.   [2] IV. II. xvi.   [3] IV. VIII. xxxi.   [4] IV. VIII. lxix.
[5] IV. X. vii.   [6] III. IV. lii.   [7] IV. X. vi.   [8] V. II. xv.
[9] V. II. xx. This visit was paid in the company of Alexander Stewart, see Allen, I, p. 63.   [10] IV. IX. lvi.

a banquet not far from the fire, so that the hem of his gown began to scorch. One of the guests, noticing this, said to him, 'I want to tell you something.' The other replied, 'If it is at all gloomy I don't want to hear it at a feast, where everything should be jollity and merriment.'

'It is not particularly merry.'

'Then let us leave serious things till the banquet is over.'

When he had dined festively he said, 'Now tell me what you wanted.' The other showed him his gown with a great piece burnt out of the back. Then he began to be angry at not having been told in time: 'I wanted to tell you,' said the other, 'but you wouldn't let me. Serious things after the feast.'

IV. VIII. ii: *Vinaria angina* [Wine-sickness]. I myself knew a man in Rome, a pretty good scholar, who really died of this illness. He was called Hermicus, and he was a Spaniard. This man went down with a fever; now he was stout above measure, and for that reason short of breath (*spirituosus*). An Englishman called Christopher Fisher went to visit him as he lay in bed. 'Why Hermicus,' he said, 'are you going to listen to the doctors prescribing their idiotic remedies? This trouble is best washed away with good wine', and he sent out for a four-year-old wine from Corsica. He gave this to the sick man to drink, telling him to be of good cheer. The patient was persuaded and took a big draught, but soon his breath was cut off and he began to die. Some people are naturally silent and drink makes them talkative, others are turned dumber than any fish, without danger to their health. I wish this wine-sickness were less common among the Germans.

IV. VII. xiv: *Campana superbia* [Capuan pride] [After quotations to show that Campania—capital, Capua—had a reputation for arrogance and prosperity in ancient times]. I will not say anything about the manners and morals of the people of Campania in our own time, but I will say that when I passed through Campania I found no trace whatever of that *cru* of world-wide fame. Not a drop of Falernian, Calenian, Massician, Setian, Cecubian, Surrentinian. In fact we were very nearly choked to death by wine in the city they now call Capua. We filled the whole bottle with crushed sugar. The victory was to the wine, sourer than any vinegar. They use boiled-down must, which otherwise does not last until the next vintage. And where are all those celebrated wines, whose name and region have been blotted out by time? We had a good drink of dust. And so nature lets nothing go on for ever.

IV. VIII. xxiv: *Myconiorum more* [The Myconii are the gate-crashers of the ancient world]. You may see a continuation of the Myconian behaviour today among the Irish. The distinguished William Mountjoy once told me an amusing story about this, not a fable indeed but something he himself had seen. An unknown Irishman, walking into the king's palace at breakfast time, sat down uninvited at the table with the king's household. They looked at this bird of passage, and asked where he came from. He told them his country. They enquired what office he held at the court; none, says he, but I want one. Astonished at his impudence, they ordered him to get up and leave. So I will, says he, but after breakfast. Well, there you are; the Irishman stuck to his guns and gained the day by his very brazenness. Their anger turned to laughter, and they asked the fellow in the end how he had the face to push himself into the king's household, unknown and a foreigner as he was. Why, he said, I knew the king was rich enough to stand me a breakfast.

IV. VIII. xxvii: *Trochi in morem* (Like a hoop). Hesychius says this refers to a man who cannot keep a straight course, but is driven round in a circle. This once happened to me at Schlettstadt as I was travelling to Bâle. We fell in with a horseman who led us for a long time through the wood, and then I asked him if he really knew the way. He said he did. When it went on and on, I said 'We must have gone wrong. For we have been riding in this wood for three hours, and usually we can get through it in one.' No need to say more; it turned out that we were very nearly back at our starting point.

SELECT BIBLIOGRAPHY

Erasmi Opera Omnia, ed. J. Leclerc. Leiden, 1703–1706. (A modern edition is in progress.)

Opus Epistolarum Des. Erasmi Roterodami, ed. P. S. and H. M. Allen. Oxford, 1906–41.

(These are referred to as LB and Allen respectively).

Erasme: Dulce bellum inexpertis, ed. Yvonne Rémy et René Dunil-Marque-breucq. Brussels, 1953.

TRANSLATIONS INTO ENGLISH
(a) LETTERS

Epistles of Erasmus, ed. F. M. Nichols. London, 1901–18. (To 1517 only.)

Extensive translations of letters may be found in:

Froude, J. A. *Life and Letters of Erasmus*. London, 1894.

Thomson, D. F. S. and Porter, H. C. *Erasmus and Cambridge*. Toronto, 1963.

(b) COLLOQUIES

Bailey, N. *The Whole Familiar Colloquies of Erasmus of Rotterdam*. London, 1887.

Thompson, Craig R. *The Colloquies of Erasmus*. Chicago 1963. *Ten Colloquies of Erasmus*. New York, 1957. (Paperback.)

(c) THE PRAISE OF FOLLY

Wilson, J. (1688), trans. ed. H. M. Allen. *The Praise of Folly*. Oxford, 1913.

Hoyt Hudson (trans.). *The Praise of Folly*. Princeton, 1941.

Dean, Leonard F. (trans.). *The Praise of Folly*. Chicago, 1946.

(d) THE ENCHIRIDION

A Book called in Latin Enchiridion Militis Christiani and in English the manual of the Christian Knight. London, 1905. (Text of 1533.)

Battles, F. L. *The Enchiridion*. Abridged version in *Advocates of Christian reform*, ed. M. Spinka. London, 1953.

Dolan, J. P. *Erasmus, Handbook of the Militant Christian*. Indiana, 1962. (Abridged.)

Himelick, R. *The Enchiridion of Erasmus*. Indiana, 1963.

(e) OTHER WRITINGS

Born, L. K. (ed). *The Education of a Christian Prince*. Columbia U.P., 1936.

Paynell, T. (1559), ed. M. J. Hutton. *The Complaint of Peace*. New York, 1946.

Olin, J. *Christian Humanism and the Reformation: Desiderius Erasmus, Selected Writings*. New York, 1965.

BIOGRAPHY, ETC.

Allen, P. S. *The Age of Erasmus*. Oxford, 1914.

Allen, P. S. *Erasmus: lectures and wayfaring sketches*. Oxford, 1934.

Harbison, E. H. *The Christian Scholar in the Age of the Reformation*. New York, 1956.

Huizinga, J. *Erasmus of Rotterdam*, trans. F. Hopman. New York, 1923.

Phillips, Margaret Mann. *Erasmus and the Northern Renaissance*. London, 1949. New York, 1965.

Pineau, J. B. *Erasme, sa pensée religieuse*. Paris, 1924.

Renaudet, A. *Erasme: sa pensée religieuse, d'après sa correspondance (1518–1521)*. Paris, 1926.

Renaudet, A. *Etudes érasmiennes (1521–1529)*. Paris, 1939.

Renaudet, A. *Erasme et l'Italie*. Geneva, 1954.

Smith, Preserved. *Erasmus*. New York, 1923 and 1961.

INDEX

adages *(cont.)*
   Spartam nactus es, hanc orna, 100–7
   Summum cape, et medium habebis,
    74 n.
   Suum cuique pulchrum, 74
   Trochi in morem, 166
   Una hirundo non facit ver, xii
   Ut fici oculis incumbunt, 144–6
   Vinaria angina, 165
   Virum improbum vel mus mordeat,
    140–1
Aldine Aristotle, the, 124 n.
Aldine Press, viii, xiv, 9, 10
Aldus, Manutius, 6, 9, 13–14, 28, 30
Aleander, Jerome, 14
Allen, P. S., x, xvii, 140 n., 147, 162 n.,
   164 n.
Ammonius, 146 n.
anchor and dolphin, as symbol of
   Aldine Press, 6–9, 17
Antipolemus, 100 n., 136
Aphthonius, 14
Apostolius, 14
Aristides, 14, 43
Aristophanes, 3, 23, 48, 72, 101, 141
Aristotle, xii, 1, 7–8, 11, 14, 23, 44 n.,
   51–3, 57, 76, 80, 84, 142, 163
Athenaeus, 14, 78
Aulus Gellius, 1, 5, 16, 142

Bâle, 30, 166
Bembo, Peter, 6
Biblical references, x, 39, 47, 80, 84,
   90–1, 121–2, 127–8, 133, 135,
   139, 158
Bibliotheca Erasmiana, vii n.; list of
   editions of *Sileni Alcibiadis,* 77 n.;
   editions of *Bellum,* 99 n.
Blount, Charles, 162
Bolgar, R. R., *The Classical Heritage,*
   xiii n.
Bont, Dr, 140 n.
Botzheim, John, xvii n.

Carneades, 42
Cato, 1, 17, 152–3
Catullus, 18, 48 n.
Charles VIII of France, 103
Chrysippus, 23
Cicero, 11, 18, 27, 48 n., 100, 122 n.,
   139, 147

Clearchus, 23
Colet, John, 147
Columella, 1, 152–3
Cumae, 164

Demetrius Physicus, 58
Democritus, 53
Demosthenes, 30
de Nolhac, P., *Erasme en Italie,*
   99 n.
Didymus, 23
Diogenes Laertius, 15, 114, 122 n.
Diogenianus, 23, 75
dolphin, *see* anchor
Dominicans, the, 134
Domitius Calderinus, 32
Drummond, R. B., paraphrase of
   Scarabeus aquilam quaerit, 47 n.
Dunil-Marquebreucq, René, 100 n.
Dutch similes, 163–4

Egnatius, Baptista, 14
'Epitomes', x
Erasmus, on uses of the absurd, 142–3;
   on anarchy, 145; on ancient
   literature, restoration of, 20 ff.;
   on arbitration, 131–3; Aristotelian teaching, distrust of, 73, 80,
   123–4 n.; on Christ, 79–80, 139–
   40; on His commandment of
   love, 121–2, 127; on the contemporary Church, 34, 46–7, 65,
   81, 86–97, 145, 163; on com-
   promise, 131–3; on critics of the
   Adages, 25 f.; on debt, 35; on
   deceptive appearances, 78–9; on
   elective monarchy, 40 n.; on envy,
   19–20; on excuses for idleness,
   77; on extortion, 45–6, 136; on
   feast days, 76–7; on greed, 34,
   73, 163; on Holland, 32–3 n.; on
   hypocrisy, 74; on ingratitude,
   141; on kings, folly of, 36–7; his
   Latin style, xix n.; on learning,
   defence of, 34, pitfalls of, 123; on
   mankind, natural and divine
   attributes of, 108–10; on manuscripts, loss and corruption of,
   22–3, 31; on Mendicant Orders,
   134, 145–52; on neighbours,
   152–4; on the Papacy, 91–5,